THE

PUBLIC LETTERS

OF

THE RIGHT HON.

JOHN BRIGHT

EDITED BY

H. J. LEECH

SECOND EDITION

WITH ADDITIONS AND A MEMOIR

LONDON

SAMPSON LOW, MARSTON & COMPANY

Limited

St. Dunstan's House

FETTER LANE, FLEET STREET, E.C.

1895

KRAUS REPRINT CO.
New York
1969

KRAUS REPRINT CO.
A U.S. Division of Kraus-Thomson Organization Limited

Printed in U.S.A.

PREFACE TO FIRST EDITION.

THIS collection of letters, which Mr. Bright has written during his political career, has been obtained by a search through the files of several newspapers. Covering a space, as it does, of five-and-thirty years, many of the letters it contains will be new to the bulk of the public ; and although this can hardly be claimed for a large portion of the letters, it may be submitted that they are all valuable communications, worthy of being collected and arranged so as to be available for reference and for general perusal.

Most of the letters deal with political questions. The collection would have been simplified if it had included such communications only ; but in that case some very interesting letters of a public, though not of a political, nature would have had to be omitted, and it has seemed to me a better course to insert every letter I could find.

An exception to this rule has been made in the case of the letters included in the Brougham correspondence of 1843. On the 15th of February in that year Lord Brougham wrote to Mr. Bright, asking for a disclaimer of the " atrocious falsehood " published in the Anti-

Bread-Tax Circular, to the effect that he had importuned a League deputation to entrust him with a motion in the House of Lords. Mr. Bright, in reply, defended the League generally, and disavowed the authorship of the report. A correspondence, consisting of three letters on either side, followed ; but as the whole of the correspondence relates principally to the charges which had been brought against Lord Brougham in the Anti-Bread-Tax Circular, I have not considered it necessary to include it in this volume.

A special interest attaches to these letters from the fact that, with the exception of his speeches, they are the only medium Mr. Bright has used for bringing his opinions before the world. He has neither written books nor contributed to reviews, and it is to his letters that we have to look for whatever of literary effort he has put forth.

I have to express my indebtedness to Mr. Thomas Moss, of Levenshulme, Manchester, who had made a collection of Mr. Bright's letters from the newspapers for several years, and who, hearing of what I was doing, readily placed his list at my disposal, and thus enabled me to include in this collection a number of letters I had failed to find. I also desire to acknowledge the assistance of my friend, Mr. J. Irlam, of Walkden, Lancashire, by whom the idea of making the collection was first suggested to me, and who has rendered me considerable help in the work.

I think it necessary to state, in justice to Mr. Bright, that he is in no degree responsible for the publication of this volume. He has, it is true, given his consent to it, but so far from his having originated the work in any way, the collection was made and completed before any communication on the subject was made to him. Appreciation of the style and contents of the letters, and regard for the character and services of Mr. Bright, have led to the production of the book, and it is given to the world in the belief that it will prove an acceptable addition to the literature of the country; comprising, as it does, the written declarations of one who is confessedly a master of the English language, and containing ideas which have helped to mould the political thought of a nation.

H. J. LEECH.

Manchester, January 17th, 1885.

PREFACE TO NEW EDITION.

THE first collection of Mr. Bright's letters was published at the beginning of 1885, and, consequently, did not contain those communications from him upon public questions which continued to be written from that time until the close of the year 1888. The present edition has been issued in order to make the collection complete. In particular it contains the letters written during the Home Rule controversy, which have a special importance from the fact that, with the exception of two speeches, they were the only public pronouncements made by Mr. Bright upon that subject.

A few letters which appeared in the first edition, and which, as they contained no statement of opinion, may be looked upon as unimportant, have been omitted from this collection. The addendum to the first edition, consisting of Mr. Bright's manifesto to the working men of Rochdale in 1842, has also been omitted.

H. J. L.

Manchester, August, 1894.

CONTENTS.

PARLIAMENTARY REFORM.

THE UNITED STATES.

INDIA.

THE LAND QUESTION.

CONTENTS.

MEMOIR.

JOHN BRIGHT was born on the 16th of November, 1811, at Greenbank, Rochdale, where his father, Jacob Bright, carried on the business of a cotton spinner, and whither he had removed a few years before from Coventry. In the latter town the Bright family had lived about a century, their previous place of settlement having been in the county of Wiltshire.

They had belonged, for generations, to the Society of Friends. It has been asserted that one of them, Abraham Bright, an ancestor of John in the last century, married a Jewess. The statement rests, apparently, on the sole ground that the maiden name of the lady was Martha Jacobs, and does not therefore make great demands upon belief. Nevertheless, when Mr. Bright at Manchester in 1878 denounced Lord Beaconsfield and declaimed against the possibility of this country being dragged into a war with Russia by " a Minister who had not one drop of English blood in his veins," the supporters of the Premier inveighed hotly against his assailant on account not only of the alleged narrowness and bad taste which prompted the taunt, but also of the inconsistency of the speaker, seeing that, as they asserted, through his relation to Martha Jacobs, he was himself a descendant of Israel.

Upon another interesting point of Mr. Bright's ancestry there is no doubt. He was descended through his great-grandmother on his father's side from John Gratton, of Monyash, in Derbyshire, a Quaker preacher in the 17th century, of great power, eloquence and activity, who travelled in several English counties and in parts of Scotland and Ireland for the propagation of his religious convictions, and in the course of his ministry suffered fines innumerable and an imprisonment of five years and a half, from which he was liberated in 1686 by that singular friend of toleration, King James the Second. The affection with which the memory of this devoted man was cherished by his descendants is exhibited in the name "One Ash," applied to the house made famous by Mr. Bright's occupancy. The term was justified by the single ash tree which at one time grew in the neighbourhood of the house, but to the family it had a deeper significance, being reminiscent of the Monyash where John Gratton had his home.

Mr. Bright's mother, the daughter of a tradesman of Bolton-le-Moors, of the name of Wood, was the second of three wives married by Jacob Bright. The issue of the union were eleven children, seven sons and four daughters, of whom John Bright was the second, although by the early death of the firstborn he became the eldest when he was three years old. Mrs. Bright is said to have been a woman of remarkable qualities, "fond of reading and poetry," and of "a singularly clear and logical mind." She died in 1830.

At an early age Mr. Bright was sent as a day scholar to the boarding-school of Mr. William Littlewood, of Townhead, Rochdale. In 1822 he was sent to the Friends' school at Ackworth, near Pontefract, where he remained for a year. He then went for two years to Mr. William Simpson's school at York, afterwards, on account of the unsuitability of the York air, removing to a school at Newton, near Clitheroe, where he stayed a year and a half. He left school for good when he was three months over fifteen years of age.

His removals from one school to another indicate the desire of his parents to give him the best education that could be got within the pale of the Society. Quaker schools have generally a high reputation for the character of their teaching, and those to which Mr. Bright was sent would be likely to be the first of their kind. The period during which he was at school did not, it is true, permit of his becoming a scholar. "My limited school time," he wrote in 1886, "scarcely allowed me to think of Greek, and I should now make but slow steps in Latin, even with the help of a dictionary." But the probability is that he received a good, sound education.

Immediately on leaving school he entered his father's business, where he had the opportunity of acquiring the qualities of self-reliance, judgment and application. During the time that he was there the Rochdale Literary and Philosophical Society, of which he was a member, stimulated his studies and developed in him the habit of composition and of oratorical effort. In 1833 he had the advantage of a European tour, and in 1836 went upon a prolonged journey in which he visited the most notable places in Southern Europe, Egypt, Smyrna and Palestine.

In the course of the ten years which intervened between his leaving school and his second tour, he was led to take an interest in public questions. It was natural that a mind trained like his should have been moved by the strong, vitalizing influences which made themselves felt in that great time of awakening when, after a protracted night of political and social wrong, the sky brightening with the first streaks of a glorious dawn, was sending strange thrills of hope and delight into the hearts of men, and stimulating them to passionate efforts of patriotic endeavour. His attention was first engaged by the great controversy on Catholic Emancipation, created by the sudden change of policy of the Wellington administration in 1828, which produced an excitement in the country as tremendous as that caused by Mr. Gladstone's adoption of Home Rule in 1886. The agitation on Parliamentary Reform aroused in him even a keener interest. He told his constituents at Birmingham in 1866 that in the year 1832 "his young

heart was stirred with the trumpet-blast that sounded
from their midst." His sentiments in the direction of
advanced Liberalism became so strong that he was
impelled when only twenty-five years of age to issue an
anti-Tory manifesto addressed to "the Radical Reformers of the Borough of Rochdale." An agitation
in 1841 against a church rate in Rochdale enabled him
to win his spurs as a public speaker and reformer by
delivering an address against the rate in the parish
churchyard to an assembly of several thousand persons.
He had made his first Anti-Corn Law speech at a
meeting at Rochdale in February, 1839. In the same
year he had married Elizabeth, daughter of Mr.
Jonathan Priestman, of Newcastle-upon-Tyne. Mrs.
Bright died in 1841. The event was charged with
destiny to himself, and was full of importance to the
Corn Law movement and to the nation, for while, as he
has said, all that was left on earth of his young wife,
" except the memory of a sainted life and of a too brief
happiness, was lying still and cold in the chamber
above," Mr. Cobden paid him a visit of condolence,
and before leaving, addressed to him these memorable
words, "There are thousands of homes in England at
this moment where wives, mothers, and children are
dying of hunger. Now when the first paroxysm of your
grief is past I would advise you to come with me, and
we will never rest till the Corn Law is repealed." The
impressive appeal received the response that was
desired, and shortly afterwards there was formed that
close association between the two men which became so
eventful in results.

They presented a rather remarkable combination. It
was a union of two heads with a single heart, a partnership in which there was one sympathy and one purpose,
combined with many diverse qualities of character and
mind. In several respects they represented entirely
opposite types; but their spirits were fused and their
views harmonized to such an extent that, during the
whole time they were in Parliament together, they only

voted twice on different sides of a question. Upon one point a similarity existed between their natures, which is remarkable because of the rarity of the distinction in public men. This was the absence in both of them, to an extraordinary degree, of the sentiment of personal ambition. This, and the unselfishness of motive guiding their public action, made the fullest co-operation between them easy, and caused their combined labours to have the directness and consistency of those of a single individual.

In 1842 Mr. Bright threw himself entirely into the work of the Anti-Corn Law League and proved an invaluable accession to its ranks. He had not then developed those finer traits of oratory with which he later impressed the country, but he had already become a public speaker of the first rank. Possessing a voice of extraordinary compass and volume, and endowed with the richest musical cadences, with a pleasing countenance and an impressive presence, he had more than the physical qualities necessary to success on the platform. In addition he displayed a charming fluency of expression, ability to treat a subject with freshness, and aptness in illustration. Above all there was in him an ardour and depth of feeling that made him pathetic in appeal or impassioned in declamation as the occasion required, and enabled him both to soften the hearts of his hearers and to rouse them to a pitch of excited enthusiasm. The great middle class, which was the backbone of the League, perceived with delight that out of its midst had arisen a man gifted so wonderfully with the powers requisite for carrying on the work it had undertaken. The fame of the orator spread from meeting to meeting and gave an immense impetus to the movement. In conjunction with Mr. Cobden he travelled in the years 1842-3 from town to town throughout the land rousing the people and educating them in the principles of Free Trade. Mr. Cobden was a most convincing reasoner. "I recollect well," his colleague has said, "how at every meeting he attended

I could see the truth, as it were, spreading from his lips, and permeating the minds of all those who heard him, till you could see in their countenances and eyes that they had got hold of a new truth that they would keep for ever." The efforts of the pair were irresistible. The giant Monopoly reeled under their blows and made only feeble and blundering attempts at resistance. Some idea of the despair they created in the minds of the Protectionists may be gathered from the fact that at one of their open-air meetings in the market-place of a country town in the South of England, the farmers of the neighbourhood assembled on horseback in the vicinity and galloped round the crowd, striking their top-boots loudly with their heavy riding whips in order to drown the voices of the speakers and thus render inaudible arguments which they knew could not be answered.

The history of the League has often been related and need not be repeated in detail here. In 1845 the country had been won over to a thorough reprobation of the principles of protection, though owing to the restricted franchise and the anomalies of the electoral system, a large majority still existed in Parliament to support the discredited system. Then came famine to add the terrors of its presence to the demand for the abolition of the bread tax, and at the critical moment there was found in Sir Robert Peel a statesman who knew how to put the exigencies of party and the interests of a class below the needs of a nation. In 1846 he repealed the Corn Law, amid the execrations of some of his followers, but sustained by the belief, beautifully expressed by him, that he should "leave a name sometimes remembered with expressions of good-will in the abodes of those whose lot it is to labour, and to earn their daily bread by the sweat of their brow, when they shall recruit their exhausted strength with abundant and untaxed food, the sweeter because it is no longer leavened by a sense of injustice." The immediate consequence of his high-minded action was that he was driven from power, but he was abundantly recompensed by the knowledge that, as Mr. Cobden said, if he had lost office he had gained a country.

A natural sequel of Mr. Bright's political activity was that he should have a seat in Parliament. A vacancy occurring in 1843 in the representation of the City of Durham, he was induced to come forward as a candidate. At the election he was defeated by his opponent, Lord Dungannon, but the latter being unseated on petition, another election ensued, when Mr. Bright was returned. In this Parliament, which had been elected in the summer of 1841, the Tories had a majority of over seventy members, a strong reaction having taken place since the time immediately following the passing of the Reform Act of 1832, when Peel found himself with barely one hundred and fifty followers in the House of Commons. In regard to the character of its representatives it differed very little from the unreformed Parliaments, except that it contained members—mostly Whigs or Radicals—from the manufacturing towns of the northern and midland counties. There were, it is true, in the electoral system no longer any purely mythical constituencies like Old Sarum, but there were still thirty-eight very small boroughs, which returned two members each ; the counties were the undisturbed preserves of the great landed families, and the masses of the people were deprived of the suffrage.

Amongst the members of the Parliament which Mr. Bright now entered, there were some interesting personalities. On the Whig side, linking the House of Commons of that day with a distant past, sat George Byng, who had represented Middlesex continually since 1791. Mr. Byng had sat for several years in the same Parliaments as Burke and Sheridan, and had often heard those famous orators. He had heard, too, the shrill voice of Charles James Fox, the sonorous eloquence of Fox's great rival, and the fervid rhetoric of Grattan, and had witnessed those triumphant feats

in debate which the keen and powerful wit of Canning
could achieve. Compared with these the speakers of
his later days must have seemed tame and common-
place ; yet there were two sitting on the same side of
the House as himself who were not unworthy to be
mentioned in comparison even with the giants of his
youth. These were Macaulay and Shiel. Macaulay
at this time had lost some of the fire which glowed in
his speeches on the Reform Bill and the slave trade,
but had increased his facility for picturesque detail,
and was still vehement in thought, language and
manner. Possessing a fluency which made him the
terror of reporters, and a mind crowded with facts and
ideas, there seems good reason to believe that had he
cultivated those outward graces of expression which
add so much to the delivery of a speech, he would
have been an orator of unrivalled reputation. Shiel
was a master of that polished, ornate, epigrammatic
style of speaking in which Irishmen seem to excel,
which Grattan displayed in its perfection a hundred
years ago, and which in our days has delighted the
House of Commons from the lips of Patrick J. Smyth.
Mr. Gladstone has described Shiel's voice as resembling
the sounds produced by a tin kettle when striking
against different objects, but declared that he was, notwithstanding, a great orator, with a very vivid imagination, and an enormous power of language and of
strong feeling. O'Connell, who also sat amongst the
Whigs, was an orator of a different stamp from Shiel,
his strong full voice, with its rich brogue, giving utterance to language that was like his figure, broad and
massive, and redolent of the racy Irish humour that
was expressed in his face. Near him was the colossal
form of Joseph Hume, the Radical leader, who, though
little above the middle height, was built on an immense
scale, with tremendous chest and shoulders, enormous
feet, clad in buckskin leather boots, and a mighty head
covered with bushy, dark grey hair, and who on estimate nights, in his broad Scotch accent, would speak

from ten to thirty times in the course of an evening. Also among the Whigs were Sir William Molesworth, the historian ; " Tom " Duncombe, the best-dressed man in the House, an ardent Radical, though a very fashionable person ; Lord Leveson, better known by his later name of Lord Granville ; Charles Villiers, representing then, as he does now, the borough of Wolverhampton ; Lord Howick, still living until lately as Earl Grey ; Milner Gibson, Richard Cobden, Joseph Brotherton, the member for Salford—winning everybody's esteem by the modesty and goodness of his disposition, and anticipating a reform of nearly fifty years later by his persistence in moving the adjournment of the House at midnight—and the gifted, much loved Charles Buller, the former pupil of Carlyle, who described him as " the genialest Radical I ever met," a giant in stature, but delicate in health, soon to die at the age of 42, and be apostrophized by Bulwer Lytton in " St. Stephen's,"—

" Farewell, fine humorist, finer reasoner still,
Lively as Luttrell, logical as Mill."

The two foremost men in the party were Lord Palmerston and Lord John Russell. They were very unlike each other, the tall and handsome form of Lord Palmerston presenting as great a contrast to the small and insignificant appearance of his colleague, as did the dashing and reckless nature of the one to the caution, steadiness and timidity of the other. Neither of them was an orator, but Palmerston had the faculty of always being asked to say exactly what he meant and a power of retort which made him dreaded in debate, while Lord John was very lucid in statement, ready in reply, and a master of fluent and copious speech. Accustomed as we have been now for many years to see the undisturbed supremacy of one man in either of the great parties, it seems strange to us to look upon the spectacle of these two changing places with each other in the highest offices of the State, and throwing the premiership and the leadership of the party from one to

the other in rapid succession. The reason is that their
ability and great experience put them about upon a
level, but beyond all other competitors, and there was
no jealousy between them. When one was tripped up,
the other took his place, and the fallen comrade then
immediately sprang to his feet and played the second
fiddle with delightful complacency. In their youth
they had both been very ardent Liberals and had
supported with enthusiasm Catholic Emancipation
and Reform, but in their later years neither had much
sympathy with the projects of the advanced wing
of their party. But while Palmerston was obstinate in
his opposition, Lord John was open to conviction, and
thus escaped some of the obloquy which fell to his
colleague's share. Palmerston's efforts in opposition to
the slave trade deserve honourable recognition, and the
constant zeal which Lord John displayed on behalf of
education is one proof that he was the possessor of
sound, liberal principles.

On the Tory side of the House the most commanding
figure was Sir Robert Peel. He was then Prime
Minister and at the zenith of his career, though the
crowning proof of his statesmanship was yet to come.
In the prime of life, at the head of a great party,
possessing unrivalled power as a Parliamentary debater,
and pre-eminent ability and experience in the management of the House of Commons, his position was such
as to dwarf that of every other member of the House.
He stands out from amongst the Parliamentarians of that
day as the one unquestionably great man of the time.
The ascendancy he enjoyed over the House of
Commons was the result of a variety of reasons, but
the place he holds in history is due to his statesmanship,
to his reforms in police, in the Criminal law, currency
and finance, and to his great measures for the emancipation of the Catholics, the relief of Dissenters, and the
freeing of trade, which show that he was no mere party
strategist, but that he held himself to be, and acted as,
the steward of the nation.

Amongst his followers were Sir James Graham and Lord Stanley, "the Rupert of Debate," both recruits from the Whigs, as was also the top-booted Sir Francis Burdett, typical English squire, who had been an enthusiastic reformer, and whose harangues on that topic in the House caused such sensation that—

> " Pitt's burly squires resign'd their port, and ran
> To hear the dangerous but large-acred man."

Lord Ashley, the future Earl of Shaftesbury of philanthropic renown, also sat on these benches, and young Lord John Manners, the present Duke of Rutland. There might also occasionally be seen, when the more important business of the turf did not prevent him being present, the tall, manly form of Lord George Bentinck, now just turned forty years of age, a glint of scarlet beneath the white overcoat very often indicating that he had come straight to the House from a run, for he was an enthusiastic fox-hunter. Every athletic exercise, indeed, secured his interest, and he was proficient in all—a bold rider, a good shot, an expert on the cricket field and on the river. But the turf possessed his deepest affection. In 1841 he refused an offer of a seat in the Government rather than relinquish in any degree his racing pursuits, which were so keen that in 1844 he had no less than forty horses running in public and about a hundred altogether. It is rather remarkable that the same force which had seized upon the young Quaker manufacturer, had snatched him from the obcurity of private life and thrown him into the glare and distinction of a public career, should be working in an opposite direction upon the sporting aristocrat, and be destined to separate him from all his favourite occupations and condemn him to the uncongenial work of leading a political party.

But so it was. The declaration of Sir Robert Peel in favour of Free Trade left the Protectionists without a leader, and Lord George Bentinck was singled out as the man best fitted to fill the vacant place. His

opposition to Free Trade was uncompromising and had
in it something of the sportsman's attitude of mind. " I
keep horses in three counties," he said, " and they tell
me that I shall save 1500*l.* a year by Free Trade. I
don't care for that. What I cannot bear is being sold."
He displayed an unselfish fidelity to what he believed
to be his duty which it is impossible not to admire.
Just at the time when his chances of success were most
brilliant he sold his magnificent stud for 10,000*l.* and
devoted himself wholly to political work. He had the
mortification of seeing the Derby won in 1847 by a
horse bred out of his favourite mare Crucifix, which he
had sold with the rest of his stud. He continued,
however, his political labours with unflagging zeal and
with considerable success both as a speaker and party
manager until his death, which occurred at the early
age of forty-six, and which was brought about, there
can be little question, by the close devotion to sedentary
occupations which his new *rôle* forced upon him. His
lieutenant was the brilliant young Jew who had entered
the House a few years before, and whose maiden
speech had been signalized by shouts of derisive
laughter from his auditors, provoking from the speaker
the defiant prediction that though he was silenced then,
the time would come when they should hear him. The
time had now arrived. He was rapidly rising to be one
of the first speakers in the House, and not many years
were to elapse before he was to lead the Tory party in
the Commons, to be the object of its admiration and
confidence, to guide it by his wisdom and encourage it
by brilliant epigram and startling paradox through the
long years of its exclusion from power, wielding a
flashing rapier that inspired his doughtiest opponents
with respect, ever confident, skilful, courteous, and
making headway against successive defeats by indomit-
able courage, by invincible resolution and by the infinite
resources which genius can command. On the same
side of the House as himself, but separated from him by
an immeasurable distance of principle, purpose and

character, was his future rival, the youngest henchman of Sir Robert Peel, then the rising hope of the Tories, but destined to be the set star of Liberalism, destined also to become the greatest Parliamentarian of the nineteenth century, to surpass Palmerston in the magnitude of his ascendancy over his party and to put into the shade Peel's legislative achievements. The young member for Newark was now Vice-President of the Board of Trade, in a few months he was to be President of the Board, and within three years to be Secretary for the Colonies. The eyes of men were beginning to be fixed upon him with hope and confident expectation, for although but thirty-four years of age, he had already given proofs of the possession of some of those marvellous powers, the display of which has made him, during the last thirty years, the supreme figure in Parliament.

Mr. Bright can hardly have been free from the ambition to match his powers of speaking against some of these redoubtable champions. He delivered his maiden speech shortly after taking his seat, the occasion being a Free Trade debate on a resolution moved by Mr. W. Ewart, August 7, 1843. He spoke with vigour and effect, though much of what he said must have been strongly objectionable to a large number of those who listened to him. Free, unsparing criticism was launched at members of the Government. Lord Stanley was described as having displayed " profound ignorance " on the question, Mr. Gladstone was rebuked for the " flimsy excuses " he had put forward during the debate, and Sir Robert Peel was reminded of "the source from which he had sprung." But there was no denying the force and pungency of his remarks ; he was, moreover, always impressively in earnest, and sometimes undeniably eloquent, and his delivery being such as to satisfy the taste of even that critical assembly, it was obvious when he sat down that in the new member the House had acquired a debater of uncommon power. His success was highly gratifying to his friends, and

was, no doubt, satisfactory to himself, whatever truth
there may be in the assertion made by Mr. Justin
McCarthy in his biography of Peel, that Mr. Bright
detested the House of Commons though he prevailed in
it.

His attitude towards the landed party during the
early years of his Parliamentary career was one of
marked hostility, and found expression in occasional
passages of scathing declamation. "You," he declared
during the session of 1844, "you, the magnanimous
aristocracy of Britain, you own the soil, you boast of
ancestry, you amuse yourselves with much painting on
the panels of your coaches—and yet you make laws in
this House to enrich your own class at the expense of
millions, to whom you deny all political power, and to
whom you give no protection whatever." This was out-
spoken sentiment and procured him some hatred, which
was increased when he attempted to lay his hands upon
the sacred fabric of the Game Laws. This he did in
1845 by moving for the appointment of a Select Committee to inquire into the operation of the system. The
Committee was obtained, and after a number of meetings issued a report, but nothing further ensued, and
Mr. Bright some years later complained of the little
support he had received from the farmers on the question. His action probably had for its chief effect that
of accentuating his own position. It is evident that he
was rapidly progressing towards the position which Mr.
Gladstone said he afterwards acquired, of being "the
great, standing, habitual bugbear of the country."

It was about this time that a compulsory limitation
of the hours of labour in factories was proposed by Lord
Ashley. Mr. Bright strenuously opposed the measure,
being averse both as a manufacturer and an economist
to State interferences in the hours of labour. He dis-
claimed any want of sympathy with the workpeople,
but insisted that reductions in the hours of labour
should be obtained by voluntary arrangement, and
maintained that the evils which were said to have been

produced by the Factory System had been grossly exaggerated.

In 1847 he was married to Miss Margaret Elizabeth Leathem, daughter of Mr. William Leathem, of Heath House, Wakefield. From this marriage there were seven children, John Albert, Mary Harriet, William Leathem, Anna Elizabeth, Margaret Sophia, Leonard, and Philip. Leonard died in his sixth year, and was buried in the churchyard of St. Tudno, Llandudno. The eldest son, John Albert, succeeded his father in the representation of Central Birmingham. From the first marriage there was one daughter, Helen.

Mr. Bright was elected member for Manchester in 1847, along with Mr. T. Milner Gibson, and in the autumn session delivered in the House of Commons the first of that series of great speeches which did so much to educate English opinion as to the existence of injustice and wrong in the government of Ireland. About the same time he took up the question of the government of India, and threw considerable light on that subject also. Other questions which secured his advocacy were the abolition of flogging in the army, the abolition of the death punishment, of church rates and of the paper duty, and the extension of the franchise.

At the beginning of 1854 the outbreak of war between England and Russia led to a course of action on his part, which, while it brought him at the time much unpopularity, called forth nevertheless his power of oratory to such a degree as to greatly heighten and extend his reputation. And as the wisdom of the policy he advocated commended itself more and more with the lapse of time to the conscience and judgment of the people, it had the effect of helping to establish him afterwards in the position of a public guide and counsellor.

An idea exists that his oposition to the Crimean war was due entirely to his strong objection to war in general, and was not the result of a consideration of

b

the circumstances of the case. This notion, however, does injustice to the position he assumed on the question. He told Lord Palmerston in the House of Commons that he was not afraid of discussing the war with him on his own principles, that he understood the Blue Books as well as the noble lord, and that the war could not be justified out of those documents. These were the grounds on which by logical argument he opposed the war. He did not discuss the question on the abstract principle of peace at any price. What he did was to insist that in deliberating on the question of war, it was the duty of those who advocated it to show that the interests of the country were clearly involved ; that the objects for which the war was undertaken were probable or at least possible of attainment ; and that the end proposed to be accomplished was worth the cost and sacrifices which they were about to incur. Maintaining that these points had not been proved, he declared the war to be unjust, and denounced it with the passionate energy of which his nature was capable. It is quite true that his horror of war, due to a large extent to his Quaker training, intensified his opposition. The subject presented itself to his mind stripped of the illusions with which it is clothed in its appearances to the common imagination. In one of those noble passages which are frequently found in his speeches on this question, he exclaimed, "He (Lord Palmerston) may · perchance never see that which comes often to my vision, the interminable ghastly procession of our slaughtered countrymen, to which every day fresh lists of victims are added. I see these things. I speak in apprehension of them." It was this grave appreciation of the realities of war that made him so determined an opponent of a policy which appeared to him from the evidence of facts to be without justification.

Yet, while intensely convinced of the iniquity of the Crimean war, he was not betrayed into futile, unmanly expostulations against it. Throughout the whole of that fierce and passion-stained controversy, in which was arrayed against him most of what was intellectual and all that was savage and brutal in the country, he preserved unimpaired the calmness and dignity of his demeanour. His firmness was not shaken by clamour or rudeness of opposition. As the dispute grew hotter and the outcries of insulted patriotism increased in volume, his reasoning took a keener edge, his pathos a deeper note, his declamation a more imperious tone. Like a brave and expert swordsman, who displays the greatest self-possession and skill in fence at the most desperate moment of the combat, the diction of his speeches became more beautiful and the illustrations more choice and artistically wrought as the hopelessness of his cause and the opposition to his views increased. It was shortly after the battles of Alma and Balaclava, when the nation was intoxicated with military pride, and his own unpopularity was manifested by the burning of his effigy in the streets of Manchester, that he delivered in the House of Commons a speech urging a settlement of the war, which in its calm, yet powerful logic, its exquisite touches of pathetic allusion, its superb and glowing, yet always restrained rhetoric, is a model of artistic composition. The effect of this speech, which burned throughout with suppressed passion, was such as there is no record of having been witnessed before or since in the House of Commons. They who assailed the speaker at the beginning of his address with angry interruptions listened to him later on with awe and unwilling admiration ; many were subdued to tears ; the ministry, described as an " incapable and guilty administration," were filled with confusion and dismay ; and when the orator concluded by declaring that though his were "a solitary voice, raised amid the din of arms and the clamours of a venal press," he should have the consolation that no word of his had tended to promote the squandering of his country's treasure or the spilling of one drop of his country's blood, the profound and painful silence that ensued testified more powerfully than the most tumultuous applause to the greatness of the triumph he had achieved.

On this as on the other occasions of his opposition on that question, Mr. Bright was in a minority when the voting took place, but it was a great thing for him to have succeeded in compelling his protest to be received with attention. Nor did his words, like most of those spoken in Parliamentary contest, have a mere ephemeral existence, for now, after the fiery controversy has long ago been hushed to rest, and the bulk of what was uttered in it has been consigned to the dust-heap of oblivion, the brave, eloquent voice, charged with feeling, and nerved by righteous conviction, peals audibly and sweetly across the gulf of forty years which separates that period from ours.

The defeat of Lord Palmerston's Government in March, 1857, upon a resolution moved by Mr. Cobden condemning their policy towards China, led to a dissolution of Parliament, when the constituencies showed their confidence in the Prime Minister by returning a majority of his supporters. Mr. Bright was travelling on the Continent to recruit his health when the debate on Mr. Cobden's resolution took place, and had therefore no share in the overthrow of the Ministry. But it was well known that his sympathies were with his friend, and on account of that and his action on the Crimean war, a determined attempt was made to prevent his return for Manchester. The opposition to him was successful, for at the election he and his colleague Mr. Milner Gibson were rejected by a majority of nearly three thousand votes in favour of Sir John Potter and Mr. J. A. Turner. He had personally taken no part in the election, owing to his ill-health, and it was at Florence that the news reached him of his defeat. From there he wrote a manly letter of thanks to his supporters, and of farewell to the constituency. The event caused a sensation in the country, and was the subject of regret to all shades of politicians. So far as he himself was concerned the misfortune was soon remedied, but to

Manchester it was an irreparable disaster, and subsequently became a subject of bitter mortification and regret to the inhabitants of that city.

He remained only four months out of Parliament, for in August, 1857, a vacancy occurring in the representation of Birmingham, he was invited to become a candidate, and having consented, was returned without a contest. His connection with the great Midland borough was mutually satisfactory, and continued until his death.

His re-appearance in the House of Commons in the session of 1858 was signalized by two speeches on the government of India. The question touched his imagination, and bringing that faculty into play in order to reveal the grandeur and interest of the subject, he appealed on behalf of "the countless millions, helpless and defenceless, deprived of their natural leaders and their ancient chiefs, and who were looking with only some small ray of hope to that omnipresent and irresistible Power by which they had been subjected," and aroused the nobler motives of his fellow-members by inviting them to "a glory not 'fann'd by conquest's crimson wing,' but based upon the solid and lasting benefits which it was in the power of the Parliament of England to confer upon the countless populations of India."

The most important questions which occupied his attention during the next few years were the American War, Parliamentary Reform, and Ireland. On the first of these he took up a position of decided approval of the cause of the North, declaring himself on the side of that policy which gave hope to the bondsmen of the South. His finest effort on this question was the speech he delivered in the Birmingham Town Hall on the 18th of December, 1862. Feeling ran very high in this country at the time in relation to the internecine struggle. The majority of the Liberal party and of the working classes were staunch in their adherence to the cause of the North, but the South had many sym-

pathizers, and of these some were men of high position
and of great influence.   Recent successes of the Con-
federate States had given rise to a belief in their ultimate
triumph, and a disposition to recognize them as an
independent Power had been widely exhibited.   Mr.
Bright devoted himself on this occasion to the task of
demonstrating the right of the Americans to maintain
the integrity of their Republic.   If any doubt existed of
the fact that he held war, under certain circumstances,
to be admissible, it is dispelled by this speech.   He maintained in it that the revolt of the South ought to be put
down, which, of course, was a justification of the war.   He
placed the war on a higher basis still.   "Is not this
war," he demanded, "the penalty which inexorable justice
exacts from America, North and South, for the enormous
guilt of cherishing that frightful iniquity of slavery for
the last eighty years?"   He demanded the sympathy
of Englishmen for the North in their efforts to prevent
the erection of a new State of which slavery was
"blasphemously set up to be its chief corner-stone,"
and repudiated with indignation the claims of "that
portentous and monstrous shape" to be received into
the family of nations.   His address was an impassioned
appeal to the conscience of the nation, and concluded
with a passage of nervous and stately eloquence, aflame
with generous feeling, rich in imaginative colouring,
and containing a declaration of conviction which has
now the solemnity of a prophetic utterance.   "The
leaders of this revolt," he cried, "propose this monstrous
thing—that over a territory forty times as large as
England, the blight and curse of slavery shall be for
ever perpetuated.   I cannot believe, myself, in such a
fate befalling that fair land, stricken as it now is with the
ravages of war.   I cannot believe that civilization in its
journey with the sun will sink into endless night to gratify
the ambition of the leaders of this revolt, who seek to—

'Wade through slaughter to a throne,
And shut the gates of mercy on mankind.'

I have a far other and far brighter vision before my gaze. It may be but a vision, but I will cherish it. I see one vast Confederation stretching from the frozen North in unbroken line to the glowing South, and from the wild billows of the Atlantic, westward to the calmer waters of the Pacific main—and I see one people, and one law, and one language, and one faith, and over all that wide continent, the home of freedom, and a refuge for the oppressed of every race and of every clime."

The great popularity which Mr. Bright enjoyed amongst the Americans up to the time of his death was well earned by this and other speeches on the Civil War. In the hour of need he was their greatest friend, and in their time of prosperity they did not forget him. The regard in which he was held in the Commonwealth across the seas is probably greater than that ever possessed by any other Englishman.

In the movement in favour of Parliamentary Reform, which began about 1859 and ended with the passing of the Reform Bill of 1867, Mr. Bright played a leading part. The speeches he delivered on the question from time to time had the effect of rousing the country, and Lord Cranborne only expressed the general feeling when he said that the measure introduced in 1867 by the Conservatives was a triumph not for them but for the member for Birmingham. In the struggle on the second reading of the Bill in 1866, when took place the last fight of oligarchic privilege against the establishment of a popular suffrage, he entered the lists against the foremost champions of the existing order, and employing against them the weapons of wit and sarcasm, covered them with ridicule. It was then that he delighted the country with the brilliant simile of the Cave of Adullam applied to the Dissentient Liberals, by which he achieved a stroke of superb satire and enriched the language by imparting a new meaning to an old word. He was now no longer a prophet in the wilderness, but a successful leader whose cause was winning all along the line, and it was with just pride that he declared that the political gains of the previous twenty-five years were his political gains, if they could be called the gains in any degree of any living Englishman.

No sooner was the Reform question safe than the condition of Ireland claimed his attention. The disturbed state of that country requiring the passing of a Coercion Bill, he took the opportunity afforded him by the discussion of the measure in the House of Commons to utter a grave warning as to the necessity of a thorough consideration of Irish wrongs and necessities. Addressing Mr. Gladstone, then Chancellor of the Exchequer, and Mr. Disraeli, the leader of the Opposition, in almost tutorial language, he sketched the possibilities in the direction of Irish legislation if they ".. with their intellects, with their far-reaching vision," should thoroughly examine the question and determine to make Ireland a strength and not a weakness to the British Empire. He then, with startling directness, asked Mr. Gladstone whether the Irish question was above the stature of himself and his colleagues. If it was, he said, he called upon them to come down from the high places which they occupied, and try to learn the art of legislation and government before they practised it. Governments have before and since that time been the objects of invective and satire in Parliament, but never, probably, did a private member rebuke and tutor powerful administrations with the dignified force of this plain-spoken monitor. In little more than a year later Mr. Gladstone had concentrated his astonishing energies on the subject of Ireland, and given a practical answer to the question put to him by unfurling the flag of religious liberty, and attacking one of the most prominent injustices in that country.

In the meantime Mr. Bright had visited Ireland and had powerfully directed public attention to the needs of the country by delivering there a series of speeches full of sympathy with Irish sentiment and of reprobation of their misgovernment. In our time a great illumination has taken place on the subject, and

only the ignorant or the victims of inveterate prejudice
will now ascribe the woes of Ireland to the effect of the
iniquities and shortcomings of her people. But thirty
years ago the public mind was less advanced, and it was
a real enlightenment for a politician of the first rank
to point out, as Mr. Bright in these and subsequent
speeches did, the truths which underlay the question,
and the connection which existed between misgovernment and discontent. How strongly he felt on the
subject is shown by the tenor of his utterances upon it.
There were rare occasions when the virility which
marked his ordinary speech gave place to something
more impressive, when his genius, exercising its full
power, touched a loftier note. But it was not on common topics that he displayed this supreme quality of
the orator. The character and circumstances of the case
had to be such as stirred his own nature to its depths,
and it was then and only then that issued forth the
clear vibrating tone that had the power to touch the
hearts of men. The prospect of a vast American
Commonwealth consecrated to freedom inspired one
such passage, and the occasion of another was the
desolation of English homes by a war which he
regarded as unnecessary. A third instance was when,
standing on the soil of Ireland and reviewing her
history, her misfortunes and her wrongs, he described,
in terms of surpassing beauty, the phenomenon which
to England is a shame and reproach and to America a
perpetual crown of honour. "You will recollect," he
said, "that when the ancient Hebrew prophet prayed
in his captivity, he prayed with his window opened
towards Jerusalem. You know that the followers of
Mohammed, when they pray, turn their faces towards
Mecca. When the Irish peasant asks for food, and freedom, and blessing, his eye follows the setting sun ; the
aspirations of his heart reach beyond the wide Atlantic,
and in spirit he grasps hands with the great Republic of
the West."

But it was not to give utterance to mere sentiment,

however generous or sympathetic, that Mr. Bright
undertook the discussion of the Irish question. He
provided also suggestions of practical statesmanship, of
which one, proposing a system of State-aided land
purchase, after being neglected for seventeen years, was
adopted by the Government of the day, and put into
operation upon a limited scale, with what is generally
admitted to be eminently satisfactory results. The
disestablishment of the Irish Church, which was another
of his proposals, was carried out at an earlier date, and
he had the satisfaction of living to hear acknowledgments
of the wisdom and justice of the measure even from
within the pale of the Church which had been thus
dealt with.

On the return of the Liberals to power in 1868, Mr.
Gladstone invited Mr. Bright to join the administration he was forming. There is no doubt of the
genuine reluctance which Mr. Bright entertained towards the proposition. Mr. Gladstone has stated that
the task of inducing him to assent to the proposal was the
most difficult he remembers, that the subject was debated
between the two from eleven o'clock at night until one
in the morning, and that it was only at the last moment
Mr. Bright was persuaded to set aside his repugnance.
The office he was asked to accept was that of Secretary
of State for India, but this he resolutely declined from
a fear of being unequal in strength to the duties it
would impose, and because of the close connection
between the Department and the Army. He declared
his preference for the Board of Trade, and was in
consequence appointed President of that Department,
with a seat in the Cabinet. He had held the office
little more than a year when he was prostrated by
an illness which compelled him to retire from public life
for a time, and in December, 1870, he resigned his office.
A prolonged retirement re-established his health ; he
returned to Parliament in April, 1872, re-entered Mr.
Gladstone's Cabinet in August of that year as
Chancellor of the Duchy of Lancaster, and occupied

the post until the resignation of the Liberal Ministry in February, 1874.

During the existence of the Beaconsfield Administration he engaged in the discussion of most of the public questions which occurred during that time, and in particular delivered several notable speeches on the burning question of English policy in the East of Europe. In again opposing a war with Russia in the interests of the Turk he was in a very different position from that in which he stood during the Crimean war. He was now supported by a united Liberal party, and was assisted and almost overshadowed by a mighty ally in the person of Mr. Gladstone, who by a display of energy and ability which would have been remarkable in a younger man, aroused in the country an enthusiasm against interference on behalf of Turkey that carried everything before it. In view of the changed condition of things Mr. Bright declared that "now he could afford to be tranquil, and in some degree a spectator, because he saw the policy he had preached successful and triumphant." The line of policy he advocated was not, indeed, identical with that taken by Mr. Gladstone. It was one of strict non-intervention, while Mr. Gladstone proposed a course which, under certain circumstances, would have required, in order to be consistently carried out, the armed interference of England in the East. But they were both agreed in opposition to English aid being given to Turkey, which was the disposition of the Beaconsfield Government, and were able to act together in complete harmony throughout the whole of the controversy.

On the return of the Liberals to power in 1880 Mr. Bright again undertook the office of Chancellor of the Duchy of Lancaster, but resigned it in July, 1882, on account of the bombardment of Alexandria. In his explanation of the step to the House of Commons he stated that it was a well-known fact that he had for forty years endeavoured to teach his countrymen that the moral law is intended not only for individual life,

but for the life and practice of States in dealing with
one another. In the case of Egypt he said his
conscience was satisfied that here had been a manifest
violation both of international law and of the moral
law, and therefore it was impossible for him to continue
longer in the Cabinet.

There was no great sentiment existing in the country
at the time against the bombardment of Alexandria,
but while Mr. Bright's condemnation of the act failed to
elicit any material response from the people, there was
a general feeling of acquiescence in the course he had
taken. It was felt to be natural and proper that one
who had opposed and denounced war as he had done
should not be mixed up in aggressive military opera-
tions. There was also a feeling that in retiring from
the Ministry he was leaving an uncongenial occupation
to resume what was his true *rôle*. His career in office
had been quiet and uneventful, and it was considered to
be a gain to the country to have him placed once more
in the position of a free and independent counsellor of
the nation. It was probably also a relief to himself to
be thus free, and thenceforward until his death he
remained a private member of Parliament, giving, up
to the period of the great wrench of 1886, a loyal and
hearty support to his party.

While in office it had been a great satisfaction to
him to support the Irish land measures introduced by
the Government. He was as earnest as ever in
advocating remedial legislation as the true method of
dealing with Irish discontent, and when the House of
Lords rejected the Compensation for Disturbance Bill
in 1881, he severely rebuked them in a speech at
Birmingham, in which he made the famous declaration,
often since quoted, that "force is not a remedy." His
abhorrence of crime, however, prevented him from
opposing repressive measures when they were necessary.
He supported the Bill for the suspension of the Habeas
Corpus Act in 1881, with some warnings as to the real
source from which the evils of Ireland sprang. His

action with respect to this measure exposed him to the reproaches of the Irish Nationalist Party, which were rendered more bitter by a passage in his speech on the Bill declaring that the Irish leaders had to a large extent demoralized the people whom they professed to serve. The breach thus caused was made wider by subsequent events. Mr. Bright gave increased offence to the Nationalists by his speech on the second reading of the Land Bill, when with characteristic courage he reminded the people of Ireland that although changes in the law were necessary, something more would be required in order to establish the prosperity of their country. " I do not see why," he said, " if there was that spirit amongst the Irish classes—I am not speaking of the poor labourer, but of the middle classes—why in the name of common sense is it that during the last hundred years there has not been a single manufactory of any importance established and sustained in Ireland ? Why is it that water runs from Lough Corrib into Galway Harbour, and there is nothing done with it ? If it were in America, it would be used. If it were in Great Britain, it would be used. Why is it not used in Ireland ? It is not a sufficient answer to say that the land laws are bad. Our land laws are bad. But what we have done has been in the teeth of a system of land laws which is in some respects even worse than that of Ireland." There was nothing to which the Nationalists could object in this language except, perhaps, its unwelcome candour, but by two subsequent speeches Mr. Bright put himself in a position of marked hostility towards the representatives of Ireland. In the first, which was delivered at Birmingham in 1883, he asserted that some of the Conservative members in the House of Commons seemed to be abandoning the character and conduct of gentlemen, and appeared willing to repudiate the authority of a majority of the constituencies. In addition to that, the Conservatives, he said, were found in alliance with an Irish rebel party, the main portion of whose funds, for the purposes of agitation, came directly from the avowed enemies of England, and whose oath of allegiance was broken by association with its enemies. Sir Stafford Northcote made the first portion of these words the ground for a resolution in the House of Commons that Mr. Bright had committed a breach of privilege. Some of the Irish members naturally took part in the discussion which followed, and Mr. T. P. O'Connor declared that Mr. Bright himself was "a converted rebel." The resolution was negatived, but two years later a fresh offence exposed Mr. Bright to another impeachment of the kind. A banquet was given in London to Earl Spencer in July, 1885, and Mr. Bright, in proposing the health of the chairman on the occasion, displayed some of that straight and forcible hitting which has so often aroused the admiration of his friends and the terror and wrath of his foes. "Who," he asked, "are the assailers of the noble earl? They are to be found in some of those who profess to be the representatives of Ireland. Now, these men—I speak of those who have brought these hideous charges against Lord Spencer—are disloyal to the Crown, and directly hostile to Great Britain. They obstruct all legislation which is intended to discover, or to prevent or to punish crime. They have insulted and denounced every man in Ireland concerned with the just administration of the law. They have attacked the Viceroy in a manner hitherto unknown. They have attacked the judges. They have displayed a boundless sympathy for criminals and for murderers."

The condemnation naturally provoked the resentment of those against whom it was directed, and that eminent purist, Mr. Philip Callan, undertook to bring the matter before the House of Commons in the form of a resolution declaring that a breach of privilege had been committed. In the absence of Mr. Gladstone it fell to the lot of Lord Hartington, who was leading the Liberal party in the House of Commons for the time, to defend his colleague, which he did in the straightforward manner characteristic of him. He could not believe, he said, that the motion was brought forward with the general assent of the members of the Irish party, as, having habitually indulged themselves in liberties—nay, license—of speech, they would hardly go whining to that house to complain because a great orator had expressed opinions about some of them which were generally allowed to be true.

The incident has almost the appearance of the shadow of a coming event, though neither Mr. Bright nor Lord Hartington could then have the suspicion that within twelve months they would be drawn together in an alliance against not only the forces of Irish Nationalism, but even against the bulk of the party of which they were honoured leaders. How far the decision of either of them was influenced by the attitude of the other upon the Home Rule Question we do not yet know, but there is little doubt that there was a strong affinity between the once reputed most aggressive and dangerous Radical in the country and the heir to the traditions and possessions of the Whig House of Cavendish. Truthfulness in statement, sincerity of disposition, and an unfailing common sense were the characteristics, to a rare degree, of both; the political creed of the younger had been moulded by the elder's teachings, and there was, on either hand, a Conservative tendency by nature. The preception of these qualities in each other was sufficient to bring about a mutual attraction, and that such attraction existed is evident. Mr. Bright's advice may have had some effect in inducing Lord Hartington to relinquish a resolution, at which he appears to have arrived thirty years ago, to retire from Parliament. On his confiding his intention to Mr. Bright, mentioning as one reason his want of practice in public speaking, the latter reminded the young member of the services which his family had rendered to the public, and encouraged him to believe that if he would endeavour to continue those services himself, there was no position of influence in the House of Commons to which he might not fairly aspire. Ten

years later Lord Hartington was nominated for the
leadership of the Liberal party and was supported by
Mr. Bright, who on the occasion added another to the
many proofs he has given of his penetration and the
accuracy of his judgment. His description of Lord
Hartington was that he had a strong head, and would
run so straight that the Liberal party might entirely
rely on him.

The agreement of Lord Hartington and himself on
the question of Home Rule enabled them to maintain
unimpaired their political comradeship to the end. But
at the outset their usual positions were reversed, the
younger of the two taking the initiative in this case.
Lord Hartington decided quickly, and threw in the
whole of his influence against the Home Rule policy at
the very beginning of its inception, and there can be
little doubt that the firm and steady attitude of opposition maintained by him was the main cause of the
formation of a Liberal Unionist party inside the House
of Commons, although it would be unjust to overlook
the great weight that was flung into the scale by the
defection from Mr. Gladstone of so pronounced a
Radical and of a politican so influential as Mr.
Chamberlain. Mr. Bright, on the other hand, deliber-
ated long, and it may be imagined with painful care,
before making up his mind to actively resist the new
departure of the Liberal leader. No official statesman
had ever inspired him with the kind of regard he felt for
Mr. Gladstone. "There never was the head of a
Government," he said in 1881, "more capable, more
anxious to do good, than Mr. Gladstone." For twenty
years their aims had been one. They had sat in the
same Cabinets, they had supported the same measures,
and had shared, without rivalry, the affection and
veneration of the Liberal party. To oppose a policy
coming from such a source, over whose supporters were
unfurled the banners of freedom and justice, which was
welcomed with effusion by the great majority of the
Irish people, and which every day secured fresh crowds

of enthusiastic adherents from amongst English Liberals, was to him no light thing. Fate could scarcely have offered him any more terrible ordeal than that, in his old age, he should come into conflict with the party to which he had given a life's affection and service, and which had rewarded him with its implict confidence and reverential regard. His hesitation was therefore natural. The caution, too, which was characteristic of him made him wait until he was perfectly sure of his ground before committing himself. His first public pronouncement, which was made in the form of a letter to Lord Hartington's Chairman in the Rossendale division, was very guarded. In this declaration he simply commended Lord Hartington's "consistent and courageous conduct" upon the two Irish Bills introduced by Mr. Gladstone, insisted on the right of Liberal members to take an independent action upon them, and condemned the introduction of measures of such vast importance without any sufficient preparation of the public or the party mind to accept them. He took no part in the long debate on the second reading of the Home Rule Bill, contenting himself with giving a silent vote against it. When at length, however, he spoke, there were no signs of doubt or misgiving in his tone, and from that fact his long silence seems to indicate a self-restraint and self-effacement which very few men in his position could have practised.

At the general election of 1886 he was returned without a contest for the Central Division of Birmingham, and on July 1st he delivered a speech to his constituents in recognition of the honour which had been conferred upon him. On this occasion he unsparingly condemned the Home Rule policy in the clear, resolute, convincing style with which the people were familiar. He spoke in the old tone and with as much power and lucidity as he had ever displayed. In a rather remarkable passage he somewhat haughtily repudiated the assumption that he was a mere follower of Mr. Gladstone. "During more than twenty years," he said, "I have acted in Parliamentary life alongside the action of the still eminent leader of the Liberal party. I have not been a follower of the leader of the Liberal party, I have been one of those happy to a large extent to work alongside of him."

The report of the speech appeared in the newspapers on the very morning of the first elections for the English boroughs, and although it would be absurd to impute the successes of the Unionists on that and succeeding days to its influence alone, there is good reason to believe that it powerfully contributed to those results. The eve of the general election found a great number of Liberals still wavering in their minds upon the question of the hour, but disposed to give their party the benefit of the doubt, and to rely, though with many qualms, upon the wisdom and statesmanship of their distinguished leader. Upon these the denunciation of the new policy from the lips of the great Tribune of the people fell with overwhelming effect, and the enormous and unprecedented abstention of Liberals from the polls marked the force of the blow.

With this striking proof of his prowess the old warrior retired from the fight. Once subsequently he delivered a speech of minor importance at a Liberal Unionist gathering, but he never again addressed a popular, political audience, nor was he ever heard in the House of Commons after 1885. His further contributions to political discussion were through the medium of letters addressed to correspondents and published in the newspapers, which are included in this volume.

The end was now near. In May, 1888, he caught a severe cold while travelling from London to Rochdale, and having incautiously ventured out before recovery, was thrown into a violent illness, which was complicated by a recurrence of the constitutional complaint to which he was subject. He partially recovered from the attack,. but had a serious relapse in November. He rallied again, and for a few months enjoyed tolerable health, but in March he grew worse, and it soon became evident that the symptoms were fatal. The last stage of his illness was peaceful and painless, and he passed quietly away at half-past eight in the morning of Wednesday, March 27, 1889. He was buried on the following Saturday in the graveyard attached to the Friends' Meeting House, Rochdale.

It is scarcely necessary to point out the singular unity and completeness of the life here briefly depicted in some of its phases. It was a beautiful, and for a politician a unique career, marked by simplicity, by freedom from self-seeking, and by fidelity to a lofty ideal of patriotism. It followed a plain, undeviating path, and found, unsought, fame and honour. Courage and manliness were amongst its prominent features. The caricatures which for many years represented Mr. Bright in the style of the stage Quaker, meek, effeminate and self-righteous, were puerile in conception and monstrously untrue. The essence of the principles of Quakerism was in the depths of his nature, and made him devout, earnest, truthful, sincere, but for the rest he was a typical Englishman, with a strong prejudice, it is true, against unnecessary war, but fit to be reckoned as a characteristic member of " an old and haughty nation, proud in arms." He was accustomed to give and take blows, and had essentially the warrior spirit. His eloquence was the natural outcome of his nature. Exercise and study had something to do with the form of it, but in his case it was emphatically true that the style was the man. His oratory had elements of grandeur because he was grand himself. When not eloquent his language had the charm of simplicity and clearness, and in those points his speeches will serve as models for imitation. None may catch his imperial tone, but it is within the power of diligence to copy him in his other less striking though still admirable qualities. The fact that while simple in his style, he was always choice and refined in the expression of his thoughts, whatever audience he was addressing, should be a lesson to that class of popular speakers which thinks to prevail greatly by means of slang, and seems to hold the opinion that the degradation of a language is a necessary step towards the better government of the country where it is spoken. Loving purity of speech himself, Mr. Bright paid his hearers the compliment of supposing that they had the same taste, and spoke accordingly. Yet his speeches were free from flattery to an extent probably never seen in the public utterances of any other popular speaker. Even upon occasions when to most men a little adulation would have seemed in place, the note that was heard from him was often that of caution, warning or admonition. His conduct was built upon the same lines. He was willing to serve, but not to fawn upon the democracy. Through all the dangers and temptations which beset a popular leader, he preserved his integrity, and it is because he was true to himself that he remains so stimulating an example to others. And that his example will be cherished we may be certain so long as greatness of character has the power to attract the admiration and regard of men.

FOREIGN POLICY, PEACE AND WAR.

THE PUBLIC LETTERS

OF THE

RIGHT HON. JOHN BRIGHT.

———•◆•———

MR. BRIGHT'S OPPOSITION TO LORD PALMERSTON'S FOREIGN POLICY.

ADDRESSED to one of Mr. Bright's constituents, who had written to him expressing his disapproval of his vote against Mr. Roebuck's resolution on the foreign policy of the Russell Government.

Mr. Roebuck's resolution was moved on the 24th of June, 1850. It had reference to the foreign policy of the Government, of which Lord John Russell was Premier and Lord Palmerston Foreign Secretary, and was as follows :—" That the principles which have hitherto regulated the foreign policy of her Majesty's Government are such as were required to preserve untarnished the honour and dignity of this country, and at all times best calculated to maintain peace between this country and the various nations of the world." Mr. Roebuck moved this resolution as a vote of confidence in the Government in reply to an adverse vote in the House of Lords, on the 17th of June, on Lord Stanley's motion, censuring the Government for undue interference in the affairs of Greece. The debate in the Commons lasted four nights. It was remarkable for the brilliant defence which Lord Palmerston made for his policy, and ended in a majority of forty-six for the Government. Among those who spoke in support of the Government was Mr. Alexander Cockburn, afterwards Lord Chief Justice, and the most notable speeches against the resolution were those of Mr. Gladstone and Sir Robert Peel. The latter spoke on this occasion for the last time in the House of Commons. On the following day occurred the lamentable accident which terminated his life.

London, July 3, 1850.

SIR,—I have your letter of yesterday, and regret to find that my vote on a recent occasion has not been such as to meet your views. I cannot, of course, expect on all occasions to find myself in harmony with all the electors of Manchester; but I am most anxious that my votes should be found in accordance with my honest convictions and with the sentiments I expressed in Manchester before and at my election.

The question at issue in the late debate was mainly this : Shall the foreign minister of this country be permitted to interfere in the affairs of other countries in cases where the direct interests of the country do not require it ? Shall he advise, and warn, and meddle in matters which concern only the domestic and internal affairs of other countries ? I say that such a policy necessarily leads to irritation, and to quarrels with other nations, and may lead even to war ; and that it involves the necessity of maintaining greater armaments, and heavier expenditure and taxation than would otherwise be required. It is a policy, therefore, which I cannot support under any pretence whatever. It is contrary to all I have ever declared in the Free Trade Hall, and in the many speeches in which I have touched upon this subject; and it is contrary to the principles on which I was elected.

With regard to the particular vote, I have only to say that, in giving it, I followed my own convictions, and acted upon opinions long since and constantly avowed.

I venture to think that no good could arise to Manchester from its representatives acting on any other principle ; and I would not for a moment sit in Parliament for Manchester, or for any other constituency, if it was to be understood that I am to forget my own character and long-held principles, and what I believe to be the true interests of the country, to abandon all these, and vote as the necessities of *party* may require, at the crack of the treasury whip.

You speak of an alliance with Lord Stanley, and seem to forget that the resolution on which I voted was moved by Mr. Roebuck, a friend of the present Government. It was not a resolution condemning the Government, moved by an opponent, but a resolution approving the Government policy, moved by one of their friends. I was asked to approve it ; honestly, I could not do it. You may say that I might have been absent ; but the question appeared to me of so grave a character, that I felt I could not shrink from deciding upon it. I took the only honest and manly course, and I am prepared to abide the consequences. To represent Manchester, on such terms as an independent mind can accept, is a position of honour which I hope I can fully appreciate ; but to sit in Parliament as the mere instrument of *party* is no object of hope and ambition with me.

It is possible my conduct may be blamed, and my motives called in question by some, but I will rely in confidence on all I have done in public life during the last ten years as my answer to those who suppose me careless of the interests of freedom, whether at home or abroad. I have the satisfaction, too, of having voted with my colleague in the representation of Manchester,[1] and of his judgment, and principles, and political honesty, I have the highest opinion. I voted, too, with Mr. Cobden, whom few men will suspect of a want of political sagacity, or a disregard of the true interests of liberty and of his country. I voted, too, with Mr. Hume,

---

[1] Mr. T. Milner Gibson.

of whose character and labours for the public welfare I need say nothing. I voted, too, with that statesman,[1] since then so suddenly taken from amongst us, whose good disposition towards the existing Government none could doubt, and whose sacrifices in recent years have been such as to make his name sacred among his countrymen, and if on this point there be any distinction among them, most of all to be revered by the inhabitants of your city.

I am fortified, then, by the association of men for whose judgment, and principles, and character, I have the most profound regard,—by the knowledge that I have acted in accordance with every pledge, and with every opinion expressed in times past to my constituents—and more than all by the consciousness that my vote has been recorded against a policy calculated to engender ill-will between nations, and therefore, in reality, hostile to the true interests of liberty, both at home and abroad.

I have not the pleasure of being personally acquainted with you, but as you are the only person, among all the constituency of Manchester, who has written to me in condemnation of my vote, I take the liberty of writing to you at some length, in justification of the course I have taken.   I am, very respectfully,

JOHN BRIGHT.

To Mr. John Heywood, Manchester.

THE WAR WITH RUSSIA.

Written to Mr. David Urquhart, and read at a public meeting convened by that gentleman at the Corn Exchange, Manchester, on April 19th, 1854, to discuss the question, " With whom are we at war ? " In opening the meeting Mr. Urquhart said it was his sense of alarm that had prompted his audacity in calling the meeting, and he thanked them for approving of that audacity by their attendance.

[1]   Robert Peel.   Died July 2, 1850.

Rochdale, April 18, 1854.

DEAR SIR,—I have to thank you for your note of the 15th inst., inviting me to a meeting to be held in Manchester to-morrow. I am not astounded at your audacity in calling the meeting ; on the contrary, I believe in your sincerity. I regard your resolution to appeal openly to your countrymen as courageous and proper. If I agreed with you on this Eastern question ; if we had one starting-point—if our sentiments in regard to it were in harmony—I should feel it my duty to be at your side. But the fact is that we differ widely on almost every point, except in the condemnation of this war ; and I do not think I should do anything for the cause of peace by appearing to go with you, when, in truth, there is little agreement between us. I believe the war to be altogether unnecessary, and that nothing can be said either for its justice or its expediency. I believe, further, that after having permitted the country by a series of blunders to drift into war, the ministers who have chiefly spoken on the subject, with the exception of Lord Aberdeen, have misrepresented the facts of the case, and have thereby misled public opinion.

With regard to the professed objects of the war, I believe them to be impossible of attainment, and that Russia, in her wildest dreams of ambition, never imagined so many calamities to Turkey as have been brought upon that devoted country, in a single year, by the friendship which our Government has professed towards her. It is a melancholy circumstance that the English public—not examining, and not reflecting, accepting, with a childlike simplicity, the declarations of statesmen, whose only present bond of union is a partnership in the guilt of this war, and relying on the assertions of a press more anxious for a trade in newspapers than for truth—should give their sanction to proceedings as much opposed to their own interests as they are to every principle of morality. Our countrymen fancy they are fighting for freedom because the

Russian Government is a despotism : they forget that the object of their solicitude is no less a despot ; that their chief ally but the other day overthrew a republic, and imprisoned or expatriated the members of a freely-elected parliament ; that they are alternately coaxing and bullying Austria, whose regard for freedom and justice Hungary and Italy can attest, to join them in this holy war, and that the chief result of their success, if success be possible, will be to perpetuate the domination of a handful of the followers of Mahomet over many millions of Christians throughout the provinces of European Turkey.

There was a time when it was fashionable to have sympathy for Greece. Now, Athens is to be occupied by English and French troops if a strong anti-Turkish feeling is manifested there. Five years ago English Liberals wished success to the insurrections in Italy and to the war for independence in Hungary ; now, the efforts of the Greeks for freedom are pronounced ill-timed, as if we, who are sending our fleets and armies to perfect their subjugation to the Turks, were the best judges of the moment when their fetters should be struck off. The people, or a portion of them, are drunk with a confused notion of fighting with Russia ; they confound the blowing up of ships and the slaughter of thousands with the cause of freedom, as if there were any connection in matters wholly apart.

I cannot hope to change this feeling, and fear you cannot. Time and experience alone will convince them, perhaps when too late, that a great national crime lies at their door. The time will come when history will record what English treasure was expended, and what English blood was shed, for an object in which England had no real interest, and for an object, too, which the very statesmen who advised it knew could not possibly succeed. I have spoken my sentiments on this painful question in the House of Commons—my constituents are generally acquainted with them—and therefore I feel it the less needful for me to take part in the meeting to-morrow.

I am, with great respect,
Yours, &c.,
JOHN BRIGHT.

David Urquhart, Esq., Manchester.

THE WAR WITH RUSSIA.

Mr. Absalom Watkin, of Manchester, having invited Mr. Bright to a meeting about to be held in that city in support of a " patriotic fund," and having stated that in his opinion the existing war was justified by the authority of *Vattel*, Mr. Bright replied in the subjoined letter.

Rhyl, North Wales, October 29, 1854.

MY DEAR SIR,—I think, on further consideration, you will perceive that the meeting on Thursday would be a most improper occasion for a discussion as to the justice of the war. Just or unjust, the war is a fact, and the men whose lives are miserably thrown away in it have clearly a claim upon the country, and especially upon those who, by the expression of opinions favourable to the war, have made themselves responsible for it. I cannot, therefore, for a moment, appear to discourage the liberality of those who believe the war to be just, and whose utmost generosity, in my opinion, will make but a wretched return for the ruin they have brought upon hundreds of families.

With regard to the war itself, I am not surprised at the difference between your opinion and mine, if you decide a question of this nature by an appeal to *Vattel*. The " law of nations " is not my law, and at best it is a code full of confusion and contradictions, having its foundation on custom, and not on a higher morality ; and on custom which has always been determined by the will of the strongest. It may be a question of some interest whether the first crusade was in accordance with the law and principles of *Vattel* ; but whether the first crusade was just, and whether the policy of the

crusade was a wise policy, is a totally different question.   I have no doubt that the American war was a
just war according to the principles laid down by writers
on the " law of nations," and yet no man in his senses
in this country will now say that the policy of
George III. toward the American colonies was a wise
policy, or that war a righteous war.   The French war,
too, was doubtless just according to the same authorities ; for there were fears and anticipated dangers to be
combated, and law and order to be sustained in
Europe ; and yet few intelligent men now believe the
French war to have been either necessary or just.   You
must excuse me if I refuse altogether to pin my faith
upon *Vattel*.   There have been writers on international
law, who have attempted to show that private assassina-
tion and the poisoning of wells were justifiable in war ;
and perhaps it would be difficult to demonstrate
wherein these horrors differ from some of the practices
which are now in vogue.   I will not ask you to mould
your opinion on these points by such writers, nor shall
I submit my judgment to that of *Vattel*.

The question of the present war is in two parts—first
was it necessary for us to interfere by arms in a dispute
between the Russians and the Turks ? and secondly,
having determined to interfere, under certain circumstances, why was not the whole question terminated
when Russia accepted the Vienna note ?   The seat of
war is 3000 miles away from us.   We had not been
attacked—not even insulted in any way.   Two independent Governments had a dispute, and we thrust ourselves into the quarrel.   That there was some ground for
the dispute is admitted by the four powers in the proposition of the Vienna note.   But for the English
Minister at Constantinople and the Cabinet at home the
dispute would have settled itself, and the last note of
Prince Menschikoff would have been accepted, and no
human being can point out any material difference
between that note and the Vienna note, afterwards
agreed upon and recommended by the Governments of

England, France, Austria, and Prussia. But our Government would not allow the dispute to be settled. Lord Stratford de Redcliffe held private interviews with the Sultan—did his utmost to alarm him—insisted on his rejection of all terms of accommodation with Russia, and promised him the armed assistance of England if war should arise.

The Turks rejected the Russian note, and the Russians crossed the Pruth, occupying the Principalities as a " material guarantee." I do not defend this act of Russia : it has always appeared to me impolitic and immoral ; but I think it likely it could be well defended out of *Vattel*, and it is at least as justifiable as the conduct of Lord John Russell and Lord Palmerston in 1850, when they sent ten or twelve ships of war to the Piræus, menacing the town with a bombardment if the dishonest pecuniary claim made by Don Pacifico were not at once satisfied.

But the passage of the Pruth was declared by England and France and Turkey not to be a *casus belli*. Negotiations were commenced at Vienna, and the celebrated Vienna note was drawn up. This note had its origin in Paris, was agreed to by the Conference at Vienna, ratified and approved by the Cabinets of Paris and London, and pronounced by all these authorities to be such as would satisfy the honour of Russia, and at the same time be compatible with the " independence and integrity " of Turkey and the honour of the Sultan. Russia accepted this note at once,—accepted it, I believe, by telegraph, even before the precise words of it had been received in St. Petersburg. Everybody thought the question now settled ; a Cabinet Minister assured me we should never hear another word about it ; "the whole thing is at an end," he said, and so it appeared for a moment. But the Turk refused the note which had been drawn up by his own arbitrators, and which Russia had accepted. And what did the Ministers say then, and what did their organ, the *Times*, say ? They said it was merely a difference about words; it was a pity the Turk made any difficulty, but it would soon be settled. But it was not settled, and why not? It is said that the Russian Government put an improper construction on the Vienna note. But it is unfortunate for those who say this, that the Turk placed precisely the same construction upon it; and further it is upon record that the French Government advised the Russian Government to accept it, on the ground that " its general sense differed in nothing from the sense of the proposition of Prince Menschikoff." It is, however, easy to see why the Russian Government should, when the Turks refused the award of their own arbitrators, re-state its original claim, that it might not be damaged by whatever concession it had made in accepting the award; and this is evidently the explanation of the document issued by Count Nesselrode, and about which so much has been said. But, after this, the Emperor of Russia spoke to Lord Westmoreland on the subject at Olmutz, and expressed his readiness to accept the Vienna note, with any clause which the Conference might add to it, explaining and restricting its meaning; and he urged that this should be done at once, as he was anxious that his troops should re-cross the Pruth before winter. It was in this very week that the Turks summoned a grand council, and, contrary to the advice of England and France, determined on a declaration of war.

Now, observe the course taken by our Government. They agreed to the Vienna note; not fewer than five members of this Cabinet have filled the office of Foreign Secretary, and therefore may be supposed capable of comprehending its meaning: it was a note drawn up by the friends of Turkey, and by arbitrators self-constituted on behalf of Turkey; they urged its acceptance on the Russian Government, and the Russian Government accepted it; there was then a dispute about its precise meaning, and Russia agreed and even proposed that the arbitrators at Vienna should amend it, by explaining it, and limiting its meaning, so that no question of its intention should henceforth exist.   But, the Turks having rejected it, our Government turned round, and declared the Vienna note, their own note, entirely inadmissible, and defended the conduct of the Turks in having rejected it.   The Turks declared war, against the advice of the English and French Governments—so, at least, it appears from the blue-books; but the moment war was declared by Turkey, our Government openly applauded it.   England, then, was committed to the war. She had promised armed assistance to Turkey—a country without government, and whose administration was at the mercy of contending factions; and incapable of fixing a policy for herself, she allowed herself to be dragged on by the current of events at Constantinople. She " drifted," as Lord Clarendon said, exactly describing his own position, into the war, apparently without rudder and without compass.

The whole policy of our Government in this matter is marked with an imbecility perhaps without example. I will not say they intended a war from the first, though there are not wanting many evidences that war was the object of at least a section of the Cabinet.   A distinguished member of the House of Commons said to a friend of mine, immediately after the accession of the present Government to office, " You have a war Ministry, and you will have a war."   But I leave this question to point out the disgraceful feebleness of the Cabinet, if I am to absolve them from the guilt of having sought occasion for war.   They promised the Turk armed assistance on conditions or without conditions.   They, in concert with France, Austria, and Prussia, took the original dispute out of the hands of Russia and Turkey, and formed themselves into a court of arbitration in the interests of Turkey; they made an award which they declared to be safe and honourable for both parties; this award was accepted by Russia and rejected by Turkey; and they then turned round upon their own award, and declared it to be " totally inadmissible," and made war upon the very country whose

Government, at their suggestion and urgent recommendation, had frankly accepted it. At this moment England is engaged in a murderous warfare with Russia, although the Russian Government accepted her own terms of peace, and has been willing to accept them in the sense of England's own interpretation of them ever since they were offered ; and at the same time England is allied with Turkey, whose Government rejected the award of England, and who entered into the war in opposition to the advice of England. Surely, when the Vienna note was accepted by Russia, the Turks should have been prevented from going to war, or should have been allowed to go to war at their own risk.

I have said nothing here of the fact that all these troubles have sprung out of the demands made by France upon the Turkish Government, and urged in language more insulting than any which has been shown to have been used by Prince Menschikoff. I have said nothing of the diplomatic war which has been raging for many years past in Constantinople, and in which England has been behind no other Power in attempting to subject the Porte to foreign influences. I have said nothing of the abundant evidences there is that we are not only at war with Russia, but with all the Christian population of the Turkish empire, and that we are building up our Eastern Policy on a false foundation—namely, on the perpetual maintenance of the most immoral and filthy of all despotisms over one of the fairest portions of the earth which it has desolated, and over a population it has degraded but has not been able to destroy. I have said nothing of the wretched delusion that we are fighting for civilization in supporting the Turk against the Russian and against the subject Christian population of Turkey. I have said nothing about our pretended sacrifices for freedom in this war, in which our great and now dominant ally is a monarch who, last in Europe, struck down a free constitution and dispersed by military violence a national Representative Assembly.

My doctrine would have been non-intervention in this case. The danger of the Russian power was a phantom; the necessity of permanently upholding the Mahometan rule in Europe is an absurdity. Our love for civilization, when we subject the Greeks and Christians to the Turks, is a sham; and our sacrifices for freedom, when working out the behests of the Emperor of the French and coaxing Austria to help us, is a pitiful imposture. The evils of non-intervention were remote and vague, and could neither be weighed nor described in any accurate terms. The good we can judge something of already, by estimating the cost of a contrary policy. And what is that cost ? War in the north and south of Europe, threatening to involve every country of Europe. Many, perhaps fifty millions sterling, in the course of expenditure by this country alone, to be raised from the taxes of a people whose extrication from ignorance and poverty can only be hoped for from the continuance of peace. The disturbance of trade throughout the world, the derangement of monetary affairs, and difficulties and ruin to thousands of families. Another year of high prices of food, notwithstanding a full harvest in England, chiefly because war interferes with imports, and we have declared our principal foreign food-growers to be our enemies. The loss of human life to an enormous extent. Many thousands of our own countrymen have already perished of pestilence and in the field; and hundreds, perhaps thousands, of English families will be plunged into sorrow, as a part of the penalty to be paid for the folly of the nation and its rulers.

When the time comes for the " inquisition for blood," who shall answer for these things ? You have read the tidings from the Crimea ; you have, perhaps, shuddered at the slaughter ; you remember the terrific picture—I speak not of the battle, and the charge, and the tumultuous excitement of the conflict, but of the field after the battle—Russians in their frenzy or their terror, shooting Englishmen who would have offered them water to quench their agony of thirst ; Englishmen, in crowds, rifling the pockets of the men they had slain or wounded, taking their few shillings or roubles, and discovering among the plunder of the stiffening corpses images of the "Virgin and the Child." You have read this, and your imagination has followed the fearful details. This is war,—every crime which human nature can commit or imagine, every horror it can perpetrate or suffer ; and this it is which our Christian Government recklessly plunges into, and which so many of our countrymen at this moment think it patriotic to applaud! You must excuse me if I cannot go with you. I will have no part in this terrible crime. My hands shall be unstained with the blood which is being shed. The necessity of maintaining themselves in office may influence an administration ; delusion may mislead a people ; *Vattel* may afford you a law and a defence ; but no respect for men who form a Government, no regard I have for "going with a stream," and no fear of being deemed wanting in patriotism, shall influence me in favour of a policy which, in my conscience, I believe to be as criminal before God as it is destructive of the true interest of my country.

I have only to ask you to forgive me for writing so long a letter. You have forced it from me, and I would not have written it did I not so much appreciate your sincerity and your good intentions towards me.

Believe me to be very sincerely yours,

JOHN BRIGHT.

Absalom Watkin, Esq., Manchester.

TURKISH RULE IN EUROPE.

Read at a meeting held in the Rochdale Town Hall, on the 4th of September, 1876, to protest against the Turkish atrocities in Bulgaria.

Inverinate House, Lochalsh, Scotland,
September 1, 1876.

DEAR SIR,—Your letter has just reached me late

this evening. I have no time to write anything for the meeting. The question is not one to be treated hastily, and I almost fear to say anything about it. More than twenty years ago I explained my views of the Eastern or Turkish difficulty. The Government of the day differed from me, as did the vast majority of the nation, and the war with Russia was entered upon. Some of its results we now know. It is said to have cost England 40,000 lives and 100,000,000*l.* of money. It cost all the parties to the war more than half a million of lives. Since then it has cost us 10,000,000*l.* a year in increased military expenses, or 200,000,000*l.* in all, and in loans to the Turkish Sultan it has probably cost England another 100,000,000*l.* sterling. The money account thus comes to four hundred millions (400,000,000*l.*) sterling; the loss of life was enormous. The policy of that day was popular, and the result is what I have described. I was assailed and insulted in and by almost all the newspapers in the kingdom because I condemned the war and the policy which led to it.

The present Government accepts the policy of the Government of 1854. It is now understood throughout the world to be the main if not the one supporter of the Turkish rule in Europe. If it had acted with Russia and the other Powers, it is almost certain the Servian war would not have taken place; and but for the confidence caused by the support of England, the Turks would not have dared to have committed the horrid crimes of which they have been guilty in Bulgaria. In these crimes there is nothing new. They are familiar to all who know anything of Turkish history. What is new is that the English Government cannot see the crimes till an English newspaper describes and denounces them; and that an English Minister, speaking for himself and his colleagues, treats them as of small account, and as the common incidents of insurrection and war. I am not sure that a Minister truly representing English opinion would not have withdrawn the Queen's Ambassador from Constantinople, and have

C

refused longer to receive a Minister from Turkey at the Queen's Court. The Government of England should clear itself of all partnership in the interest and the policy of the Turkish Government. It is a partnership in no degree necessary to our interests, and degrades us in the estimation of every Christian nation. Every town should have its meeting, and protest against our country being stained and disgraced by a participation in the policy and crimes of the Turkish Government. I do not think this can reach you before your meeting is held, but it is some relief to have written it.

I am, very truly yours,

JOHN BRIGHT.

Mr. R. Hope Brown, Rochdale.

THE EASTERN QUESTION.

Written in reply to a communication from a number of Bristol working men, asking Mr. Bright's opinion, whether it would be patriotic on their part to engage in a demonstration on behalf of the Christian population of Turkey.

Rochdale, November 25, 1876.

DEAR SIR,—You need not fear being unpatriotic in objecting to war for Turkey or against Russia on account of Turkey. I advise you to protest against war in connection with the Eastern Question, and in any interference on the part of England, to urge that we support the propositions offered by Russia as the best that can be done for the Christian populations of the Turkish provinces in Europe. You should condemn this foolish and wicked jealousy of Russia, which springs from ignorance among our people, and is fostered by writers in the press. It suits those who live out of the 25,000,000*l.* spent annually, and for the most part wasted on our monstrous armaments, to keep up this feeling, and the influential among them are constantly acting on the proprietors, editors, and writers of the London newspapers. Working men everywhere should resist this feeling and influence. It is their blood which is shed in war ; the destruction of capital and the injury to industry and trade fall upon them with crushing weight. But for the wicked wars of past times, which now we all see to have been wicked, the working classes of this country might have been surrounded by the comforts of home and blessed with education, as are the families of what is termed the middle classes in our English society. In every city and town the working men should denounce the idea of this threatened war, and they should condemn the minister whose loose and reckless tongue makes peace more difficult to secure. I hope Bristol will not be behind other towns in expression of opinion on this great question.

I am, very truly yours,

JOHN BRIGHT.

Mr. W. H. Godfrey, Pennywell Road, Bristol.

THE POLICY OF LORD BEACONSFIELD'S GOVERNMENT ON THE EASTERN QUESTION.

Read at a conference of representative working men, held on the 4th of May, 1878, in the Concert Hall, Liverpool, to consider the crisis as affecting labour.

At this time England seemed in imminent danger of being plunged into war with Russia. The vote of credit for 6,000,000*l*. had been given, the fleet had gone to the Dardanelles, the reserves had been called out, the Indian troops were on their way to Malta, and it seemed possible that at any moment hostilities might begin.

Rochdale, May 2, 1878.

DEAR SIR,—I cannot come to your meeting to-morrow, but I am glad to hear that you are to meet.

After my speech on Tuesday evening at Manchester, I have not much to write. I ask your friends to notice three points, to two of which I referred at Manchester. I charge the Government with constant deception practised on the House of Commons and the country, by professions of a wish for peace whilst engaged in acts which are distinctly provocative of war. I charge them, further, with constantly interposing obstacles in the way of any arrangement with Russia or the other European Powers for the settlement of the Eastern Question on any basis favourable to the freedom of the oppressed Christian population of the Turkish provinces in Europe.

There is a third charge which may be brought against them, as seen in the action of their party organization in London and in many of the large towns in England. Through that party organization they attempt to suppress the expression of opinion of thoughtful and peaceful citizens, through the ordinary means of public meetings, by an exhibition of violence and rowdyism from which, for many years past, the country has happily been free; and they are willing to accept this violence and riot as the voice of the English people.

This Government is no friend to freedom at home or to peace abroad; and, to add to its other offences, it now introduces into its contemplated European warfare an armed force of Mahometans from India, whose numbers have not been voted by Parliament, and the cost of whose maintenance and employment has not been given in any Parliamentary estimate.

The people of England will begin to ask themselves if they have gone back to the times of Charles I., and if the prevalent idea of English freedom and of constitutional principles and practice is only a dream. I wish I could speak to every working man in the kingdom, and to all the members of your trade societies. I would urge them to meet and speak at this moment of supreme interest, it may be of supreme peril. The country and its dearest interests are in evil hands, and it is possible for a Cabinet by the same policy to betray both crown and people.

I am, very respectfully yours,
JOHN BRIGHT.

Mr. J. W. Julian, Liverpool.

ENGLAND AND RUSSIA.

Read at a Conference of Delegates from various working men's associations, held at the St. James's Hall, Leeds, on the 4th of May, 1878, to take into consideration the subject of peace or war, and to express the opinions of working men on that question.

May, 1878.

DEAR SIR,—If the trades' societies would speak out for peace, there would be no war. There are men and classes to whom war is sometimes gain ; to the working men it is only loss. Hitherto they have had little voice in determining whether war should be entered into. They have had to bear the sufferings inseparable from it, and their blood has been mainly shed at the bidding of monarchs and statesmen. Now, in a question of this kind the voice of the working classes is powerful, if not omnipotent ; and if the sufferings of war are again to be endured, their silence at this supreme moment would throw no light responsibility upon them. I would advise you to take some means whereby the famous and unanswerable speech of Lord Derby shall be widely circulated among the householders and electors in the districts represented by the members of your Conference. Lord Derby's name and character, his late high position and great office in the Government, and his perfect knowledge of the whole question now before the country, will give immense force to his arguments and opinions.

Wishing you all success in your attempt to defeat the war policy of the Government,

I remain, &c.,

JOHN BRIGHT.

ENGLAND AND RUSSIA.

The following letter was written to a Cheltenham gentleman :—

One Ash, Rochdale, October 26, 1886.

DEAR SIR,—I thank you for your friendly letter, and for your good wishes. As to foreign affairs, I believe all our fears and jealousy of Russia are misplaced. Russia has not made war upon us. England made the Crimean War, which cost Russia some hundreds of thousands of lives. Russia, in my opinion, has no dream, even, of invading India ; and our fear of her arises from our position as conquerors in our Indian empire. We seize and annex Burmah, and we menace Russia if she approaches Afghanistan. We deny Russia the right of entering the Mediterranean from the Black Sea, and we treat her as an enemy, to be always suspected and guarded against. That Russia should in some degree retaliate is not unlikely or unnatural. There is no other country in Europe that would be more friendly with us than Russia would be if England would be friendly with Russia. These views are not easily accepted by those who defended the Crimean War, but something has been learned from that great crime and that great calamity, and I hope no Minister will again be able to drag us into another contest. I wish millions of our people would consider this great question, it might save much to them and their children. Again thanking you for your kind letter,

I am, very respectfully yours,

JOHN BRIGHT.

THE WAR IN EGYPT.

In September, 1882, the Rev. Thomas Rippon, of Warrington, in a letter to Mr. Bright, discussed the question of war in the abstract, holding that " peace at any price " was an untenable position, and that the Egyptian war seemed a righteous one from that standpoint. He reminded Mr. Bright of the prevailing opinion of his countrymen that his was a policy of " peace at any price," without reserve, and that it was that alone which led him to give up office. He also called his attention to a letter which appeared in the previous week's *Spectator*, in which the writer said "Mr. Bright gave up office and association with an admired leader, solely because he believed the war to be a departure from national morality, and therefore from the principles of the Liberal party;" together with the editor's note thereon, that "Mr. Bright did not oppose the Egyptian war in particular, but all wars."

Mr. Bright replied to the letter as follows:—

Cassencary, Creetown, N.B.,
September 25, 1882.

DEAR SIR,—The *Spectator* and other supporters of this war answer me by saying that I oppose the war because I condemn all war. The same thing was said during the Crimean war.

I have not opposed any war on the ground that all war is unlawful and immoral. I have never expressed such an opinion. I have discussed these questions of war, Chinese, Crimean, Afghan, Zulu, Egyptian, on grounds common to and admitted by all thoughtful men, and have condemned them with arguments which I believe have never been answered.

I will not discuss the abstract question. I shall be content when we reach the point at which all Christian men will condemn war when it is unnecessary, unjust, and leading to no useful or good result. We are far from that point now, but we make some way towards it.

But of this war I may say this, that it has no better justification than other wars which have gone before it, and that doubtless when the blood is shed, and the cost paid, and the results seen and weighed, we shall be generally of that opinion.

Perhaps the bondholders, and those who have made money by it, and those who have got promotion and titles and pensions, will defend it, but thoughtful and Christian men will condemn it.

I am, &c.,
JOHN BRIGHT.

Rev. Thomas Rippon, Warrington.

PEACE AND WAR.

Read at a " Peace Conference of Christians," held at Philadelphia in 1876.

Rochdale, ninth month 22, 1876.

DEAR FRIEND DANIEL HILL,—I cannot come to your conference, and I do not feel that I can write anything that will be of service.

There seems nothing cheerful to write on the subject of peace or war, except this—that the influences in favour of peace are now becoming so strong that with millions of men in arms in Europe, still peace is the rule ; and nations are not so much in the hands of monarchs and ministers as they have been in past times.

When the boundaries of nations and races are well adjusted, and when the hindrance to trade created by hostile tariffs is removed, I think the time will have come when the intelligence and Christian feeling and the true interests of nations will overcome the motives and passions which lead to war.

We may hope that in Europe there will arise a monarch or a statesman of sufficient authority and influence to lead his own country, and to induce other countries, to unite in some resolute effort for a great reduction of armaments.

We may hope, too, that as duelling is gradually being condemned for the adjustment of differences between private persons, so war may be condemned as a practice fitted only for savage nations, and wholly disgraceful and infamous when waged by nations pretending to civilization and professing the religion of the Prince of Peace.

I wish your conference a good result, although I am not able to take any part in it.

I am, sincerely thy friend,
JOHN BRIGHT.

WAR.

In the autumn of 1879, Mr. Alexander H. Urquhart, of Manchester, wrote to Mr. Bright, asking his opinion on war, and particularly whether he would do away with war and armies altogether. Mr. Bright wrote in reply as follows :—

One Ash, Rochdale, August 18, 1879.

DEAR SIR,—I have not time to write fully upon the question. It is one on which men should make up their minds as to their own personal duty. So far men have defended war as if it were a natural condition of things which must always continue. It might be true that war could not always be avoided, and that in some cases it might be justifiable, and yet, granting this, it might be shown that nineteen out of every twenty wars which might have been waged ought to have been avoided, and were criminal in the highest degree. I believe that all our wars since the time and accession of William III. might have been avoided on principles which do not require the absolute condemnation of war in every possible case that may be suggested or imagined. We need not discuss the question as you put it. We shall change the policy and the aspect of our country and of the world, if we leave the demon of war to the cases in which there seems to Christian and rational men no escape from the miseries he inflicts upon mankind. I would advise you not to trouble yourself with the abstract question. The practical question is the one which presses, and when we have settled that, there will remain very little of the mischief to contend about or to get rid of. If you wish to know the best argument against war, I would recommend you to read Jonathan Dymond's "Essays on the Principles of Morality," or his "Essay on War." You may obtain them from Mr. Harris, 5, Bishopsgate Street Without, London.

I am, yours, &c.,

JOHN BRIGHT.

INTERNATIONAL ARBITRATION.

The following letter was addressed to Mr. William Jones, Secretary of the London Peace Society :—

London, August 30, 1887.

DEAR FRIEND WILLIAM JONES,—I am glad to hear that you are going to the United States on what I may term a peace mission. You will find many friends of peace on the other side of the Atlantic—more perhaps than you will leave on this side, for our people have seen nothing of war among them during this century; they know something of taxes the result of war, but they have seen nothing of the bloodshed in war.

There is talk of a permanent Arbitration Treaty between England and the United States ; the project is a reasonable one, and discussion on both sides may bring it about.

I think if the Government of the States were willing, and were in any way to signify their willingness, to become a party to such a treaty, there is a force of good men with us to induce our Government to consent to it. If this can be done, it will be a grand step forward in the world's march, and would be followed, at some not distant time, by some other nations willing to escape from the sore burden of these military armaments.

You will doubtless see many intelligent and leading men in the States, and will learn something of their feelings on this matter. They may receive you as a trustworthy representative of the moral and peace-loving people in England, and I hope your interview may do something in the direction that you and I so greatly desire.

I find that nearly 200 members of our House of Commons are addressing a memorial to the Government at Washington to suggest an arbitration treaty such as I have decided ; more, far more I hope, than this number will be ready to urge the acceptance of such a treaty upon our Government if the action at Washington should meet with any favour and success.

England and the States will remain two nations, but I would have them always regarded by themselves as one people.

An Arbitration Treaty, honestly made and adhered to, would tend much to this blessed result.

I wish you a pleasant voyage and some good results of your labours.

I am, always, sincerely yours,

JOHN BRIGHT.

Mr. William Jones, 47, New Broad Street, London.

FREE TRADE

THE FRENCH COMMERCIAL TREATY OF
1872.

Written in reply to a letter from Mr. Nathaniel Poole, of Coventry, who enclosed a resolution passed at a public meeting at Coventry, and who said he was directed to ask whether there was any hope of the artisans of Coventry obtaining fair play in the fierce race of competition between France and England. If her Majesty's Ministers, he said, knew or considered "the vast amount of misery and wretchedness these continued one-sided and anti-free-trade treaties inflicted upon seven thousand industrious men and women in Coventry," he thought they would hesitate before they brought so great an evil upon them.

Llandudno, November 22, 1872.

SIR,—It is to be regretted that you and your friends should distress yourselves about the new treaty, and prefer, as I conclude you would prefer, to have no treaty at all. If there were no treaty, the French Government would not reduce their import duties, some of them they would probably raise, and the English Government would not impose new or higher duties on importations from France. The treaty, therefore, which fixes the limit of the French tariff, but which does not prevent its amendment in the direction of lower duties, and which in no degree affects the duties we impose on foreign goods, can inflict no injury on Coventry or on any other manufacturing town in the kingdom. The treaty may not be a wise treaty on the part of France, but it is impossible that it should be injurious to England, for under its provisions England does not bind herself to do anything which she would not willingly and wisely do if the treaty were not in existence. If, under the treaty, the French tariff is in any degree lower than it would be without the treaty, then by so much are we the gainers by it.

Our Government would have been delighted to have signed a treaty under which the French tariff would have been as liberal and as sensible as our own, but it can only act for England, and not for France. If I am not mistaken, you were against the treaty of 1860, and on the same grounds, doubtless, you are against the renewed treaty of 1872. You think the special interests of Coventry should have been cared for at the expense of the general population of the kingdom. But Lord Granville is not the Minister for Coventry only, but for the United Kingdom, and he and his colleagues must act for the general good, and not for any special interest or trade which clamours for protection at his hands.

In the protest you have sent me, you say that " while the French were fighting in 1871, the trade of Coventry was exceptionally good," that is, when you had no competition your trade was very good ; and what you want now is, that our tariff should prevent foreign competition with you in this market, and give you the prosperity at the cost of your customers, which you had last year, caused by the calamities of the French. I am sorry, if not surprised, that there are any working men in Coventry who still think duties for protection are just and good for English industry after the experience of the last twenty-five years. Surely it is something of a discredit to Coventry that, almost alone among all the towns of the United Kingdom, she should ask the Government to place her upon that " outdoor relief " which is intended by the system of special duties for the protection of special trades. I do not believe the workmen of Coventry are less able to fight the battle of competition than are the workmen of Bradford, or

Birmingham, or Rochdale ; and when the cry of protection is so thoroughly worn out in your ancient city that it can no longer serve a local political purpose, I suspect we shall hear no more of it even from you.

I am sorry to trouble you with so long a reply. In future I must ask you to forgive me if I am silent.

I am, respectfully yours, ·

JOHN BRIGHT.

Mr. Nathaniel Poole.

FREE TRADE AND THE PRICE OF FOOD.

At a ward meeting in Leeds in October, 1874, a Conservative speaker said "the people were no better off now relative to the price of bread than they were before the repeal of the Corn Laws and other protective laws." This statement was forwarded to Mr. Bright, and elicted the following reply :—

Corriebruck House, Pitlochry,
October 12, 1874.

DEAR SIR,—Your letter has been sent on to me, and I have only time to acknowledge the receipt of it. Your opponent must be a man profoundly ignorant or strangely perverse, or he would have a different opinion of the effects of Free Trade in corn. He, perhaps, does not know that last year 12,000,000 quarters of wheat were imported, worth in this market last year nearly 40,000,000*l.* sterling, and that great quantities of other grain were also imported ; that not less than 500,000 tons of potatoes, with great quantities of cattle, and meat, and cheese, and butter were imported ; that, in fact, 80,000,000*l.* sterling in value were imported, nearly all of which it was the object of the Corn Law and other protective laws to exclude from the country. More than half the working men of England, with their families, are fed on bread which comes from abroad, and it is obvious that the continuance of the protective system as applied to agriculture would have spread famine among

D

the people, and would have plunged the nation into anarchy.

I have not time to write more to you, and I feel certain that to add to what I have said would be of no use to your opponent, as he must be very ignorant, and I fear quite unable to reason on a matter of this nature. If you turn to the newspapers from 1839 to 1846, or to the debates in Hansard, you may obtain all the facts and arguments you require.

I am, respectfully yours,
JOHN BRIGHT.

A PROTECTIVE POLICY IN THE ENGLISH COLONIES.

At a banquet given at Melbourne in June, 1877, in honour of Mr. John Young, the Cnnadian representative at the Industrial Exhibition held at Sydney in that year, some of the speeches turned on the subject of Free Trade, and Sir Charles Gavan Duffy, Speaker of the Victoria Legislative Assembly, said that seeing that the tendency of opinion in that colony was in favour of Protection of some sort, he consulted three eminent gentlemen in England—John Bright, John Stuart Mill, and Thomas Carlyle. He said to John Bright : " All my life will be spent in Australia. I am a Free Trader, as you know. They are going to have a protective policy there. Am I to retire therefore from public life ? " John Bright, a practical man, said, " If there are particular industries that can flourish in that country, and if it is the determination of the people to encourage them, I would grant bonuses on certain industries liberally, in order to promote them ; or I would come to an agreement with the Protectionists to protect a certain number of articles for a certain number of years, and let them try their experiment."

Mr. A. Langton, of Melbourne, a Free Trader, who was present at the banquet, wrote to Mr. T. B. Potter,

M.P., and asked him to call Mr. Bright's attention to these remarks, and in reply to the letter which was sent him, Mr. Bright wrote as follows :—

Rochdale, July 31, 1877.

DEAR MR. POTTER,—I thank you for sending me Mr. Langton's letter of the 10th of June, from Melbourne. By the same mail I have three other letters on the same subject on which Mr. Langton has written to you: one from the Secretary of the Free Trade League of Victoria; one from Sir Charles Gavan Duffy; and one written at Suez by Mr. John Young, of Montreal, to whom the dinner at Melbourne was given.

I need not tell you that I am surprised and amused at the stir which so small a matter has caused among our friends on the other side of the globe.

I recollect meeting Sir Charles Gavan Duffy on his visit to this country ; but I have not the least recollection that we had any conversation on the subject of Protection, or on the policy of the province of Victoria on that question. If any such conversation occurred, I can say with confidence that my views have been entirely misunderstood and misrepresented by Sir Charles. The words he put into my mouth are much like in meaning what I think I have seen in some of the writings of Mr. John Stuart Mill, and it may be that Sir Charles may have inadvertently attributed to me what he has heard from Mr. Mill, or read in some of his works.

If a Government voted a sum of money to support a steamboat enterprise which was deemed of great service to the country, but which, from its novelty, or its risk, private capitalists would not undertake, I should say that in doing this no sound principle would be broken, and that the public interest might possibly be wisely served. So, if a Government thought that if a new culture might be introduced into the country, such as the grape or tea, it might appropriate a sum of money to make that experiment, leaving its future progress or fate entirely to the industry and disposition of the people. But to enact a tariff imposing heavy duties on most important articles of import, to establish an oppressive and costly system of custom-houses, to build up special interests before their time, or industries which might never thrive in the free air of competition, at the expense of taxation upon the whole people, levied partly at the custom-houses, and partly by the high prices which are sought to be obtained on the home-made and protected article, is a policy so unsound and so injurious that I am greatly surprised that any one in the least acquainted with me or with my life should have supposed it possible that I should have given it my support.

Englishmen form colonies at a distance from the mother country. They throw off many of the superstitions which are still to a large extent cherished in England. In respect of Protection by means of a prohibitive or restrictive tariff, the colony of Victoria clings to a superstition of error which we in England have abandoned. Our experience is conclusive as to the wisdom of our policy. Victoria is young, and thinks she knows more and better than we know. But when she finds herself, not at the head, but at the tail of the great Australian communities as to her success and the growth of wealth, she may discover that industry has no greater enemy than a protective or restrictive tariff.

If you will kindly send this letter to your correspondent, Mr. Langton, it will not be necessary for me to write to Sir Charles Duffy or to the Secretary of the Free Trade League of Victoria.

Believe me, &c.,
JOHN BRIGHT.

FREE TRADE AND ARMAMENTS.

Written in reply to a letter suggesting that Mr. Bright should assist in the formation of an International Free Trade League.

Rochdale, March 18, 1878.

DEAR SIR,—I thank you for your letter. You greatly over-estimate the force of any influence I may possess. The formation of an International Free Trade League is a grand idea, which some of our Free Trade friends have often suggested ; but the difficulty is great, if not insuperable. The difference of language is in itself one great difficulty, and the jealousy between nations is another. For myself I am too far on in life to be able to undertake any great work of this kind. My lamented friend, Mr. Cobden, did something towards it, or attempted something ; but wars and national jealousies have barred the way against the growth of his beneficent ideas. Just now Europe is disturbed, the chief disturber being our own Government. The war between Russia and Turkey is over, and England is the Power which threatens to reopen the contest on a wider field. So long as our people are so ignorant as to their true interests, and so long as a war party of any considerable influence exists among us, I fear we shall do little to encourage other nations to enter the Free Trade path. To abolish tariffs is the only way which leads to the abolition of great armies. Free Trade between nations would give the nations peace ; but war, anxieties, and menaced conflicts make it impossible for the nations calmly to consider their true interests. If any opportunity offers, I hope I shall be ready to do anything in my power in furtherance of the policy you suggest.

I am, yours,

JOHN BRIGHT.

Mr. J. R. Morrison, Hampstead.

FREE TRADE AND WAR.

Written in answer to an invitation to attend the Peace Congress held in September, 1878, at Savona. The Advocate, Pietro Sbarbaro, to whom the letter was written, was Professor of Law in the University of Macerata, and prime mover in the commemoration of

Alberigo Gentili, who from his chair in Oxford first propounded the doctrine of international arbitration.

Rochdale, September 23, 1878.

DEAR SIR,—I cannot write to you at any length on the interesting subject of which you have spoken to me, and I fear my short letter will not reach you in time for your Peace Congress.

The situation of Europe at this moment is deplorable ; its nations are groaning under the weight of enormous armies and burdensome taxation. They are at the same time disjoined in interests and sentiments by tariffs, which form an insurmountable barrier between the peoples of the different States, and prevent that reciprocity of interests which would make it impossible for their statesmen to drag them into war.

How can wars be avoided and standing armies dissolved ? This is the great question for Europe, and for every nation of Europe. In my own view the directest way—I was going to say the only way—to this great end lies in Free trade between the peoples of Europe. If tariffs were abolished, or even if they were made very moderate, the nations would trade freely with each other, their commerce would increase enormously, and they would bit by bit become like one grand nation, their commercial interests would multiply on such a scale, and their natural knowledge and intercourse would become so intimate, that the ambition of monarchs and of statesmen would be impotent to drive them to war.

The treaty between France and England, negotiated eighteen years ago by Mr. Cobden, has entirely changed the sentiments of the two nations to each other, and if the tariff of France were as free as that of England, the two States would, through their interests, become as one. If the tariffs of Europe were abolished, Europe would not fear war, and her armies would in a short time be reduced.

Monopoly in commerce, high tariffs, protection of the

trading classes at the expense of society and the consumers, such are the allies of great armies and the grand obstacle to a general and lasting peace in Europe. Destroy the tariffs, or reduce them greatly, and standing armies will be dissolved, for then almost every pretext on which they are kept up will have disappeared.

For the disbanding of great armies and the promotion of peace I rely on the abolition of tariffs, and on the brotherhood of the nations resulting from free trade in the products of industry.

Let us try to impress on public opinion the conviction that the protectionist system, the system of high tariffs, and the monopoly which some classes are eager to keep, to the detriment of the people, are the principal cause and the most powerful support of standing armies and of frequent wars. If this idea could prevail in Europe, then indeed should we be able to welcome the dawn of that day in which armies will no longer be considered necessary, and high tariffs a crime against the interests and the happiness of the people.

I am, with great respect, yours, &c.,

JOHN BRIGHT.

To Professor Pietro Sbarbaro, Bologna.

PROTECTION IN THE UNITED STATES.

One Ash, Rochdale, January 21, 1879.

MY DEAR MR. FIELD,—I never write for reviews or any other periodicals. It is so long since I have written, that my hand has lost its cunning, if it ever had it. I do not think anything an Englishman could say would have any effect upon an American protectionist. The man who possesses a monopoly by which he thinks he gains is not open to argument. It was so in this country forty years ago, and it is so with you now. It is strange that a people who put down slavery at an immense sacrifice are not able to suppress monopoly, which is but a milder form of the same evil. Under slavery the man was seized, and his labour was stolen from him, and the profit of it enjoyed by his master and owner. Under protection the man is apparently free, but he is denied the right to exchange the produce of his labour except with his countrymen, who offer him much less for it than the foreigner would give. Some portion of his labour is thus confiscated. In our protection days our weavers and artisans could not exchange with American flour. They exchanged with an English farmer, who gave them sometimes only half the quantity the American would have given them. Now, your farmer is forbidden to trade with the Englishman, and must give to an American double the quantity of grain and flour for many articles he is constantly requiring that he would give if your laws did not forbid his trade with England.

A country may have democratic institutions, its government may be republican, and based on a wide suffrage, and yet there may be no freedom to men for that which is the source of life and comfort. If a man's labour is not free, if its exchange is not free, the man is not free. And whether the law which enacts this restriction be the offspring of republican or autocratic government and power, it is equally evil, and to be condemned and withstood by all who love freedom and understand what it is.

Nations learn slowly—but they do learn ; and therefore I do not doubt that the time will come when trade will be as free as the winds, and when freedom and industry will do much to put down great armies and the peril and suffering of war. But I am writing you almost an article instead of a short note—as if I would teach you, which would be an impertinence. If you could teach your farmers, and ask the " solid South " to help them and you, you might soon succeed.

Believe me, always sincerely your friend,

JOHN BRIGHT.

Cyrus W. Field, Esq., New York.

THE CONDITION OF ENGLAND UNDER FREE TRADE.

Written to Mr. Abraham Sharp, who was chairman of a meeting of working men held at Bradford in March, 1879, in favour of Free Trade.

132, Piccadilly, April 1, 1879.

DEAR SIR,—I thank you for your note and the newspaper. The meeting seems to have been a very good one, but the report of the speeches is not good. The "reciprocity" notion is exactly adapted to catch the considerable class of simpletons who have no memory and no logic. But for this lack of memory and of reasoning power they would know that the "distress" in this country was ten times greater in the period from 1839 to 1842 than it has been from 1877 to the present time, or than it is at this moment, although in the former period we had protection, as much as Parliament and the law could give. They would know, also, that in the United States, the most "protected" nation in the world, the distress during the last five years has been more prolonged, more widely spread, and far more intense than in this country. If your "reciprocity" neighbours could reason, surely these facts would help to convince them of the silliness of their views.

You wish to learn something of the distress of the former period. I recommend you to read a volume written lately by my friend, Henry Ashworth, of Bolton. Its title is "Cobden and the League." Any bookseller will get it for you. If England could be reduced this year to the condition it was in after the bad harvests from 1839 to 1842, we should have insurrection and anarchy all over the country, and the simpletons who are writing pamphlets and delivering lectures in favour of protection would be flying for their lives. If your working men ask for protection and reciprocity after what they have seen and known during the past thirty years, it is clear that neither facts nor arguments nor experience can be of any service to them. I am not afraid that this heresy and lunacy will make much way amongst them.

I am, very respectfully yours,

JOHN BRIGHT.

Mr. Abraham Sharp.

FREE TRADE AND THE DEPRESSION IN TRADE IN 1879.

Addressed in May, 1879, to the editor of the *North American Review*, who had asked his opinion as to the nature and extent of the so-called movement in favour of Protection in England.

May, 1879.

MY DEAR SIR,—I have no difficulty in replying to your letter of the 31st ultimo. Do not think there is any chance of a return in this country to the doctrines of protection. We export everything but agricultural produce. To protect our manufactures is manifestly impossible. From another cause the protection of our land produce is not more possible. Half our population exists on imported food. To limit this import by customs duties in order to raise the price of home-grown food is a proposition that cannot be entertained for a moment. Such a scheme offered to Parliament and the country would destroy any Government and any party.

We are passing through a time of commercial depression. Its causes are apparent to those who examine and consider the facts of recent and past years ; but in times of trouble ignorant men seize upon unlikely and impossible propositions and schemes for relief. There is no special remedy for this malady. Time, patience, the working of natural laws, the avoidance and cessation of the half-madness of the past, and a general economy will bring about a cure, not without some or much suffering, but without failure. We adopted Free Trade in the year 1846, but our landowners and farmers and multitudes of our people did not comprehend the principles we taught, and a new generation is on the stage, ill acquainted even with the facts of forty years ago. There has been no great distress since our corn law was abolished, and now when trouble has come for a time, some of the sufferers, and some of the quack doctors, who are always ready to perscribe for the public, cry out for protection as if we had never tried it before, and as if it had been found a specific in other countries. There is no danger of our going back to protection. The present trouble will pass away. It has been aggravated by the evil policy of our Government, and that also will pass away, and the simpletons who are looking for relief to an exploded doctrine and practice will relapse into that silent obscurity which becomes them.

It is a grief to me that your people do not yet see their way to a moderate tariff. They are doing wonders unequalled in the world's history in paying off your national debt. A moderate tariff, I should think, would give you a better revenue, and by degrees you might approach a more civilized system. What can be more strange than for your great, free country to build barriers against that commerce which is everywhere the handmaid of freedom and of civilization?

I should despair of the prospects of mankind if I did not believe that before long the intelligence of your people would revolt against the barbarism of your tariff. It seems now your one great humiliation. The world looks to you for example in all forms of freedom. As to commerce, the great civilizer, shall it look in vain?

Believe me, very sincerely yours,

JOHN BRIGHT.

THE DEPRESSION IN TRADE IN 1879 AND ITS CAUSES.

Written in reply to a letter asking Mr. Bright to support a motion in the House of Commons for an inquiry into the causes of the depression in trade.

132, Piccadilly, London,
June 26, 1879.

DEAR SIR,—Mr. Chaplin is about to move for an inquiry by Royal Commission into the existing agricultural distress, and I do not see how or why such an
inquiry should be granted without including in it a
more general inquiry as to the present depression in
other branches of industry. Some people still have
faith in Parliamentary Committees and Royal Commis-
sions on matters of this kind; I confess that I have
none.

A few years ago we had a panic about the scarcity
and price of coal, and a Parliamentary Committee sat
upon it and about it. The Committee led to nothing.
More recently we had a Committee on the Fall in the
Value of Silver, and the inquiry led to nothing. Just
now we have a Committee on Co-operative Stores, and
it will lead to nothing, except to show generally the
uselessness of such inquiries. If Mr. Chaplin gets his
Committee or Commission it will lead to nothing,
except to prove that, with free imports of corn, bad
harvests are bad for farmers, and that the omnipotence
of Parliament fails when it seeks to control the seasons;
and that, therefore, Parliament cannot step in by
legislation materially to mitigate the admitted sufferings
of the farmers.

As to the present depression of trade, we owe some
of it to the bad harvests, which have impoverished
many farmers, who are not an inconsiderable portion of
our home-trade customers; we owe much of it to
famines in India and China, and to the commercial and
manufacturing distress which has prevailed in almost
every country, and not least in those countries which
have sought to secure themselves by high protective
duties. If our harvest this year is unfavourable, I fear
the recovery we all hope for will be delayed; if it is
abundant, which seems not probable, we shall soon see,
not symptoms only, but proofs of a revival.

In the United States, with a great harvest last year,

trade is reviving. We followed them in their depression, but not to so deep a depth, and we shall follow them in their recovery. These great changes are not in the power of Congresses or Parliaments; they are in the ordering of nature, and we must accept them, always endeavouring not to aggravate them by our own follies.

There is one great consolation in our present condition; the food of our people is cheap. But for the free imports the price of bread would be more than double, the price of sugar would be three times its present price, the price of cheese and bacon would be double, or nearly so, and of the price of labour it may be said that it would be much lessened by a greater prostration of every industry in the country not immediately connected with the growth of food. The freedom of our imports will enable us to pass through the present time of depression with less suffering than at any former period of disastrous seasons.

As to Parliament and its inquiries, I have seen much of it and of them. If Parliament would keep out of foreign broils; if it would conduct the government of the country at an expenditure of sixty millions instead of eighty millions in the year; if it would devote its time and labours to questions of home interest rather than to those which involve the sacrifice of the blood and treasure of our people in remote lands, we might have hope and faith that Parliament could serve the nation in times of depression, and we should find that such times of suffering would visit us more rarely.

If an inquiry, such as you refer to, is granted, I hope it may do some good, if it only shows once more how useless such inquiries are. I need not tell you that the friends of Free Trade can have no objection to Commission or Committee if the Government wishes to appoint one.   I am, respectfully yours,

JOHN BRIGHT.

Mr. Frederick Blood,
32, Charlotte Street, Birmingham.

FREE TRADE—ITS PROGRESS AND RESULTS.

Mr. Russell, a working man, residing in Glasgow, who described himself as having been an enthusiastic member of the Anti-Corn-Law League, wrote to Mr. Bright in July, 1879, asking his opinion as to the existing wide-spread depression in trade. Mr. Russell said there could be no doubt about the excellence of the principle of Free Trade abstractedly considered, but, he added, the good effects of the principle in a commercial point of view could only be felt when other nations met us in the same spirit.

Mr. Bright, in reply, wrote :—

One Ash, Rochdale, August 1, 1879.

DEAR SIR,—There are two passages in your letter that I must dispute. You speak of depressed trade from 1839 to 1843 as being nothing like that which now exists.   If you will read Mr. Ashworth's book, " Cobden and the League," you will learn that the distress now is not to be compared with that of the former period. This I can confidently assert from my own knowledge, but Mr. Ashworth gives abundant proofs of it.

You say that in our agitation, now nearly forty years ago, we urged that a necessary consequence of Corn Law repeal would be that "war would cease, and that there would be no more commercial and agricultural depression."

We never said this. We said that Free Trade greatly tends to promote peace between nations, and that commercial depression caused by the Corn Law on the occasion of every bad harvest would be prevented. Before 1846, and during the thirty years of Corn Law, there were five or six parliamentary committees on agricultural distress ; during more than thirty years of free imports of corn, until this session, there has been no such committee appointed or asked for ; and now all sensible men know that the commission to be appointed is a mere delusion held out to cajole the farmers.

War has not ceased. *We* made the Russian war in 1854, and since then the armaments of Europe have much more than doubled. Free Trade—imports of corn—cannot make Englishmen or Scotchmen sensible or moral. But with regard to France, every man must know that our relations with France have been much more friendly since Mr. Cobden's treaty came into force ; and that now we are on most friendly terms with the nation with whom in past times we have most frequently contended on the battle-field.

.As to Germany and its tariff, its military expenditure demands more taxes ; and by offering higher duties to her manufacturers, higher taxes are made less unwelcome to many of her people. I am not aware of any movement towards Protection in Italy, or Belgium, or France. In France the cause of Free Trade is far more powerful now than at any former period. America has had her tremendous civil war; but for that and her enormous debt Protection would have been dead and buried long ago ; and nobody surely expected or said that the repeal of our Corn Law could make or prevent a civil war on the great question of slavery in the United States.

Why don't you and your friends ask why American commercial distress has been much deeper and more prolonged than our own ? Yet America has all the good which Protection can give her.

We are suffering from many bad harvests at home, from famines and poverty in India and China, from depression in North and South America, from like suffering in Germany, from war in the east of Europe, and from the extravagance and inflation of the years preceding the present bad times. And, after all, our people as a whole suffer infinitely less than in the three years from 1839 to 1842 ; and our farm labourers, who were to be specially ruined, are receiving nearly double the wages, and of that which wages can buy, that they received in the three years to which I have referred.

If you use your faculties as well now as you did in the days of the Free Trade contest, you will not doubt the wisdom of our present policy.

I am, respectfully yours,

JOHN BRIGHT.

Mr. Wm. Russell, Glasgow.

CANADIAN POLICY WITH REGARD TO FREE TRADE.

Written to a gentleman in New York. Sir John Macdonald, who was appointed Premier of Canada in the beginning of 1879, signalized his accession to office by adopting a policy of protection to native industries. Some months later he visited this country and endeavoured to raise a loan for the construction of a railway through Canada to the Pacific.

Rochdale, August 16, 1879.

DEAR SIR,—The policy of the Canadian Government seems to me injurious to the inhabitants of the Dominion, and, if persisted in, will be fatal to its connection with the mother country. To shut out the manufacturer of England is bad enough, but at the same time to seek to borrow money from her on a guarantee for a loan is a scheme and a policy so impudent that it cannot succeed. The great railway project of Canada can only add to the debt of Canada, and this can only cause heavier taxes, and will be made the excuse for still higher protective duties on imports, so that England's generous but foolish help to the colony, if further given, will tend directly to cripple the trade between them. I believe the present policy of the Canadian Government is inflicting a wound on the union between the colony and England from which, if it be not speedily reversed, great changes must come. I watch the progress of the protection malady in the States and in Canada with great interest. I cannot think it will continue very long.

Your letters will do something to weaken its hold upon those affected by it.

I am, very respectfully yours,

JOHN BRIGHT.

FREE TRADE BETWEEN ENGLAND AND THE UNITED STATES.

Written to Mr. Alfred Gray, Secretary of the Agricultural Board of the State of Kansas, acknowledging receipt of a copy of one of Mr. Gray's agricultural reports.

One Ash, Rochdale, January 3, 1880.

DEAR SIR,—I have received the volume you have kindly forwarded to me. It contains much apparently exact and interesting information on agricultural affairs and on land in your State. There is a growing desire here to know more of your progress, and there are signs that emigration is on the increase. There is, too, among both farmers and landowners, a great fear that you will beat them in their own markets. I am inclined to think that the panic will subside, and that if we have good seasons our agriculture will return at least to a moderate prosperity. I hope your world and ours may help each other. We take everything you have to sell freely, without customs duties, except tobacco and spirits, and on these our duties are only for revenue, for we have equal duties on spirits, and we prohibit the growth of tobacco, while you charge with extravagant duties nearly everything you take from us and that we can or could send you. If in commercial matters and in agriculture you could annex the United Kingdom, it would be a great and good thing for both.

Believe me, truly yours,

JOHN BRIGHT.

E

PROTECTIONIST PROPOSALS.

On Tuesday, the 15th of March, 1881, Mr. Hermon, member for Preston, delivered a speech in the Area of the Corn Exchange of that town, in which he advocated a return to Protection. A Preston gentleman sent a copy of the speech to Mr. Bright, and received the following reply :—

132, Piccadilly, March 18, 1881.

DEAR SIR,—I have read Mr. Hermon's speech to which you refer me. I am not amazed at the ignorance it displays, or its misrepresentation of facts. He does not tell us how he proposes to protect by new tariff duties the factory-workers or the mill-workers of Preston. His constituents are exporters of cotton goods to all quarters of the globe ; they compete with all foreign manufacturers in all foreign markets. How can he protect them by re-imposing duties on the import of cotton goods, which they so largely export ?

Does he intend to give a bounty out of the general taxes on all goods they export, as he says " he would give a bonus on every acre of land that a farmer of this country chooses to till and crop with corn " ?

He proposes to give out of the taxes a bonus, how much he does not say, but so much per acre on all land growing corn, doubtless to enable the farmers to pay a higher rent than the land is worth, and to limit our supplies of corn from the United States, Canada, and other countries !

Mr. Hermon did not tell his audience that between the harvests of 1879 and 1880, that is in the year after the bad harvest of 1879, *out of every four loaves of bread eaten by the people of the United Kingdom three loaves came from abroad,* and that in no other year in his lifetime or in mine have our people been fed so cheaply or on bread of such excellent quality.

What must Mr. Hermon think of the mental condition of his constituents when he ventured to utter to them the confused nonsense of his speech, and what must every intelligent elector of your town think of a representative in Parliament who has not advanced a step beyond the benighted ignorance of forty years ago?

If you wish to see this question of Free Trade and our trade well discussed, I advise you to pay sixpence for the little book published by Messrs. Cassell, Petter, and Galpin, of London, entitled "Free Trade and English Commerce," written by Mr. Mongredien. I wish every elector in Preston could have it and read it, and I may recommend it to Mr. Hermon as a book out of which he may begin to learn something of correct facts and sound arguments on the question of Free Trade, and on the results of our policy as adopted by Sir Robert Peel and Mr. Gladstone since the year 1841. I have not time to write you at greater length. The little book I have mentioned will tell you the truth on the facts and results of our Free-Trade policy.

I am, very truly yours,
JOHN BRIGHT.

THE FRENCH AND AMERICAN TARIFFS.

In March, 1881, Mr. Ephraim Rigg, of Drighlington, near Leeds, addressed to Mr. Bright a few questions on the subject of Free Trade *versus* Foreign Tariffs, and received the following reply:—

London, March 29, 1881.

DEAR SIR,—I have not time to answer your letters at length. If you will read the little book to which I referred in my letter on the speech of the Member for Preston, you may learn much from it—more than I can tell you in any letter I can write.

We all regret that France, the United States of America, and other countries continue to maintain their high tariffs; it is, we believe, a misfortune to them and injurious to us; but we can only legislate for our own country and not for them. If you think that, *not being able to sell freely*, we should mend ourselves by *giving up the power to buy freely*, I must leave you to that opinion, only expressing my wonder at it. But you will perhaps say that we can force other nations to reduce their tariffs if we impose a tariff against them. You forget, probably, that we have tried this in past times, and that it has wholly failed. Sir Robert Peel taught this nearly forty years ago, and he believed, as I believe, that the best defence we can have against the evils of foreign tariffs is to have no tariff of our own.

You speak of France. The French Senate is in favour of more protection. The Chamber of Deputies is disposed to Free Trade and a more liberal policy. The Free Trade party in France is more powerful than in past times, and it is not certain that the proposed treaty will be less favourable to trade between the two countries. As to America, how will you compel its Government to reduce their tariff? By placing duties on American exports to England? If so, on what exports? On cotton for the mills of Lancashire, or on corn for the food of all our people? The American Protective Tariff makes it difficult or impossible for Americans to become great exporters of manufactures. If you fight them at the Custom Houses, you can only assail them by duties on cotton or on corn, and this surely will not benefit Lancashire or the West Riding. When the debt of the United States is much reduced, when their revenue is in excess of their wants, then their tariff will be reformed and their import duties will be reduced.

If you doubt what Free Trade has done for England, go back to your histories, and read what was the condition of our working men and their families for the first forty years of this century, when everything was supposed to be protected, and compare it with what it is now.

For some years past manufacturers and farmers have suffered greatly, and workmen have suffered much, but they have not seen one-tenth of the part of the distress which afflicted them during the forty years of the high duties from 1800 to 1840. The country suffers now, not from our purified tariff, and not wholly, or in chief part, from foreign tariffs. It suffers from want of sunshine—from the short harvests of several years ; and till we have again good harvests we must suffer and endure. Parliament cannot give sun and heat for our fields, and it will be no compensation to re-impose import duties and to deny us the right to purchase freely what we need from foreign nations.

I am, very respectfully yours,

JOHN BRIGHT.

Mr. E. Rigg, Drighlington, near Leeds.

RECIPROCAL TARIFFS.

A gentleman from Bradford, having written to Mr. Bright on the effect upon that town of a Free Trade policy, received the following reply :—

One Ash, Rochdale, April 15, 1881.

SIR,—I cannot reply at length to letters like yours. Only last week, I think, a letter from me on the subject on which you have written was published in your newspapers. I can only refer to it.

The home trade is bad mainly or entirely because our harvests have been bad for several years. I believe the agricultural classes—owners and occupiers of land in the three kingdoms—have lost more than 150,000,000l. sterling through the great deficiency of our harvests. This great loss must inevitably and seriously depress all our other industries. It is not Bradford alone that has suffered, the whole cotton trade of Lancashire has suffered greatly, and much of all this is to be attributed to the condition of our great farming interest, and this again to the unfavourable seasons of several recent years.

The remedy will come with more sunshine and better yield from the land ; without this it cannot come. To imagine that your suffering springs now from hostile tariffs is absurd, because you have had great prosperity with the same tariffs ; but to suppose your case will be improved by refusing to buy what you want from foreigners, to punish them for not buying freely from you, seems to me an idea and a scheme only worthy of the inmates of a lunatic asylum.

To return to protection, under the name of reciprocity, is to confess to the protectionists abroad that we have been wrong and that they are right, and protection will henceforth be the justified policy of all nations. If protection is needful and good, surely at this moment it is needful for our farming class, and yet who dares to propose another sliding-scale or a fixed duty on the import of foreign corn ? Bradford must be watchful and patient, to look out for new markets or new products for her looms, and to endure a temporary reverse, to be followed, I trust, at no remote period, with a revival of prosperity. Bradford has had a good innings since 1860 ; she gained more than other towns from Mr. Cobden's treaty with France. Great success and great expansion of business are followed by depression, to be followed, I hope and believe, by a return to a fair measure of prosperity. But our recovery depends more on the produce of our harvests than on foreign tariffs, or on the changes in the fashion of dress to which you refer.

I am, respectfully yours,
JOHN BRIGHT.

Mr. W. G. Lord, 1, Norfolk Street, Bradford.

THE FRENCH TREATY.

Written to the Secretary of the National Trades' Defence League in reference to a resolution passed at a meeting in Birmingham on the 3rd of August, 1881, protesting against the conclusion of any treaty of commerce with France which did not materially reduce the high duties hitherto levied by France upon British manufactures, and which did not also provide for

England's withdrawal from such treaty upon giving twelve months' notice to do so.

House of Commons, August 10, 1881.

DEAR SIR,—The French treaty, as a matter of course, if negotiated at all, will be liable to termination by either of the parties to it giving due notice to the other party. As to our having a treaty at all or not, I hope you will allow the Government to do what is best in the matter. We cannot expect to deal with the French tariff as if it was our own. Each Government has its own people and interest to care for, and all that can be done is what the two Governments can agree upon. We may fail in doing anything good, but we shall do our best, and may possibly succeed. I hope if this negotiation fails, they who ask to have no treaty except such a one as is impossible will not turn round upon the Governments and blame them for not accepting an arrangement which might have been of great value to some branches of our varied industry. I think you may trust the Government to do what, under the circumstances of the case, is the best for the country.

I am, respectfully yours,

JOHN BRIGHT.

RECIPROCITY IN TRADE.

Mr. Thomas Barrow, of Kegworth, near Derby, who was the first traveller for a well-known carpet firm, under the Cobden treaty in France, wrote to Mr. Bright, in September, 1881, stating his experience in French trade—namely, that as soon as the French adopted steam-power for their manufactures, we should not be able to compete with them, their labour being obtainable at such a low rate. He therefore asked Mr. Bright whether he did not consider in the case of France that we should adopt a system of reciprocity.

Mr. Bright replied as follows :—

One Ash, Rochdale, September 2, 1881.

SIR,—I do not know what you mean by a system of reciprocity ; if you mean that we are only to trade freely without duties at our ports with nations who will do the same with us, then I am against reciprocity as a stupid and impossible proposition.

If you mean that we are to put on duties at our ports with the notion that we shall compel other nations to take off their duties, then I am against it, from the conviction that such a plan must fail, as it has done in all past time. For thirty years before our Free Trade times this plan was made use of and offered to foreign ports, and it entirely failed, as it would fail if again offered.

If you begin to put on duties at our ports, the protectionists of all other nations would say we were adopting their policy and admitting that our Free-Trade policy was unsound, as we had repented and begun to adopt theirs.

The true course for England is to open her ports as widely and completely as possible, whatsoever may be the tariffs of other countries.

I am, respectfully yours,
JOHN BRIGHT.

Mr. T. Barrow, Kegworth, Derby.

PROTECTION DUTIES.

Written to a gentleman at Newport, Isle of Wight, in reply to questions on the subject of protective duties.

One Ash, Rochdale, November 20, 1881.

DEAR SIR,—If you keep a particular trade employed at the cost of taxing persons engaged in other trades, what is it but a system of relief, or like feeding a dog with its own tail ? Our people are not turned out of work by foreign imports. How do we employ and feed ten millions increased population since the Free Trade era—or since 1840 ? They are far better employed and paid and fed now than they were forty years ago, when they were ten millions less in number. The present state of things is one of steady and general improvement. Poor-rates are decreasing everywhere. All these ideas are delusions and falsehoods.

Yours truly,

JOHN BRIGHT.

[Read Mr. Medley's "Reciprocity Craze," published by Cassell, Petter, and Galpin, for facts.]

PROTECTION IN YOUNG COUNTRIES.

Written in reply to an Australian correspondent who had asked Mr. Bright's opinion as to a policy of protection in young countries.

Llandudno, N. Wales, November 30, 1883.

DEAR SIR,—I have but a short answer to your letter of the 17th of October.

If you impose duties on foreign manufactures, you tax all who consume them. With this tax you hope to induce your own neighbours to begin to manufacture what they had hitherto received from abroad. You succeed in this object to some, and perhaps to a considerable, extent. During this process you create and build up a new industry, which, the larger it becomes, becomes more exacting, and insists on a continuance of, even on an increase of the protecting duties under which it has been created. The system soon becomes one which taxes a multitude for the profit of a few, and the few by combination soon become so powerful that the multitude is more and more burdened, and the evil and unjust system is confirmed. Two results follow : If you have produce to export, the demand for it is lessened, for if you put obstacles in the way of your purchasing, you put them also in the way of your selling, and in the course of time your protected industries are in trouble, for they, forced into an unnatural activity, produce more than you can consume, your home market becomes glutted, and you have no foreign market to relieve it.

A protected industry is confined to its own market—its productions are necessarily so costly that it cannot relieve itself by exportation, for in foreign markets it cannot compete with other non-protecting nations. If your Government offered some definite sum of money to establish a certain manufacture as an example or encouragement to others, the evil would be small, and could be measured, and no claim or demand would be created for a general system of protection, and the public might gain or suffer only a certain and moderate loss in the experiment. This might be done in a given case, without harm, and without the departure from any sound principle.

If I were one of your community, I should steadfastly resist the introduction of any system of tariff protection —it is evil in principle, and an evil which tends to grow, and which in time, by combination, defies the efforts of honest men to abolish it.

I would trust to time and to individual efforts to open up new industries, and I should feel that in doing so I was only doing what, in the end, was most likely to do good to the community in which I was living. Your colony, from all I can learn of it, is more prosperous than Victoria. You are on a safe basis. Free Trade, or a low tariff, only for revenue, is the true policy, and will last longest. Any departure from it is evil, and tends at once to breed an interest hostile to the interest of the whole community. The experience of this country ought to convince all our colonies of the wisdom of low tariff or no tariff ; but it does not, for men are selfish and men are ignorant, and the selfish act upon the ignorant and bewilder them.

There is nothing in public affairs that tends more to make men dishonest than the system of protection. It was so in this country before our Free Trade era ; it is so now in the United States.

There is no meanness to which those who gain by tariff obstructions to trade will not stoop to continue a system by which they profit at the expense of the consuming public.

The efforts of all honest men should be directed to prevent the beginning of such a mischief, and to destroy it where unhappily it has been permitted to take root.

Your colonies should learn from us to shun our many errors, and to follow us where, after long and bitter experience, we have discovered true principles and the right path.

Yours, &c.,
JOHN BRIGHT.

Mr. Frederick Jones,
235, Pitt Street, Sydney, New South Wales.

"FAIR TRADE" PROPOSALS.

Mr. J. Gething, of Birmingham, having sent Mr. Bright a copy of a resolution passed at a Fair Trade conference held in Birmingham in March, 1884, in favour of the appointment of a Royal Commission or a Parliamentary Committee to consider the state of trade, received the following reply :—

April 1, 1884.

DEAR SIR,—I have received the copy of the "Fair Trade" resolution, and thank you for it. I cannot undertake to urge upon the Government or Parliament the inquiry you suggest, although I am certain it would result in a complete overthrow of your case. Your friends greatly exaggerate what you call "the unsatisfactory and unprofitable state of trade." I have known trade on many occasions in a far more "unsatisfactory and unprofitable" state than it is now, and I have seen a gradual restoration of activity and prosperity, which I do not doubt we shall again see.

As to the condition of agriculture, if a commission or committee could give us plenty of sunshine and hot or warm summers, I should gladly vote for it. For the produce of our farms a high or a fair price is given except for wheat. If wool is cheap, mutton is dear ; and in this respect the farmer is more than compensated.

The inquiry you suggest could not lessen injury caused by diseases which occasionally and in some localities afflict our cattle. What we want in agriculture is more capital on the land, and more skill and enterprise among those who rent and cultivate it. Parliament has made the land and its owners its special favourites for fifty years past, and can do no more in that direction. The farmer cannot now be helped by higher prices caused by the restrictions on the import of foreign corn. If produce and prices will not yield the accustomed rents, then rents must be reduced. Parliament can do nothing, and will not attempt to do anything, to sustain rents.

As to industry generally, I believe the artisan and working classes throughout the country are at this moment better fed, and clothed, and sheltered, than at any former period within our knowledge or recollection. There is still poverty and suffering, but it lessens in amount, and the spread of education and the growth of habits of temperance will, we may hope and believe, diminish the suffering and add to the comfort of our people. Your " Fair Trade " notion is a delusion which comes from an ignorance of the facts bearing on the industrial condition, or from want of power to reason from them. To establish what you call " Fair Trade " you propose to restrict our trade, to enact that our people shall not buy in the markets where to buy would be most profitable for them. In some branches of business you would restrict, in others you would not restrict, and this you call " Fair Trade." I am surprised at the want of sound reasoning in your dealings with the questions, and in your daring to give the name of " Fair Trade " to the policy which you are offering for the acceptance of your countrymen. Rest assured that "freedom of industry" is a far greater blessing than any you can confer by parliamentary tinkering with individual trades which you would subject to your " Fair Trade " theories.

As to the future, I do not doubt that if our harvests are more favourable, we shall witness a general improvement in the agricultural department of industry, and this will aid the restoration to greater activity of the various manufactures on which so large a portion of our people depend for their employment and their means of living.

I have written you a long letter in return for yours. I have not done so because I am likely to convince you, but because of the earnestness with which you have addressed me. You are, as you say, my political opponent. In the course I take on the question we have been discussing, I am not an opponent of your true interests, but your friend.

I am, respectfully yours,

JOHN BRIGHT.

FREE TRADE AND DEPRESSED INDUSTRIES.

In June, 1884, a gentleman interested in the Nottingham lace trade wrote to Mr. Bright, pointing out the injury likely to be done to that important industry by the measure then before the German Parliament—increasing the duties on lace goods to such an extent as practically to close the German market to British producers, whilst, at the same time, Nottingham manufacturers were exporting some of their machinery to Germany, where it could be worked cheaper, and whence the goods came back to injure the home market for Nottingham produce. The writer expressed doubts as to the value of the Free Trade system, under which such results were possible, and hinted that the right hon. gentleman should suggest a remedy, or use his influence with the Government for the benefit of the lace trade. Mr. Bright replied as follows :—

One Ash, Rochdale, June 19, 1884.

DEAR SIR,—I cannot give you any decided answer to your letter, for I have no definite statement of facts before me.

Free Trade intends that you should buy where you like to buy, and sell where you can sell, and that this should be and is the right of every workman and trader.

If I understand your letter, your idea is that your present customers in this country should not be allowed to exercise this right ; they must buy such goods as are made in Nottingham from the manufacturers and workmen of Nottingham, and not from German manufacturers or workmen, although, and indeed because, these offer their goods at somewhat lower prices. I cannot see the justice or reasonableness of this. The right to buy freely is as sacred a right as the right to sell freely, and the customer may justly complain if he is shut out from a cheap market and forced only to purchase in a dear one.

We export more manufactured goods than any other country in the world. We have a greater interest in freedom to buy and sell than any other country, and I should strongly object to any measure intended to tax all our people with a view of sustaining any special industry among them. If this were done for one, why not for others, and for all ? And if for some, or all, we should give the greatest encouragement to foreign nations to combine and make more strict and injurious their exclusive policy.

I know little of the conditions of your trade. It may suffer under a depression which has visited many trades of late, and must wait for the revival which will doubtless come.

The most depressed trades in England for several years past are those connected with coal and iron, and yet coal and iron are not imported into this country in any quantities to affect prices. The depression comes from causes which Governments and Parliaments cannot reach.

As to your own case, surely with as good machinery and as much skill and as much industry as the Germans you can meet them in your own or in any foreign market.

If you wish to compel me and others to give you a higher price than the article is worth in the world's market, what is it but something like a "rate in aid" that you are asking, and that all your countrymen should subscribe to support the special industry of your town? We do not ask it for the cotton industry of Lancashire, although we have our depression and difficulties.

I hope we shall see better days for all our industries. All countries have suffered, and the protected countries, I believe, have suffered more than England, whose trade is free.

I am, respectfully yours,

JOHN BRIGHT.

THE RESULTS OF FREE TRADE IN ENGLAND.

Addressed to Mr. Adam Wilde, of the Hackney Liberal Association, during the election in that borough consequent on the death of Mr. Fawcett. Professor Stuart, who was the Liberal candidate on the occasion, was subsequently returned by a large majority over his opponent.

132, Piccadilly, W., November 17, 1884.

DEAR SIR,—I observe that your Tory candidate and his friends are seeking support as Fair Traders, in opposition to Free Traders. They complain that we are allowed by our Government and our tariff to buy freely all the products of foreign countries, and that, owing to some foreign tariffs, we cannot sell our own products as freely as we wish to do. We can fix the duties in our own tariff and on our imports, but we cannot fix the duties in the tariffs of foreign countries and on their imports. All this is true enough and plain enough, but what is not plain and not true is the strange belief held by Fair Traders that being injured by not being able to sell so freely as we wish to do, owing to duties in foreign tariffs, we should remedy the evil by giving up the power to buy freely by putting duties on our own tariff.

To sell freely would be a great advantage, as to buy freely is a great advantage ; but neither to buy freely nor to sell freely, as the Fair Traders recommend, would, in my view, enormously increase the injury to our trade arising from the foreign tariffs which now obstruct our foreign trade.

Let your workmen reflect on the change in their condition which Free Trade has wrought within the last forty years since the reform of our tariff. The corn law was intended to keep wheat at the price of 80s. the quarter ; it is now under 40s. the quarter. The price of tea is now less than the duty which was paid upon it in former days. Sugar is not more than one-third of its cost when a monopoly of East and West India sugar existed. As to wages in Lancashire and Yorkshire, the weekly income of thousands of workers in factories is nearly if not quite double that paid before the time when ·Free Trade was established. The wages of domestic servants in the county from which I come are, in most cases, doubled since that time. A working brick-setter told me lately that his wages are now 7s. 6d. per day ; formerly he worked at the rate of 4s. per day. Some weeks ago I asked an eminent upholsterer in a great town in Scotland what had been the change in wages in his trade. He said that thirty to forty years ago he paid a cabinet-maker 12s. per week ; he now pays him 28s. per week. If you inquire as to the wages of farm-labourers, you will find them doubled, or nearly doubled, in some counties, and gene-rally over the whole country advanced more than 50 per cent., or one-half, whilst the price of food and the hours of labour have diminished. It may be said that milk and butter and meat are dear, which is true ; but these are dear because our people, by thousands of families, eat meat who formerly rarely tasted it, and because our imports of these articles are not sufficient to keep prices at a more moderate rate. The Fair Traders tell you that trade in some branches is depressed, which is true, though their statements are greatly exaggerated. We have had a great depression in agriculture, caused mainly by several seasons of bad harvest, and some of our traders have suffered much from too rapid extension in prosperous years. I have known the depression in trade to be much greater than it is now, and the sufferings of traders and workmen during our time of Protection, previous to 1842, when the reform of our tariff began, were beyond all comparison greater than they are now. In foreign countries where high tariffs exist, say in Russia, in France, and in the United States, the disturbance and depression of manufacturing industries are far greater at this moment than with us. Their tariffs make it impossible for them to have a larger foreign trade ; we have a wide field for our exports, which they cannot enter. We have an open market for the most part in South America, in China, in Japan, and with a population of more than 200,000,000 in our Indian Empire, and in our colonies, with the exception of Canada, and the province of Victoria in Australia. The field for our manufacturing industry is far wider than that for any other manufacturing nation in the world, and I cannot doubt that we shall gradually rise from the existing depression, and shall reap even greater gain from our policy of Free Trade in the future than we have reaped in the past. In 1846, when the cruel Corn Law was repealed, we did not convert our landowners and farmers, we only vanquished them. Even now there remains among them a longing for Protection ; they cling still to the ancient heresy, and, believing in the ignorance or forgetfulness of our working men, they raise their old cry at every election of members of Parliament. If I have any influence with your own or any electors, let me assure them that for centuries past there has been no change of our national policy which has conferred and will confer so great good on our industrious people as that policy of Free Trade which the two greatest Ministers of our time, Sir Robert

F

Peel and Mr. Gladstone, have fixed, I cannot doubt for ever, on the statute book of our country.

The recent contest in the United States has over-thrown the party of Protection and monopoly. It may prove a great blessing to the English nation on the American continent. When England and America shall have embraced the policy of free industry the whole fabric of monopoly the world over will totter to its fall.

I am, very respectfully yours,

JOHN BRIGHT.

Mr. Adam Wilde, The Morley Hall, Hackney, E.

"FAIR TRADE" PROPOSALS.

A Sheffield correspondent, who had been inquiring into the industrial condition of the working classes of Yorkshire, wrote to Mr. John Bright, pointing out that there was a growing leaning in favour of Fair Trade, and that in some quarters the working men were under the impression that Mr. Bright had modified his opinions with respect to Free Trade. Mr. Bright forwarded the following letter in reply :—

One Ash, Rochdale, Nov. 25, 1887.

DEAR SIR,—I cannot be more in favour of Free Trade than I have been in times past, nor am I, nor can I, be less in favour of it than heretofore.

The depression of trade of some recent years has afforded additional proof of the wisdom of our policy, and I believe we have suffered less than the countries which still adhere to the protective system.

Doubtless you will have observed that the Fair-traders are in an amusing confusion as to what they want. Some would tax corn, as in the old days ; others would not tax corn. Some would only tax manufactured goods, but they do not tell us which, or how much they would tax them. Some would have Free Trade only with the colonies, not appearing to know that our principal colonies—say Canada and Victoria—have heavy tariffs against English goods.

Our chief depression is in the farming industry. Our farmers, as a rule, have had farms twice too large for the capital employed upon them. Under the Corn Laws land was made to grow corn which should not have grown it, and now with low prices must cease to grow it. With free trade in corn land must depend upon its own quality, and on the capacity of those who possess it or who cultivate it.

The question of rent must depend on what tenants are willing and able to pay. You cannot ask that a rate in aid shall be levied on the breakfast table of every working man's family to enable a tenant farmer to pay a rent which the land he tills is not able to yield or to bear. The rent must settle itself, and produce and prices will enable the farmer to determine what he can undertake to pay. And if those Fair-traders in their silly and childish dreams propose again to raise the price of food by partial exclusion of foreign corn, how do they propose to protect the crowds of men and women working in the cotton and woollen trades of Lancashire and Yorkshire, and to compensate them for the various taxes which the Fair-traders are anxious to see re-imposed upon food and goods of various kinds which we import from abroad?

I should like to see a carefully drawn tariff of the Fair-traders, and Protectionists, and Monopolists who are now asking for public support. It would be an amusing exhibition of ignorance, and folly, and confusion. It would show the impossibility of going back to the system which Sir Robert Peel attacked in the year 1842, and which he utterly demolished in 1846. Since that time there is abundant evidence of the improved condition of the millions who work for their daily bread. Wages are generally higher—in many employments they are nearly or quite doubled ; and the cost of almost everything the millions buy and consume is greatly reduced, and their general condition is comfortable beyond anything that has been known in the country during the last hundred years.

There are exceptions to this picture, as there have always been seasons of depression in some or in special trades and industries ; but the picture, as a whole, is not over-coloured. If, as you perhaps fear, the working men will be persuaded to go back to the errors and mischiefs of fifty years ago, it will only show, notwithstanding efforts for their education, how far they are from comprehending their true interests.

You have observed what the Conservatives have been saying at Oxford. They return, shall I say, like a dog to his vomit. They very slowly accept new teachings and new opinions, and the old delusions still attach to them ; but they are all confusion, and know not what they ask. Excuse this long letter.

Yours very respectfully,
JOHN BRIGHT.

PROTECTION AND MILITARY EXPEN-DITURE.

Mr. Bright's attention having been called to the report of a Fair Trade meeting at Aston, where a speaker calling himself a Radical, said, in effect, that the principles of Free Trade might have been all very well a few years ago, but would not do now, he wrote as follows :—

One Ash, Rochdale, May 17, 1885.

DEAR SIR,—Your Radical friend is not for standing still, but for going back. There seem to be few men acquainted with facts, and still fewer who can reason from them. An American asked me if I thought we should return to a policy of protection. I said, " Perhaps so, but not till you return to slavery." The feeble cry is dying out, and even Salisbury and Northcote have discovered this. Our great danger now is in our foreign policy, in which Tory and Liberal administrations are about equally at fault. Unless our people can have their eyes open on this branch of political life, I think we have disaster and calamities before us. Adding millions to our military expenditure while complaining of the depression of trade and the miserable housing of the poor, is a policy rather of lunacy than of intelligent statesmanship. Our children may look out for trouble if we escape it. I hope you will have no trouble with your friends in Aston.

Yours very truly,
JOHN BRIGHT.

DEPRESSED TRADE.

A Nottingham gentleman having written to Mr. Bright, calling attention to the depression in the lace industry, and the removal of machinery from that town to Scotland and other places, Mr. Bright replied as follows :—

One Ash, Rochdale, November 29, 1886.

DEAR SIR,—I fear I can write nothing that will be of service to you in the circumstances you describe. If your manufacturers are unable to compete with their rivals in other parts of the country or in foreign countries, their business must be unprosperous, and may gradually decay if the cause of this lie in the high wages claimed and paid in your town. Unless wages in other parts can be raised it would seem to follow that your trade can only be preserved by a reduction in your wages, or by some other diminution of the cost of manufacturing, if such be possible. There have been cases in which trades have been driven from towns and districts by special circumstances causing an increase of costs in manufacturing and producing, and those acquainted with the conditions of your town and trade can judge much better than I. If trades unions, for example, insist on wages which a trade cannot pay, the particular trade may, and indeed, must suffer, must become unprosperous, and may decay and be driven to some other district where labour is free from the interference and unwise restrictions of combinations of workmen. If any given trade is being removed from your town, if machinery is being taken down in Nottingham to be set up in some other town or district, it must be known to your workmen, and they surely will not be long in discovering their true interest in the question.

The wish for protection as regards wages is like the wish for it in manufactures, and, as it has been exhibited in agriculture, it tends to blind the eyes interested in it and to cause men to refuse what is just, although at the cost of future and much greater evil.

I can only hope that any difficulties in your trade may be overcome by such reasonable concession as the case may admit of. Speaking of employers of labour in general, and of whom I am one, it has always seemed to me more pleasant to pay good wages when trade permitted than to be compelled to reduce them, though this last remedy is sometimes unavoidable. I cannot hope this letter will be of any service, but it is a brief reply to the questions on the case you put to me.

Yours very respectfully,
JOHN BRIGHT.

THE ADVANTAGES OF FREE TRADE.

On the 19th April, 1887, a member of the Glasgow Chamber of Commerce wrote to Mr. Bright as follows : " I enclose a report, but a very meagre one, of a meeting of the Glasgow Chamber of Commerce held yesterday to consider the question of Free Trade. I had expected that the meeting would have been nearly unanimous in favour of Free Trade, but this, to my surprise, was by no means the case, and it was adjourned until Monday next, when a vote will be taken on the resolution. At this meeting, and at other recent meetings of practically the same kind, your name and the name of Mr. Cobden have been freely referred to. It is alleged that you or Mr. Cobden, or both, predicted before or upon the introduction of Free Trade, as certain, that in ten years' time the whole world would follow our example, and that if not there would then be good reason to reconsider the question. It would be most interesting to know if those statements attributed to you or to Mr. Cobden are correct, and I venture to suggest that it is also important—and it may be to the public advantage—if, before the adjourned meeting on Monday, you will inform me if your views on Free Trade have undergone any change, and if you can connect the present very severe depression with the admission free into our own country of the merchandise of other countries, and who still persist in refusing our goods unless under a heavy protective duty. The prudence of retaliating, more especially upon the American and French systems of duties and bounties, is gradually forcing itself upon the conviction of many of those who, like myself, have even been born and bred in the principles of Free Trade."

Mr. Bright replied as follows :—

Reform Club, April 21, 1887.

DEAR SIR,—So far as I know, I never predicted or expected that other nations would follow us in Free Trade within ten years, nor do I believe or remember that Mr. Cobden ever said anything of the kind.

As to the reconsideration of the question, the notion is to the last degree absurd. Neither Mr. Cobden nor I, nor any man who knows anything about the question, could possibly have said or thought anything so ridiculous and childish. The more other nations accept wrong principles upon this question, the more necessary or desirable it is for us to accept and adhere to the policy of Free Trade.

Free Trade gives us freedom to buy, and increases our buying, and the more we buy the more we sell and the greater our trade, even in spite of the hindrance of foreign tariffs. Surely no man imagines that to make importing difficult, that is, to prevent our buying freely, would lessen the injury which foreign tariffs inflict upon us, and which prevent our selling freely. Is it not better to be able to buy freely, rather than by law to be unable either to buy or to sell freely ?

The reason other nations keep on their high tariffs is plain enough. The Protectionists are an organized army and the consumers are a mob. It is easier also to levy taxes, because the manufacturing classes do not complain of taxes which it is pretended are imposed for their special benefit.

The Protectionists in the United States are burdened with a large surplus revenue, and yet they refuse to lower their import duties or lessen their protection, and this is promoting a system of corruption unequalled in any other country.

If the objectors with you would read Sir T. H. Farrer's little book, "Free Trade *versus* Fair Trade," they might learn something useful if their minds are open to facts or to arguments on the Free Trade question.

Yours very truly,

JOHN BRIGHT.

PARLIAMENTARY REFORM.

PARLIAMENTARY REFORM.

Written in reply to a letter enclosing resolutions passed at a public meeting at Hawick, expressing sympathy with Messrs. Cobden, Bright, and Gibson, in losing their seats in Parliament.

Geneva, May 17, 1857.

DEAR SIR,—Your kind note, enclosing a copy of the resolutions passed at a public meeting of the inhabitants of Hawick, reached me only last evening. I lose no time in writing to say that I am very glad to find that in your town the cause of Reform, Free Trade, and Retrenchment has so may warm friends, and that you have understood and approved the policy which Mr. Cobden, Mr. Gibson, and myself have supported in the House of Commons. In the question of Free Trade little progress has been made for some years past. As to Retrenchment, the word has become almost obsolete, and the military expenditure of the country is now nearly double the amount which the Duke of Wellington and Sir Robert Peel thought necessary in 1835, although we have no more territory to defend, and although a large army is no longer necessary to maintain tranquillity in Ireland. As to Reform, whilst almost everybody professes to be in favour of it in some shape, the preparation of the particular bill to be brought forward next year is left in the hands of a minister whose hostility to every proposition for Reform since the year 1832 is notorious and undeniable. Whether on these three points, to which your resolutions refer, the country is in a satisfactory condition, I must leave the friends of Free Trade, Reform, and Retrenchment to decide.

With regard to the promised Reform, let me warn you to look not more to the question of the franchise than to the other arrangements of the measure.   It would be easy to double the number of electors, and at the same time to increase the aristocratic influence in Parliament.   To give votes without giving representatives in some fair degree in proportion to the votes, is but to cheat the people; and to give a large increase of votes without the security of the ballot will subject increased numbers of our countrymen to the degrading influences which wealth and power now exercise so unscrupulously upon the existing electoral body.   A moderate measure, and an honest one as far as it goes, is far more to be desired than one of great pretensions with some fraudulent scheme for defeating the wishes of the nation.   A dishonest apportionment of members may effectually destroy a representation, and any trick to obstruct the free action of majorities, such as that proposed in Lord John Russell's last Bill, should be strenuously resisted as calculated to undermine the very basis of representative institutions, and designed only to cheat the people of that increased power which the Bill would profess to confer upon them.

Whether I shall ever again in Parliament support the policy you approve is extremely uncertain, but I shall always retain a grateful sense of the kindness which I have received in past times, and at the present time, from the intelligent community on whose behalf you have written to me.

Believe me to be very sincerely yours,

JOHN BRIGHT.

To Alex. Laing, Esq., Hawick.

PARLIAMENTARY REFORM.

Read at a meeting held in the Town Hall, Birmingham, on the 2nd of February, 1858, in support of Parliamentary Reform.

The London circular, referred to in the letter, was an address on the subject of Reform, issued in London in January, 1858. It was signed by over thirty Liberal Members of Parliament of advanced views, and urged upon the people the desirability of insisting upon the following points :—

1. (*a*) The extension of the borough franchise in England and Wales to every male person of full age and not subject to any legal incapacity, who shall occupy, as owner or tenant in part or whole, any premises within the borough which are rated for the relief of the poor.

(*b*) The extension of the county franchise in England and Wales to all 10*l.* occupiers at least.

(*c*) The assimilation, as far as possible, of the franchises in Scotland and Ireland to those of England and Wales.

2. Protection to the voter by the ballot, on a plan similar to that adopted in the Australian colonies.

3. A reapportionment of seats that should make such an approach to an equalization of constituencies as should give in the United Kingdom a majority of members to a majority of electors.

4. Abolition of property qualification for members.

5. The calling of a new Parliament every three years.

Rochdale, February 1, 1858.

MY DEAR SIR,—Although I am unable to be upon your platform to-morrow, be assured that I shall be with you in spirit, and that I wish every success to your Reform movement. May I intrude upon you with a few lines on the great topic you are about to discuss?

I observe that in the first paragraph in your circular you ask the aid of your townsmen in the endeavour to obtain an "extension of the suffrage." Afterwards you insert the propositions of the London Committee, which I am very glad to see you have adopted. But you are probably looking to the extension of the suffrage as the main point and principal demand of the new agitation. I am as much for this extension as you can be, and therefore I can, without suspicion as to my wishes with regard to it, the more frankly warn you of a danger which I see before us. Twenty-five years ago, the Tory party, and the Whigs almost as much so, were greatly afraid of an extension of the suffrage. Now very few persons of any intelligence, even among the Conservatives, are afraid of it. The propositions made some time ago by the government of Lord John Russell and Lord Aberdeen, showed clearly that the franchise is no longer the dread of the aristocratic and ruling classes, and it is not unlikely that Lord Palmerston, if he produces a Reform Bill, will go a long way in the direction we wish to go, so far as the franchise is concerned. We can easily understand this. The franchise itself gives no real power, unless accompanied by the right on the part of all the possessors of it to elect something like an equal number of representatives. I could easily frame a bill which would give "universal suffrage" in its widest sense, and which would confirm more strongly than ever the supremacy of the English oligarchy over the English people. If your great city, with its great constituency, is only to send two men to Parliament, whilst an equal population and property in some other part of the kingdom is to send twenty men to Parliament, then, I say, your franchise is of little avail. The man who can merely shout at the hustings, or contribute to the show of hands, is, in reality, in almost as good a position as the man who votes, if the value of votes is rendered so unequal, or is nearly destroyed, by the unequal distribution of representatives among the whole body of electors. The Government and the Parliament, even the House of Lords, will consent to a large increase of electors ; and men who have not considered the subject fully will imagine they have gained much by the concession. Lord John Russell, in his many speeches on a further measure of Reform, generally, if not always, confines himself to an extension of the franchise ; and his last bill, although it would have added to the number of electors throughout the kingdom, would have done absolutely nothing to lessen the power of the order to which he belongs, or to increase that of the nation as distinguished from its privileged and aristocratic class.

It is not a matter of opinion, or of any doubt, that I am discussing. It is a question of fact and of arithmetic ; and therefore I wish to urge it strongly upon your attention. The contest on the question of Reform will be on the distribution of seats. Will the great borough of the Tower Hamlets, with its half a million of population, be content to return only two members to Parliament ? Will Finsbury, will Marylebone, will Lambeth, and the other London boroughs ? Will Glasgow, and Manchester, and Liverpool, and Birmingham, and the other leading cities of the United Kingdom, be content to dwarf themselves politically to the size of boroughs whose whole population would scarcely people one of the inferior streets ? Shall it be admitted that the more men come together, the more they are industrious, skilful, intelligent, and powerful in every other respect, the less shall be their influence in the government of their country ? This is the great question, and it rests with the people of Birmingham to do much to solve it.

Any Reform Bill which is worth a moment's thought, or the smallest effort to carry it, must at least double, and it ought to do much more than double, the representation of the metropolitan boroughs and of all the great cities of the United Kingdom. The United States of America, and Belgium, and Sardinia, comprehend this simple question. A year ago I was in the city of Genoa, and I found that it returned seven representatives to the Sardinian Parliament at Turin, seven being its fair share, calculated according to the population of the various cities and districts of the Sardinian kingdom. In this country, throughout Great Britain and Ireland, you will find that property rated to the relief of the poor follows very closely the course of population ; and the only just principle of representation is that the industry, property, intelligence, and population of the country should be, as nearly as may be, equally represented, wherever they are to be found. I am not arguing for any mathematical precision in this matter, but for such a change as shall really give the House of Commons to the nation.

The third proposition in your list adopts this principle; and I only dwell upon it because I know that reformers are too much accustomed to look upon the suffrage as if it were the all-important one, the only important point in their creed.

With regard to the ballot, it is worthy of remark that no meeting has been held in favour of Reform at which the ballot has not been strongly insisted upon. If Reform is to be granted to gratify and content reformers; if their judgment and unanimity are sufficient to justify or to force its concession, then surely the ballot cannot be denied to us, and I feel certain it will not long be refused. The ballot is not so much a principle as a convenience. It does not bestow the franchise, it guarantees that which the law has already conferred. A voter goes to the poll in a cab, because it is easier and sometimes safer for him than to struggle through an excited crowd on foot. Why should he not be allowed to vote by ballot to shelter him from the more serious annoyance he may be, and is now often subjected to, from the importunity of the threats of his landlord, his creditor, or his customer? When the 200 men in the House of Commons, who are pledged to support the ballot, or when 100 of them, or when fifty of them are in earnest, and tell the Government they are resolved to have it, and that they will leave any government that will not grant it in the hands of the Philistines on the opposite side of the House, then, and probably not till then, the ballot will be conceded. I dread to think of the consequences of a wide extension of the suffrage in our manufacturing districts should it be obtained without the ballot. It will tempt employers of labour to a hateful tyranny, and it will doom multitudes of the employed, I fear, to a not less hateful condition of political degradation.

I write this letter chiefly that I may warn you against the pitfalls that are in your path. Your cause is not in the hands of friends. Your forces in the parliamentary field are commanded by men taken from, or chosen from, your constant and natural opponents, and they lead them, not for your purposes, but for their own. I beseech you to watch well what is proposed and what is done. Be the measure great or small, let it be honest in every part. Include as many as you can in the right of the franchise, insist upon such a distribution of seats as shall give the House of Commons fairly to the industry, the property, the intelligence, and the population of the country. Demand the ballot as the undeniable right of every man who is called to the poll, and take special care that the old constitutional rule and principle, by which majorities alone shall decide in Parliamentary elections, shall not be violated.

I give my hearty support, as I have heretofore done, to the proposition contained in your circular. I lament that I cannot join in your meeting to-morrow, for I esteem it a great honour to be permitted to act with the inhabitants of Birmingham on that question which, a quarter of a century ago, they did so much to advance, and on which their potent voice is once more about to be heard.

I am, very sincerely yours,
JOHN BRIGHT.

MR. BRIGHT'S REFORM BILL.

In 1859 Mr. Disraeli, on behalf of Lord Derby's Government, introduced a Reform Bill in the House of Commons. It consisted mainly of a string of ridiculous clauses, artfully designed to give the measure an appearance of extending the franchise, but with the real object of continuing the exclusion of the working classes from the suffrage. The Bill was exceedingly

G

unpopular in the country, and on the 31st of March, the second reading was rejected in the House of Commons.

A dissolution of Parliament ensued, and the following letter, explaining a scheme for a Reform Bill which Mr. Bright had drawn up the previous year, was then written at the request of some of the friends of Reform, for the enlightenment of the country :—

Reform Club, April 9, 1859.

MY DEAR SIR,—It seems scarcely needful, after the explanations I have publicly given of the principles of my bill, to enter into any long statement as to its exact provisions. I will endeavour, however, in a few words, to place before you what I intended to propose to Parliament, if the session had not been suddenly interrupted by the dissolution which is impending.

With regard to the franchise, I propose, in counties, to extend the right of voting to all occupiers of the value of 10*l*. and upwards, with the proviso that, in every such occupancy, not less than 6*l*. of the value shall be in a dwelling-house. The object of this is to prevent the fabrication of fictitious votes by pretended lettings of land where no real tenancy may exist. I propose to extend the right of voting (possessed by freeholders of the value of 40*s*. and upwards) in England and Wales, to Scotland, and to place the elective rights of freeholders in Scotland upon the same footing as in England and Wales in every respect.

With regard to the borough franchise, I propose the present municipal franchise with two variations. The municipal franchise is now possessed by every man who is a ratepayer, whether his rates are paid by himself or by his landlord, and without regard to the value of the property he occupies, or the amount of his rating. I propose to adopt the same arrangement down to a certain point : that is, I would give the vote to all persons rated at not less than 3*l*., or occupying to the value of not less than 4*l*. per annum, whether the rates are paid by the tenant or by the landlord. Below that point, in order not to exclude any industrious and frugal man, wishful to have a vote, I would allow any person being a rated occupier, to secure his vote by undertaking to pay and by paying his own rates. This is the [only test I would apply, and I think its effect would be to exclude none but such as are not likely to have any independence, and such as are utterly careless as to the possession of a vote.

The Municipal Act requires a residence of two years and eight months before a person can be placed upon the burgess roll. This is done by a clause inserted in the House of Lords, and was a concession of the House of Commons to the apprehensions of the Peers. It assumes to be directed specially against the poor, and to be conservative in its character; whilst, in fact, it acts almost equally upon every class, lessening the number of burgesses, without being a guarantee for their independent character, or for their superiority in any respect. I propose to adhere to the present term of residence for parliamentary electors—that is, to have a twelve months' residence. This is, in fact, a sixteen months' residence, for no person can now be placed on the register, which comes into force on the 1st of December in any year, who was not in occupation of his premises on the 31st of July of the year preceding ; and if his occupation began on the 1st of August, his residence must be two years and four months before he can give a vote. Under the present law, the occupation of every person who becomes entitled to vote will vary from sixteen months to twenty-eight months, or an average of twenty-two months. Surely this is long enough, and nothing but ignorance of the law and the facts, or a dread of numbers, can induce any man to wish for any longer period of residence.

In addition to this general proposition to extend the right of voting in boroughs, I propose to give the franchise to occupiers of apartments ; that is, to lodgers, paying a rent of not less than 10*l*. per annum, subject to the same period of residence as in the case of rated occupiers, and whether the rent be paid half-yearly or at any shorter period.

To all voters, whether in counties or boroughs, I would give the ballot, and my bill provides for the appointment of a commission to decide upon the best means of securing secrecy, and expedition, and order in the taking of votes at elections ; that is, to discover the best means of voting by ballot.

I need not now enter into any details about the disfranchisement of small boroughs, and the redistribution of seats ; my schedules have been and are before the public. They who regard them as extreme and hurtful are they who wish the House of Commons to be the coadjutor of the House of Lords, rather than a fair representation of the people. I believe the time will come when my propositions on this point will be considered as moderate as I now believe them to be just.

I regret very much that I have been unable to introduce my bill to the House of Commons. I feel certain that I could have removed some misapprehensions with regard to it, created chiefly by the untruthful criticisms of the newspapers in the interest of the two aristocratic parties. I could not bring in my bill before the Government brought in theirs, and I could not with advantage have asked the House to consider it whilst that of the Government was under discussion. The ground was cleared when the great division was announced ; but on the very evening when I intended to give notice of the introduction of my bill, we were informed of the impending dissolution of Parliament, and thus all chance of proceeding with any important business was at an end.

The question of Reform is now before the constituencies. The quality and extent of the measure to be passed in the new Parliament will depend on the earnestness of the existing body of electors. I hope they may act up to the occasion.

I am, truly yours,
JOHN BRIGHT.

Samuel Morley, Esq.

PARLIAMENTARY REFORM.

At a private meeting of Radical electors, held in Carlisle early in May, 1865, it was decided to solicit the opinion of Mr. Bright respecting the position to be assumed by the party at the ensuing election, which was then imminent. In reply to the appeal addressed to him, Mr. Bright wrote the following letter :—

Rochdale, May 15, 1865.

DEAR SIR,—My opinion is that the proper course for the Liberal members is to withdraw their support from any Government which will not bring in and carry a good measure for the extension of the suffrage.

Fortunately your members are well disposed on the Reform question, and would do anything that was thought wise in the matter.

Lord Palmerston is the real difficulty. He is not a Liberal, and the failure of the Bill of 1860 was owing entirely to him. When he is out of the way, no Government can exist on our side of the House which will not deal with the question of Reform.

I hope, at the coming election, the Radical electors will endeavour to bring their members up to the point of refusing to support a Government not willing to fulfil the pledges of 1859 and 1860. When it is a question of Reform or expulsion from office, the Whig statesmen will decide in favour of Reform. This is the only effectual mode of dealing with them, and I hope it will be adopted.

I hope the electors of your city will not think it needful to make any change in your representation.

I am, very respectfully yours,

JOHN BRIGHT.

LORD PALMERSTON AND REFORM.

Written in reply to an invitation to attend a Reform meeting in Glasgow.

Pitnacree, Dunkeld, September 10, 1865.

DEAR SIR,—Mr. Dalglish has forwarded your letter

to me. I thank you for your invitation, although I do not feel myself able to accept it. If I come to Glasgow, I must go to other places. I cannot bear the weight of an agitation for Reform, and spend the winter in attending great meetings, as I did in the years 1858-9, and, therefore, I feel compelled to shun engagements which I know I should find too heavy for me. I have as much interest in the question as I have had at any time, and indeed, I know, that it is advancing with most certain steps. When the present Prime Minister[1] leaves office, no ministry will be possible of the Liberal party which will not deal with the Reform question. I am not anxious that it should be dealt with during his official life, for he is the only man connected with the Liberal party who is at once both able and willing to betray it. One sentence from his lips would have passed the Bill of 1860, and that sentence he refused to utter. His colleagues preferred their places to their honour as public men, and they consented to the greatest political fraud of our times rather than leave the treasury benches even for a season. Happily this question does not depend on the Prime Minister. He has never promoted its growth, and he cannot prevent its success. There is at work a steady and a silent force which all who are not blind may mark, and every day's delay will but add to the certainty and fulness of our triumph. I hope every Liberal constituency will so act through its representatives as to make a sham Liberal Government henceforth impossible. For what can be more degrading to a Liberal member of the House of Commons than to sit as a supporter of an administration which repudiates and has betrayed the first and greatest question or cause upon which the whole policy of the Liberal party is founded ?

I am, very truly yours,
JOHN BRIGHT.

Mr. George Newton, Glasgow.

[1] Lord Palmerston.

THE REFORM BILL OF 1866.

Read at a town's meeting held at Birmingham on the 26th of March, 1866, to consider the Reform Bill introduced in the House of Commons by Mr. Gladstone on behalf of Earl Russell's Government on the 13th of March. The last sentence but one in this letter furnishes a proof that Mr. Bright at this time sanctioned the separation of franchise and redistribution.

Rochdale, March 25, 1866.

MY DEAR MR. LLOYD,—I feel sorry that I cannot be at your meeting to-morrow night, to witness and to help the expression of the sentiments of Birmingham upon the question which is now exciting so much interest throughout the country. I cannot write as I could speak, but I must write a few lines to you.

The Franchise Bill now before Parliament is a perfectly honest Bill. It will, if it becomes law, give votes extensively to the middle classes, both in counties and boroughs, and it will overthrow the principle of working-class exclusion which was established by the Reform Bill of 1832. It will admit to the franchise so many of the working men in all important and populous boroughs that they, as a class, will no longer feel themselves intentionally excluded and insulted by the law.

In the counties it will enfranchise 200,000 men; and it may be expected in some counties to make the representation less that of the class of landlords and more that of the great body of the occupiers of houses and land within the county.

It will enfranchise, in London and in all the great cities, a considerable nnmber of young men and of artisans who live in lodgings or in parts of houses, and it will thus extend the franchise to many not included in the suffrage granted by the Reform Act.

I say the Bill is an honest Bill; and if it is the least the Government could offer, it may be that it is the greatest which the Government could carry through Parliament.

Parliament is never hearty for Reform, or for any good measure. It hated the Reform Bill of 1831-2. It hated the Bill which repealed the Corn Law in 1846. It does not like the Franchise Bill now upon its table. It is to a large extent the offspring of landlord power in the counties, and of tumult and corruption in the boroughs ; and it would be strange if such a Parliament were in favour of freedom and of an honest representation of the people. But, notwithstanding such a Parliament, this Bill will pass, if Birmingham and other towns will do their duty.

There is opposed to it the Tory party, of whose blindness and folly we have abundant proofs in all history. We have no reason now to expect for it a wiser course, and we have a small section of men who do not accept the name of Tory, but zealously does its work. These combined to form a conspiracy on which all the hopes of Mr. Disraeli and the Opposition are based. I think a more dirty conspiracy has not been seen in the House of Commons for many generations. It is directed against this Bill, and not less against Lord Russell, by whom the Liberal and popular policy of the Government has been determined.

What should be done, and what must be done under these circumstances ? You know what your fathers did thirty-four years ago, and you know the result. The men who in every speech they utter insult working men, describing them as a multitude given up to ignorance and vice, will be the first to yield when the popular will is loudly and resolutely expressed. If Parliament Street from Charing Cross to the venerable abbey, were filled with men seeking a reform bill, as it was two years ago with men come to do honour to an illustrious Italian, these slanderers of their country would learn to be civil, if they did not learn to love freedom.

This Bill appeals to the middle and working classes alike. It is a measure of enfranchisement to both of them, and they should heartily unite in an effort to make it a law. That which the Tories and "dirty conspiracy" oppose cannot but deserve the support of every Liberal man in the kingdom. If the population of the Birmingham district would set apart a day, not for "humiliation," but for a firm assertion of their rights in great meetings or in one vast gathering, they might sustain their Franchise Bill, and beat down, as by one blow, the power that threatens to bolt the door of Parliament against the people.

I hope we shall see in all the towns of Great Britain during the coming fortnight, a great support of the Government and the Bill. If the vote of want of confidence is carried against the Government, there will be a change of ministers or a dissolution of Parliament. If the towns do their duty, the Government will be safe, because the Bill will be safe, and the suffrage once more established on a more rational basis. The country can then turn its attention to the arrangement and distribution of seats, which is just as needful as a wider suffrage to give us a fair representation of the nation.

Great meetings and great petitions will not only be useful but effectual.

I am, very truly yours,
JOHN BRIGHT.

Thomas Lloyd, Esq.

THE HYDE PARK REFORM DEMON-STRATION IN 1866.

The following letter has reference to the historic Reform meeting, when the railings of Hyde Park were pulled down. The Reform League had made arrangements to hold a meeting in Hyde Park on Monday, the 24th of July, 1866, but the Government (Lord Derby's) refused to allow the meeting to be held there. At five o'clock on Monday afternoon the park entrances were all closed, 1500 policemen were placed inside, and the Foot and Life Guards were held in readiness. About

seven o'clock the Reform League procession arrived at
the gates and were refused admission, whereupon, after
protest being made, the League went to Trafalgar
Square and held a great meeting there.   A large crowd,
however, remained at the gates, and after attempting,
without success, to effect an entrance there, they attacked the railings and pulled them down for several
yards.   The police then charged the crowd, and a fight
ensued, in which several policemen were wounded and
some inspectors unhorsed.   The people poured into the
park by thousands, and although the police charged
again and again, they were unable to drive them out.
The police would have been utterly routed, if it had not
been for the intervention of the military.   The Foot
Guards with loaded guns and fixed bayonets were
drawn up near the Marble Arch, and a Horse Guards'
troop patrolled the avenues.   Eventually a meeting was
held, and resolutions condemning the Government were
passed.

Rochdale, July 19, 1866.

DEAR SIR,—I thank your council for the invitation
to the meeting intended to be held in Hyde Park on
Monday next.   I cannot leave home for some days to
come, and therefore cannot be in London on the 23rd
instant.   I see that the chief of the metropolitan police
force has announced his intention to prevent the holding
of the meeting.   It appears from this that the people
may meet in the parks for every purpose but that which
ought to be most important and most dear to them.
To meet in the streets is inconvenient, and to meet in
the parks is unlawful—this is the theory of the police
authorities of the metropolis.   You have asserted your
right to meet on Primrose Hill and in Trafalgar Square.
I hope after Monday next no one will doubt your right
to meet in Hyde Park.   If a public meeting in a public
park is denied you, and if millions of intelligent and
honest men are denied the franchise, on what foundation
does our liberty rest ?—or is there in the country any
liberty but the toleration of the ruling class ?   This is a

serious question, but it is necessary to ask it, and some answer must be given to it.

I am, very respectfully yours,

JOHN BRIGHT.

Mr. George Howell,
Secretary to the Reform League,
8, Adelphi Terrace, Strand.

THE REFORM RESOLUTIONS OF 1867.

On Lord Dunkellin's amendment being carried in Committee on the Reform Bill of 1866, Earl Russell resigned office, and Lord Derby was asked to form a ministry. As soon as the Conservatives were in office they reopened the question of Reform. The course they proposed to take was to pass a series of resolutions, and Mr. Disraeli arranged to move them on the 25th of February. They were as follows :—

"This House having, in the last session of Parliament, assented to the second reading of a Bill, entitled, 'A Bill to extend the Right of Voting at Elections of Members of Parliament in England and Wales,' is of opinion :—

"1. That the number of electors for counties and boroughs in England and Wales ought to be increased.

"2. That such increase may best be effected by both reducing the value of the qualifying tenement in counties and boroughs, and by adding other franchises not dependent on such value.

"3. That while it is desirable that a more direct representation should be given to the labouring class, it is contrary to the constitution of this realm to give to any one class or interest a predominating power over the rest of the community.

"4. That the occupation franchise in counties and boroughs shall be based upon the principle of rating.

"5. That the principle of plurality of votes, if adopted by Parliament, would facilitate the settlement of the borough franchise on an extensive basis.

"6. That it is expedient to revise the existing distribution of seats.

"7. That in such a revision it is not expedient that any borough now represented in Parliament should be wholly disfranchised.

"8. That in revising the existing distribution of seats, this House will acknowledge as its main consideration the expediency of supplying representation to places not at present represented, and which may be considered entitled to that privilege.

"9. That it is expedient that provision should be made for the better prevention of bribery and corruption at elections.

"10. That it is expedient that the system of registration of voters in counties should be assimilated, as far as possible, to that which prevails in boroughs.

"11. That it shall be open to every Parliamentary elector, if he thinks fit, to record his vote by means of a polling paper duly signed and authenticated.

"12. That provision be made for diminishing the distance which voters have to travel for the purpose of recording their votes, so that no expenditure for such purpose shall hereafter be legal.

"13. That a humble address be presented to her Majesty, praying her Majesty to issue a Royal Commission to form and submit to the consideration of Parliament a scheme for new and enlarged boundaries of the existing Parliamentary boroughs, where the population extends beyond the limits now assigned to such boroughs, and to fix, subject to the decision of Parliament, the boundaries of such other boroughs as Parliament may deem fit to be represented in this House."

These resolutions were very distasteful to the Reform party in the country, and at public meetings held to consider them they were generally condemned. Amongst others the Bradford branch of the National Reform Union declared them to be unsatisfactory and delusive, and a report of the meeting's proceedings having been sent to Mr. Bright, he wrote the following letter in reply :—

Rochdale, February 16, 1867.

DEAR SIR,—I think your resolutions very good. The course taken by the Government is an insult to the House, and a gross offence to the whole body of Reformers in the country. I cannot say what the House will do till after the meeting which is called for Thursday next.

The Administration is bitterly hostile to Reform. When in Opposition this was abundantly proved, and it is confirmed by its course since its accession to office. It has not the honesty or the courage to pronounce boldly against Reform, but it seeks to murder the cause and the question by a course contrary to Parliamentary usage and odious in the sight of all honest men. If the House joins in the guilt of this odious proceeding, it will only add to the distrust with which it is now regarded by vast multitudes of the people in all parts of the country.

You are right in holding meetings, and in every town and village meetings should be held. Already they have been held more generally, and more numerously attended than at any other time since 1832. Hitherto the effect seems little, so far as we may judge from the action of the Administration, and whether further meetings will produce any greater effect, I cannot undertake to say. But I will venture to say this, that a Government unmindful of the opinion expressed so clearly in the great centres of our population is running the country into great peril. If meetings have no effect —if the open and almost universal expression of opinion has no power on the Administration and the Legislature,—then inevitably, the minds of the people will seek other channels with a view to obtain and secure the rights which are so contemptuously denied them. If I am wrong in believing this, then history is a lie from the beginning, and we have all been mistaken in our estimate of the causes out of which many of the great and deplorable transactions it has recorded have sprung.

I understand that in Birmingham a great demonstra-- tion of opinion is contemplated, and I suppose other parts of the country will have something to say to an Administration which abdicates its function, and is ready to betray both Queen and people, that it may remain in office for another session.

I am, with great respect, yours truly,

JOHN BRIGHT.

The Secretary of the Bradford Branch
of the Reform Union.

THREE-CORNERED CONSTITUENCIES.

Written to a leading member of the Liberal party in Birmingham in reference to Lord Cairns' Amendment in Committee of the Reform Bill of 1867 in the House of Lords, providing that in constituencies represented by three members every elector should have only two votes.

Manchester, July 31, 1867.

MY DEAR SIR,—You see the vote in the Lords. It partially disfranchises Birmingham. Instead of your having *three* voices, or *two*, in a great division on a great principle, you are now to have only *one*.

Your future Tory member will pair with me or with Mr. Dixon, and there will be left only one vote for your great community. Birmingham is now reduced to the position and weight of Arundel or Calne in a great Parliamentary division, and this in the year of Reform and extension of popular power.

You will see that certain of the Whig peers have joined this childish or nefarious scheme. It is not the less dangerous on that account. I hope you will take some steps to counteract this proposition. The great towns should send deputations up to London to urge the Government to maintain the integrity of the Bill. I do not think Mr. Disraeli wishes to injure the Bill. He spoke earnestly against this scheme in the House, and I hope he will adhere to his own view on so grave a matter.

You should not for a moment dream of consenting to the audacious proposal to destroy the political weight and force of your borough.

I am, sincerely yours,

JOHN BRIGHT.

THE BALLOT.

Written to Mr. Beales, the President of the Reform League, in reply to the announcement that the League would use its organization, consisting of 430 branches, for the purposes of registration, educating the people in the use of the vote, and promoting the return to the next Parliament of members pledged to advanced Liberal principles.

August 18, 1867.

MY DEAR MR. BEALES,—I am glad to see that it is not intended to discontinue the organization and labours of the Reform League, although so great a step has been gained in the extension of the suffrage. On that branch of the question of Reform I presume you will not feel it necessary now to agitate further, so far as the boroughs are concerned. But the concession of a wide franchise is most incomplete as long as the security of the ballot is denied. As a machinery for conducting elections without disorder the arrangement of the ballot is perfect, and, if on that ground only, it should be adopted. But there is a higher ground on which all Reformers should insist upon it. The more wide the suffrage, the more there are of men in humble circumstances who are admitted to the exercise of political rights, the more clearly is it necessary that the shelter of the ballot should be granted. I am confident it would lessen expenses at elections, and greatly diminish corruption, and destroy the odious system of intimidation which now so extensively prevails, and that it would make the House of Commons a more complete representation of the opinions and wishes of the electoral body. I have a very strong conviction on this subject, and I hope all our friends throughout the country will accept the ballot as the next great question for which, in connection with Parliamentary Reform, they ought to contend. Without this safeguard there can be no escape from corruption and oppression at elections, and our political contests will still remain what they now are, a discredit to us as a free and intelligent people.

If the Reform League and the Reform Union will make the ballot their next work, they must soon succeed. I need not tell you that I shall heartily join in their labours for this great end. I hope the friends of the ballot, those who care for freedom and morality in the working of our representative system, will provide the needful funds to enable you to move on with an increasing force to a complete success.

Believe me, always sincerely yours,

JOHN BRIGHT.

Mr. Edmond Beales, Lincoln's Inn, London.

IRELAND.

THE IRISH CHURCH.

Addressed to Dr. Gray, Editor of the *Freeman's Journal,* afterwards Sir John Gray, M.P.

Rochdale, October 25, 1852.

MY DEAR DR. GRAY,—I observe from the news-papers that the friends of "religious equality" in Ire-land are about to hold a conference in the city of Dublin with a view to consider the existing ecclesiasti-cal arrangements of your country. My engagements will not permit me to be present at your deliberations, and, indeed, I am not sure that your invitations extend further than to Irishmen and Irish representatives ; but I feel strongly disposed to address you on the great question you are about to discuss—a question affecting the policy and interests of the United Kingdom, but of vital importance to Ireland.

Let me say, in the first place, that I am heartily glad that any number of the Irish representatives should have resolved to grapple with a question which, in my opinion, must be settled on some just basis, if Ireland is ever to become tranquil and content. The case of the Catholic population of Ireland—and, in truth, it is scarcely more their case than that of every intelligent and just Protestant in the three kingdoms—is so strong, so unanswerable, and so generally admitted, that nothing is wanting to ensure its complete success but the com-bination of a few able and honest men to concentrate and direct the opinion which exists. If such men are to be found among you—resolute, persevering, and disin-terested—a great work is before them, and as certainly

a great result.   They will meet with insult and calumny
in abundance ; every engine of the " supremacy " party
will be in motion against them ; they will be denounced
as " conspirators " against the institutions of the country,
when, in fact, they combine only against a grievance
which it is hard to say whether it is more humiliating in
Ireland to endure, or disgraceful in England to inflict ;
but against all this, having a right cause, and working
it by right means, they will certainly succeed.

It would be to insult your understanding were I to
imagine that you demand anything more or less than a
perfect " equality " before the law for the religious sects
which exist in Ireland—that is, for the members or
adherents of the Protestant Episcopalian, the Presbyterian, and the Roman Catholic Churches.   So entirely
is it felt that you are in the right in making this
demand, that with regard to it your opponents dare not
attempt an argument with you ; they prefer to say that
you claim something else—namely, a supremacy as
hateful as their own, and then they find it easy to
contest the matter with you, writing and speaking as
they do chiefly to a Protestant audience.   On this point
there should be no possibility of mistake ; and not only
should the demand for equality be unequivocal, but it
appears to me most desirable that some mode of attain-
ing it should be distinctly pointed out.   We may,
perhaps, imagine an " equality " which would allow the
Protestant Establishment to remain as it is, or, at least,
to continue to be a State Church, building up at its side
a Catholic Establishment ; and, to complete the scheme,
a Presbyterian Establishment also, having a batch of
Catholic prelates and of Presbyterian divines in the
House of Lords ; but, in my opinion, any scheme of
" equality " of this description would be, and must
necessarily be, altogether impracticable.

Lord John Russell, I think in 1843, expressed an
opinion that the Protestant Church in Ireland should
not be subverted, "but that the Roman Catholic
Church, with its bishops and clergy, should be placed

by the State on a footing of equality with that Church."
He adopted the term "equality," and said that any plan he
should propose would be "to follow out that principle
of equality with all its consequences." Lord Grey, in
1845, was, if possible, still more explicit, for he said,
after expressing his opinion that "the Catholics have
the first claim" on the funds applied to ecclesiastical
purposes in Ireland, "you must give the Catholic clergy
an equality in social rank and position;" and he went
even further than this, and said, "I carry my view on
this subject as far as to wish to see the prelates of the
Roman Catholic Church take their places in this House
on the episcopal bench." From this it appears that
Lord John Russell and Lord Grey, seeing the enormous
evil of the existing system, were ready to justify almost
any measure that promised political and ecclesiastical
equality, to be obtained without the subversion of the
Protestant Established Church in Ireland.

Of course, if all parties among the statesmen and the
public of the United Kingdom were agreed, funds might
be provided for the perpetual endowment and subjection
to State control of the Irish Catholic and Presbyterian
Churches, and some plan might be devised to secure
them a representation in the House of Lords; but,
happily for sound principles in civil government, and
happily for religion itself, all parties are not agreed to
to do this, but are rather agreed that it shall not be
done. The "equality" which Lord John Russell would
"follow out with all its consequences" is a dream, and
Lord Grey's bold idea of giving the Irish Catholics "the
first claim to the funds" and of placing their bishops in
the House of Lords is not less impracticable. To have
two Established Churches in Ireland, the one Protestant
and the other Catholic; to have in the House of Lords
Protestant and Catholic bishops, elbowing each other cn
"the right reverend bench," guarding the temporal and
spiritual interests of two Churches which denounce each
other as idolatrous or heretical, would be an inconsistency so glaring, that it would go far to overthrow all

reverence for Governments and Churches, if not for Christianity itself. The scheme is surely too absurd to be seriously thought of, and if there be a statesman bold enough to propose it, he will find no support in the opinion of the English public, except from that small section with whom religion goes for nothing, and churches and priests are tolerated as machinery in the pay and service of the Government.

But there is an " equality " which is attainable without inconsistency, which would meet with favour among large classes in every part of Great Britain, and which, I think, if fairly proposed, would be well received by many of the more enlightened and just Protestants in Ireland. It is an " equality " which must start from this point, that henceforth there must be no Church in Ireland in connection with the State. The whole body of English Dissenters, the United Presbyterian Church of Scotland, and the Catholic population of the United Kingdom, might be expected cordially to welcome such a proposition ; and it is difficult to understand how the Presbyterians of the north of Ireland, or the Free Church of Scotland, or the adherents of the Wesleyan Conference in England, could, with any consistency or decency, oppose it ; and I am confident that a large number of persons connected with the Established Churches in the three kingdoms, who are enlightened enough to see what is right, and just enough to wish it to be done, would give their support to any Minister who had the courage to make such a measure the great distinguishing act of his administration. But if this principle were adopted—that is, the principle that henceforth there must be no Church in Ireland in connection with the State—there would still be a question as to the appropriation of the large funds now in the hands of the Irish Established Church.

There are two modes of dealing with these funds, either of which may be defended, but one of them seems to offer facilities which do not belong to the other. The most simple plan would be to absorb the revenues of the

Established Church, as the livings become vacant, and to apply them in some channel not ecclesiastical, in which the whole population of Ireland could participate. The objections to this plan are, that it would be hard upon the Protestant Episcopalians, after having pampered them so long with a munificent support, to throw them at once on their resources; and that to withdraw the *Regium Donum* from the Presbyterians of the North, when they have no other provision made for their religious wants, would be to create a just discontent among them. There is some force in this, inasmuch as upon one generation would be thrown the burden of the creation and support of a religious organization which, in voluntary churches, is commonly the work of successive generations of their adherents, and the argument may be considered almost irresistible when it is offered to a Government which does not repudiate, but rather cherishes, the principle of a State Church. But, whatever may be the inconveniences of this plan, they are, in my estimation, infinitely less than those which are inseparable from a continuance of the present system.

There is, however, another mode of settlement which, though open to some objection, is probably more likely to obtain a general concurrence of opinion in its favour in Ireland, and to which, I think, a great amount of consent might be obtained in England and Scotland. Your present ecclesiastical arrangements are briefly these : The Protestant Episcopal Church has 500,000*l*. per annum intrusted to it, or a principal sum, at twenty years' purchase, of 10,000,000*l*. sterling. The Presbyterian Church or Churches have 40,000*l*. per annum, or, estimated at the same rate, a principal sum of 800,000*l*. The Roman Catholic Church has 26,000*l*. per annum, or a principal sum of 520,000*l*. I will say nothing about the exact proportions of population belonging to each Church, for I do not wish to give opportunity for dispute about figures. It is sufficient to say, what everybody knows to be true, that the Irish population is

Catholic, and that the Protestants, whether of the Episcopalian or Presbyterian Church, or of both united, are a small minority of the Irish people. I will admit the temporary hardship of at once withdrawing from the Protestant sects all the resources which the State has hitherto provided for them; but, at the same time, no one can deny, and I cannot forget, the hardship to which the Catholics have been subjected, inasmuch as they, the poorest portion of the people, and by many times the most numerous, have been shut out from almost all participation in the public funds applied to ecclesiastical purposes in Ireland. Is it not possible to make an arrangement by which the menaced hardship to the Protestants may be avoided, and that so long endured by the Catholics, in part at least, redressed? And can this be done without departing from the principle, " that henceforth there must be no Church in Ireland in connection with the State " ? Let an Act be passed to establish a " Church Property Commission " for Ireland, and let this Commission hold in trust, for certain purposes, all the tithes and other property now enjoyed by the Established Church; let it, in fact, become possessed of the 10,000,000*l.* sterling, the income from which now forms the revenues of that Church, as the livings and benefices become vacant. It would be desirable to offer facilities to the landed proprietors to purchase the tithes at an easy rate, in order that funds might be in hand to carry out the other arrangements of the scheme.

I have estimated the total value at 10,000,000*l.*; it might not reach that sum if the tithes were sold at a low rate; but whether it were 10,000,000*l.* or only 8,000,000*l.* would nor affect the practicability or the justice of this proposition. Let this Commission be empowered and directed to appropriate certain portions of this fund as a free gift to each of the three Churches in Ireland—to the Protestant Episcopalian, the Presbyterian, and the Roman Catholic Church. Whatever is thus given must be a free gift, and become as much the private property of the respective sects or Churches as is the property of the Free Church in Scotland, or that of the Wesleyan Methodists in England. It must no longer be a trust from the State, liable to interference or recall by the State, or the "equality" and independence of the Irish sects will not be secured.

There comes now the question of the amounts to be thus given. From some inquiries I have made I have arrived at the conclusion that if in each parish in Ireland there was a house and a small piece of land, say from ten to twenty acres, in the possession of the Roman Catholic Church, that would be all the provision that would be required or wished for, as the general support of its ministers would be derived, as at present, from the voluntary contributions of their flocks. There are, in round numbers, about 1000 parishes in Ireland. In many of them there is now a provision up to the standard above stated in the possession of the Roman Catholic Church, but I will assume that in all of them such provision would have to be made. One thousand pounds for each parish, taking one parish with another, would amply make up any deficiency, and this amount throughout the parishes of Ireland would require the sum of 1,000,000*l.* sterling to be appropriated from the general fund ; and this should be made over absolutely and for ever to the Roman Catholics of Ireland, in such hands and in such manner as the funds of their Church raised by voluntary effort are usually secured.

Under an arrangement of this kind, of course, the special grant to the College of Maynooth would be withdrawn. The Presbyterians, under the operation of this Act, would lose their annual grant of 40,000*l.* ; but, in place of it, assuming that they have an organization and a system of government which would enable them to hold and administer funds for the use of their Church, a portion of the general fund should be set apart for them, equal to the production of a revenue of like amount with that they now receive by grant from Parliament. This should also be given to them abso-

lutely and for ever, and they should become henceforth
a voluntary and independent Church.

The Protestant Episcopalians should be treated as liberally as the Presbyterians, with whom it is estimated they
are about on a par in point of numbers. Assuming that
they could and would form themselves into a Free
Episcopal Church, the Commission would be empowered
to grant them a sum equal to that granted to the
Presbyterians, and which would be about the same in
amount as that granted to the Catholics. And further,
so long as they undertook to keep the churches in re-
pair, they might be permitted to retain possession of
them at a nominal rent, for their own use only ; and
that when or where they had no congregation sufficient
to maintain the church, then the buildings should be at
the disposal of the Commission to let or sell, as might
be thought best. In the case of the Protestant Episcopalians, as with the Presbyterians and the Catholics,
whatever sum is given to them must be given absolutely
and for ever, that henceforth they may rely on their own
resources and become a voluntary and independent
Church.

The State would thus have distributed about
3,000,000*l.* of the original fund, and would have relinquished all claims upon it for ever ; and it would be the
duty of the Commission to take care that those grants
were applied, in the first instance, for the purposes and
in the manner intended by the Act. The remaining
5,000,000*l.* or 7,000,000*l.*, as the case might be, might,
and in my opinion ought, to be reserved for purposes
strictly Irish, and directed to the educational and moral
improvement of the people, without respect to class or
creed. This fund would extend and perfect the educational institutions of the country ; it would establish and
endow free libraries in all the chief towns of Ireland,
and would dispense blessings in many channels for the
free and equal enjoyment of the whole population. Of
course there will be objections started to this scheme,
as there will be to any scheme which attempts to remedy

an injustice which has lasted for centuries. The "Church party" may, and probably will, denounce it as a plan of spoliation most cruel and unholy ; but no man who proposes to remedy Irish ecclesiastical wrongs can expect to find favour with the sect whose supremacy he is compelled to assail. We must hope that State patronage has not so entirely demoralized the members of the Protestant Episcopalian sect, either in England or Ireland, as to leave none among them who are able to see what is just on this question, and who are willing that what is just should be done. I believe there are many intelligent and earnest Churchmen, and some eminent politicians connected with the Established Church, who would welcome almost any proposition which afforded a hope of a final settlement of this question.

From Scotland, and probably from certain quarters in England, we may hear of the great crime of handing over 1,000,000*l.* sterling to the Roman Catholics of Ireland. It will, perhaps, be insisted upon that to add to the means of a Church whose teaching is held to be "erroneous" is a grievous national sin ; and many will honestly doubt the wisdom of a scheme which proposes such an appropriation of a portion of the public fund. Now, there is not a man in the United Kingdom more averse to religious endowments by the State than I am. I object to the compulsory levying of a tax from any man to teach any religion, and still more to teach a religion in which he does not believe ; and I am of opinion that, to take a Church into the pay of the State, and to place it under the control of the State, is to deaden and corrupt the Church, and to enlist its influence on the side of all that is evil in the civil government. But in the plan now suggested the Irish sects or Churches would be left entirely free, as is the Free Church in Scotland, or the Wesleyan Methodist Church in England. The grant once made, each Church would possess absolutely its own funds, just as much as if they were the accumulations of the voluntary contributions and liberality of past generations of its members, and thus would be avoided the damage to religion and to civil government which is inseparable from what is called the union of Church and State ; whilst the sum granted to each Church, being equal to a provision of about 40,000*l.* per annum, would be too small to create any important corporate influence adverse to the public interest.

As to the complaint that the sum of 1,000,000*l.* is proposed to be given to the Irish Catholics, I will ask any man with a head to comprehend, and a heart to feel, to read the history of Ireland, not from the time of Henry VIII., but from the accession of William III., and if he insists upon a settlement of this question by grants to the Protestant sects, and by the refusal of any corresponding grant to the Roman Catholics, I can only say that his statesmanship is as wanting in wisdom as his Protestantism lacks the spirit of Christianity. If, for generations, a portion of the Protestants of Ireland, few in number but possessing much wealth, have enjoyed the large ecclesiastical revenues of a whole kingdom ; and if during the same period, the Roman Catholics, the bulk of the population, but possessing little wealth, have been thrown entirely on their own limited resources, and under circumstances of political and social inferiority, can it be possible, when an attempt shall be made to remedy some of the manifold injustice of past times, that any Englishman or any Scotchman will be found to complain of the impartiality of the Government, and in his zeal for Protestantism to forget the simple obligations of justice ?

But it may be objected that it is contrary to sound policy to make grants of public money to any public body, or corporation, or sect, not submitting to State control—that, in fact, a Church receiving anything from the State should be a State Church. No one is more sensible of the weight and soundness of this argument than I am ; but observe the peculiarities of this case. I start from the point that " henceforth there shall be no

Church in Ireland in connection with the State." I have to free the Protestant Episcopalian sect and the Presbyterians from their State connection ; and to make the Irish sects voluntary Churches for the future. I propose an appropriation of about one-third of existing ecclesiastical property in Ireland, with a view to soften the apparent severity of the change to the sects heretofore paid by the State, and to make some amends to that majority of the Irish population, the injustice of whose past treatment is admitted by all the world. The Protestants of Ireland have done hitherto little for themselves, because the bounty of the State has paralyzed their exertions, or made exertion unnecessary. The Catholics have done much for themselves ; but they are in great poverty, and our existing ecclesiastical legislation has been felt, and is now felt, by them to be grievously unjust. Would it not be worth the concession of the sum I have suggested, and of the deviation from ordinary rule which I venture to recommend, to obtain the grand result which is contemplated by the change now proposed ? I have said that there will be objections to this scheme and to every scheme. The grievance is centuries old, and around it are entwined interests, prejudices, fanaticism, animosities, and convictions. It is a desperate evil, and whoever waits till the remedy is pleasant to everybody may and will wait for ever. The object in view is the tranquillity of Ireland. The means are simple, but altogether novel in that unhappy country—to do full and impartial justice to her whole population. I propose to leave the Presbyterians as well circumstanced as they are now, with this exception, that all future extension of their organization must be made at their own cost ; and I would place the Protestant Episcopalians in as good a position as the Presbyterians. The Catholics only could have any ground of complaint, owing to their numbers so far exceeding those of the Protestant sects ; but in the application of the remainder, and much the largest portion of the funds, for educational or other purposes, they would participate exactly in proportion to their numbers; and I have a strong belief that, so far as they are concerned, such an arrangement as is now suggested would be accepted as a final settlement of a most difficult and irritating question.

As you know, I am neither Roman Catholic, Protestant Episcopalian, nor Presbyterian, nor am I an Irishman. My interest in this matter is not local or sectarian. I have endeavoured to study it, and to regard it as becomes an Englishman loving justice and freedom, anxious for the tranquillity of Ireland, the welfare of the empire, and the honour of the imperial government. I believe that statesmanship does not consist merely in preserving institutions, but rather in adapting them to the wants of nations, and that it is possible so to adapt the institutions of Ireland to the wants and circumstances of Ireland, that her people may become as content as the people of England and Scotland are with the mild monarchy under which we live. Some experience and much reflection have convinced me that all efforts on behalf of industry and peace in Ireland will be in great part unavailing until we eradicate the sentiment which is universal among her Catholic population—that the Imperial Government is partial, and that to belong to the Roman Catholic Church is to incur the suspicion or the hostility of the law. A true "equality" established among the Irish sects would put an end to this pernicious but all-pervading sentiment; and Catholics, whether priests or laymen, would feel that the last link of their fetters was at length broken. Supremacy on the one hand, and a degrading inferiority on the other, would be abolished, and the whole atmosphere of Irish social and political life would be purified. Then, too, Christianity would appeal to the population, not as a persecuting or a persecuted faith, with her features disfigured by the violence of political conflict, but radiant with the divine beauty which belongs to her, and speaking with irresistible force to the hearts and consciences of men.

I know not if the statesman be among us who is destined to settle this great question, but whoever he may be he will strengthen the monarchy, earn the gratitude of three kingdoms, and build up for himself a lasting renown. I am sensible that in writing this letter, and in expressing the views it contains, I run the risk of being misunderstood by some honest men, and may subject myself to misrepresentation and abuse. It is under a solemn sense of duty to my country, and to the interests of justice and religion, that I have ventured to write it. I have endeavoured to divest myself of all feeling of preference for, or hostility to, any of the Churches and sects in Ireland, and to form my judgment in this matter upon principles admitted by all true statesmanship, and based on the foundations of Christian justice. If I should succeed in directing the attention of any portion of those most deeply interested to some mode of escape from the difficulties with which this question is surrounded, I shall willingly submit to the suspicions or condemnation of those who cannot concur with me in opinion. I wish this long letter were more worthy of its purpose. As it is, I send it to you, and you may make whatever use of it you think will be likely to serve the cause of " religious equality " in Ireland.

Believe me to be, very truly yours,

JOHN BRIGHT.

THE IRISH LAND AND CHURCH QUESTIONS.

Read at a meeting held on Thursday, the 29th of December, 1864, at the Rotunda, Dublin, for the purpose of promoting an association for the following objects :—

1. A reform of the law of landlord and tenant, securing to the tenant full compensation for valuable improvements.

2. The abolition of the Irish Church Establishment.

3. The perfect freedom of education in all its branches.

The meeting was convened by the Lord Mayor of Dublin, and was addressed by the Archbishops of Dublin and Cashel, and other Roman Catholic prelates.

Rochdale, December 22, 1864.

MY DEAR LORD MAYOR,—I have to thank your committee for their friendly invitation to your approaching meeting, although I shall not be able to avail myself of it. It is difficult for me to leave home at this season, and I have an engagement to be in Birmingham about the time when your meeting is to be held.

I am glad to see that an effort is to be made to force on some political advance in your country. The objects you aim at are good, and I hope you may succeed. On the question of landlord and tenant I think you should go farther, and seek to do more. What you want in Ireland is to break down the laws of primogeniture and entail, so that in course of time, by a gradual and just process, the Irish people may become the possessors of the soil of Ireland. A legal security for tenants' improvements will be of great value, but the true remedy for your great grievances is to base the laws which affect the land upon sound principles of political economy.

With regard to the State Church, that is an institution so evil and so odious, under the circumstances of your country, that it makes one almost hopeless of Irish freedom from it that Irishmen have borne it so long. The whole Liberal party in Great Britain will, doubtless, join with you in demanding the removal of a wrong which has no equal in the character of a national insult in any other civilized and Christian country in the world.

If the popular party in Ireland would adopt as its policy " Free Land " and " Free Church," and would unite with the popular party in England and Scotland for the advance of Liberal measures, and especially for the promotion of an honest amendment of the representation, I am confident that great and beneficial changes might be made within a few years. We have on our side numbers and opinion, but we want a more distinct policy, and a better organization; and these I hope, to some extent, your meeting may supply.

I thank you for your very kind invitation to the Mansion House, and am, my dear Lord Mayor,

Yours very truly,
JOHN BRIGHT.

The Right Hon. the Lord Mayor of Dublin.

THE IRISH LAND AND CHURCH QUESTIONS.

Written in reply to some suggestions for legislation on the above subjects.

Rochdale, January 27, 1868.

MY DEAR SIR,—I have read the "proposals" over with great interest and care. They are wide, and embrace the whole Irish difficulty, and, if adopted, would at once apply a remedy to the two branches of the grand question. For twenty years I have always said that the only way to remedy the evils of Ireland is by legislation on the Church and land. But we are met still with this obstacle, even yet I fear insurmountable, that the legislation must come from and through a Parliament which is not Irish, and in which every principle essential for the regeneration of Ireland is repudiated. The knowledge of this makes me hesitate as to the wisdom of your "proposals" in their present shape. I fear the scheme is so broad, and so good, and so complete, that Parliament would stand aghast at it. To strike down an established Church and to abandon the theory of our territorial system by one Act of Parliament would be too much for Parliament, and would destroy any Government that suggested it. I can conceive a condition of things in Ireland under which such a great change might be accomplished—if Ireland were united in demanding it, and were menacing Great Britain if it should be refused; but now I suspect our rulers, though un-

1

comfortable, are not sufficiently alarmed to yield. The Tories cannot deal with Ireland. Their concession on Reform does not lead me to think they can give in on Irish affairs. The Whigs are almost as much afraid as the Tories are of questions affecting the Church and the land, and they seem to have almost no courage.

Lord Russell is old, and cannot grapple with a great question like this. Mr. Gladstone hesitates, and hardly knows how far to go. The material of his forces is not good, and I suspect he has not studied the land question, and knows little about it. The English people are in complete ignorance of Irish wrongs, and know little or nothing of the real condition of your country. This is a sad picture; but it is not coloured too darkly. There is no necessary connection between the Church and the land. To make a farmer proprietary would not involve the Government in any permanent expense, and it may be done without touching the Church question; and this, again, may be dealt with without meddling with the land. Now, the two schemes together and in one is a grand idea. Perhaps too grand for so slow a nation and parliament as ours. Many persons may be willing to get rid of the Church who are unwilling to depart from present theories with regard to the land, and some may go with you on the land and hold back on the Church. Is it supposed that for the whole scheme you can secure a larger support than for either of the two branches of it separately? This is the question you must answer. For myself, I should have no hesitation if I could persuade myself that others in sufficient numbers would follow; and, whether they follow or not, I am ready to state my general approval of your great plan, should it be brought before the public. If all the Liberal Protestants and all the Catholic population in Ireland will unite to support you, some impression may be made on English opinion and upon Parliament; but, looking to all past efforts among you, I am not very sanguine that you will succeed in bringing a strong and united pressure to bear upon our ruling class. I am expected to speak to-morrow week at Birmingham, and I intend to speak on Ireland. I am free from the trammels which fetter Mr. Gladstone, and I can speak without reserve and without fear. What I shall say will not increase your difficulties, but will, I trust, rather smooth your path with regard to English opinion. The Liberal party is not in a good position for undertaking any great measure of statesmanship. Some Whigs distrust Mr. Gladstone, and some, who call themselves Radicals, dislike him. He does not feel himself very secure as leader of a powerful and compact force. The Whig peers are generally feeble and timid, and shrink from anything out of the usual course. We want a strong man with a strong brain and convictions for a work of this kind, and I do not see him among our public men. I hope all that is wise and good in Ireland may support you, and that you may soon affect the opinion and conduct of Parliament.

I am, very sincerely yours,

JOHN BRIGHT.

THE ENGLISH PARLIAMENT AND IRELAND.

The following letter, written during the outbreak of Fenianism in Ireland, was read at a meeting of the National Association in Dublin, on Tuesday, the 6th of March, 1866. The speech to which it alludes was delivered by Mr. Bright on the 18th of February, 1866, in the House of Commons on the occasion of an intro-duction of a Bill by Sir G. Grey, on behalf of Earl Russell's Government, for the suspension of the Habeas Corpus Act in Ireland. Mr. Bright did not oppose the Bill, believing, he said, that the course which was about to be pursued, was the most merciful course for Ireland under the circumstances; but he made a powerful appeal for the removal of some of the evils under which the Irish people groaned, and denounced the way in which Ireland had been governed by this country for the previous 100 years.

London, March 3, 1866.

MY DEAR SIR,—I have received the copy of the resolution of thanks voted to me by the Committee of the National Association of Ireland. I value it very much, and ask that you will convey to the committee my gratitude for the approval they have expressed of my recent speech on the affairs and conditions of Ireland. I think there is a better prospect for your unfortunate country, and I shall gladly do all in my power to assist her own representatives and the Government in such legislation as may be required for her good. From the present administration[1] I am sure you will receive sympathy, and I cannot but hope that at an early period there will be a resolute attempt to conquer the malady which, from time to time, brings so much suffering to Ireland and so much discredit to England. I believe it is in the power of Parliament to remove all just causes of discontent with you, and I shall heartily co-operate in every effort tending to that result.

Believe me, always sincerely yours,

JOHN BRIGHT.

Peter Paul M'Swiney, Esq.'

SUNDAY CLOSING IN IRELAND.

Written in reply to a communication from Mr. T. W. Russell, Secretary of the Sunday-closing movement in Ireland, who had complained that although forty-two of the Irish members voted for the Sunday-closing Bill in the preceding session, and only ten against it, the Bill was thrown out by the English vote.

Rochdale, October 27, 1874.

DEAR SIR,—I think you have a grievance to complain of in the mode in which the House of Commons treated your Bill for closing public-houses on Sunday.

---

[1] Earl Russell's.

This seems to be one of the questions on which the opinion of the Irish members should have a special weight.

There is no great principle involved. Drapers and grocers cease from business on Sundays, and public-houses are allowed to be open only because it is supposed to be necessary for the convenience of the public ; but if the public, as represented by a great majority of the Irish members, are willing or wishful to have public-houses closed on Sundays, as the shops of other traders are closed, it seems a most unreasonable course for English members to prevent it.

I should recommend you to make a direct and earnest appeal to the Government, with a view to induce them to discourage the opposition made to the Bill.

I have no doubt that the Treasury Bench, if willing to aid you, could easily enable the Irish members, who are friends of the Bill, to pass the measure through Parliament.

By the help of the Government, and the further discussion which the Bill will receive next session, I hope you may succeed ; and I believe your success, whilst it will aid the cause of temperance, will be more beneficial to the publicans themselves than to any other class of your population.

I am, very truly yours,
JOHN BRIGHT.

Mr. T. W. Russell, Dublin.

THE IRISH LAND QUESTION.

Written to Mr. Henry Dix Hutton, who had published a pamphlet entitled " Prussia and Ireland."

Rochdale, November 11, 1867.

MY DEAR SIR,—I have read your " Prussia and Ireland " with much interest, and, as far as you go, I agree with you, but I think more requires to be done. Your plan is to help tenants to buy farms where owners are willing to sell, to lend them money on easy terms, and to take good security for the transaction. Owners are not very willing to sell, and the process of restoration, of creating an Irish proprietary, would be very slow. In my speech in Dublin a year ago I suggested another plan, not unlike yours, but more certainly operative, and with which yours might be combined. I proposed a Parliamentary Commission, empowered to buy large estates, particularly of English proprietors of Irish property, and to re-sell them in existing farms to existing tenants on terms something like those which you propose. A sum of 5,000,000*l*. thus at the disposal of the Commission would secure some large estates, and the process of creating "farmers, owners of farms," would begin at once and would go on rapidly. Your plan in fifty years would do much good, mine would do much in five years, and in twenty years or less would change the aspect of things in Ireland.

You want the change we are both in favour of, that is, we want to make the Irish farmer attached to the soil by the tie of ownership rather than by that which now exists, the necessity to have a holding in land that he may live. We want, further, to beget a new and national sentiment, to convince every Irishman now on the land that we do not intend to drive him across the Atlantic, but to remain a contented dweller on his own soil. I think my scheme would do this, would give hope and faith, and inspire him with a belief in the future, and stimulate him to effort and industry.

You will see the difference between your scheme and mine—mine is to grapple at once with the desperate malady which keeps your country in a state of chronic discontent and insurrection. Your plan may be more easily secured, but our children will only see much result from it—mine would, I think, restore confidence and banish speedily some of the despair and disloyalty which so extensively prevail. In some of our colonies, in Canada and in New Brunswick, I believe Government has bought off landlords' rights with great advantage to the people ; why not try something in Ireland ?

Thanking you for your excellent pamphlet,

I am, very truly yours,

JOHN BRIGHT.

Henry Dix Hutton, Esq., Dublin.

THE IRISH LAND BILL OF 1881.

Written to the Secretary of the Kilrea Tenant Farmers' Association.

One Ash, Rochdale, August 19, 1881.

DEAR SIR,—I have just received a copy of the resolutions passed by the tenant farmers of the Kilrea district on the subject of the Land Bill. I write to thank you and them for your friendly expressions towards myself. I believe the Bill to be a great and just measure, and that it ought to give great satisfaction to the Irish people. During Mr. Gladstone's administration the great questions of the Irish Church and Irish land have been, I hope, finally disposed of. The education question is no longer one of difficulty or of heated conflict. The Imperial Parliament has endeavoured to be liberal and just, it remains now with your people, by increased industry and by a regard to public order, to make Ireland not less prosperous and not less tranquil than England and Scotland now are.

With every good wish for you and your country,

I am, very truly yours,

JOHN BRIGHT.

THE IRISH LAND QUESTION.

Lord Kilmorey, having written to Mr. Bright for his opinions on the Irish Land Question, received the following reply :—

One Ash, Rochdale, November 11, 1887.

DEAR LORD KILMOREY,—I cannot undertake to discuss at length the propositions made in your recent letter; but I may say something of my views on the Irish Land Question. I do not agree with those who are saying so much about the dual ownership, as if there is a great importance in that phrase. The Land Act of '81 and the Land Courts have given fifteen years' leases to the tenants at a rent fixed by the Courts during the fifteen years. To me there seems no reason why, under these leases, landlord and tenant should not live in as much harmony as they have lived in past time under ordinary leases in Ireland, and as they live now in Great Britain. The difficulty arises, not from dual ownership, but from the agrarian and revolutionary agitation which has been created and continued since the passing of the Government Act of 1881. But for that agitation I believe the Act would have given a large measure of contentment and tranquillity in Ireland. As to further legislation, I cannot see the reason for any sweeping measure of purchase. The Act known as Lord Ashbourne's Act makes it easy for buyer and seller, tenant and landlord, to transfer a farm from one to the other, and thus, wherever it is desirable to be done, tenants will gradually become owners, and the Irish ownership of land will become more extended and secure. I am told the transaction or transfer is more slow and tedious than it ought to be; but surely this may be remedied, and the process of replacing present owners by tenants may go on at the same time in all parts of the country. The idea of buying up or buying out the proprietary class seems to me monstrous, unnecessary, and unjust. There are hundreds, many hundreds of proprietors in Ireland who do not wish to be bought out; they would prefer to retain possession of their ancestral mansions and estates, and have no wish to seek homes in Great Britain or elsewhere. For Parliament to insist on compulsory sale would be to gratify the disloyal leaders in Ireland. They wish to get rid of the proprietary class, and then they say, and perhaps they believe, they could unite the whole of Ireland in hostility to England. To get rid of the proprietors will be to establish a wholesale system of absenteeism, and to make the Chancellor of the Exchequer the great receiver of the rents from the great all Ireland absentee estates.   Is it possible that any sane statesman will con-sent to such a scheme, or offer to Parliament and the country so wild a policy as that involved in it? I have no affection for the system of landlordism as it has presented itself in too many cases in Ireland.   I have condemned it, and urged its reform in speeches in Parliament and on public platforms in England and in Ireland so far back as thirty years ago.   I have said there can be no security for landed property in Ireland until land as a property was made free of sale and purchase by a radical change in our laws, affecting its sale and purchase and tenure.   I have suggested means by which this great reform might be effected, but I never held the opinion that Government should step in to banish the landlords and make all tenants into owners, if not at the risk of the Imperial Exchequer.

I am of opinion that enough has been done.   Lord Ashbourne's Act is a measure sufficiently extensive and effective.   Under it, by a gradual and safe process, the desirable change may be made.   As it succeeds in different parts of the country it will naturally extend itself according to the opinions and interests of land-lords and tenants, and from year to year Parliament may vote additional sums to carry out the transfer policy so far as success may justify its extension.   Proceeding in this manner, it will not be necessary to involve the Imperial Exchequer in dangerous risks or in contests with tenants, or baronies, or poor law unions.   Nor will there be any need to take security for its advances, or an addition to duties on Irish imports, as has recently been proposed.   The process of transfer will go on at a moderate speed, and it will be seen how far the tenants who have become owners are willing and honest in the payment of the rents they have engaged to pay.   There will also be less danger of any widespread combination to throw upon the Imperial Exchequer the enormous cost which any failure of the plan of a general compulsory sale or purchase may or might involve. It is curious to witness the rashness with which some statesmen, members of Parliament, and public writers and teachers in newspapers rush in, and seize upon, and accept schemes so wild and unnecessary as are now proposed for the settlement of the Irish Land Question. I was before them all in pointing out the evil and the remedy. My remedy had in it the character of moderation, and if the Government will act upon it, the result will not fail, and they will not involve themselves in difficulties the magnitude of which they cannot measure. Let them learn something from the fate of the monstrous plan proposed by Mr. Gladstone, which, I suspect no one but himself and two or three of his colleagues ever approved, and which now almost every man is willing and eager to condemn. You will see that I am against this wild scheme. I think Parliament has gone far enough. I am for moderation in this question. I would not desire the banishment of all Irish proprietors, nor would I make my friend Mr. Goschen the universal absentee proprietor and rent collector for the whole of the landed property of Ireland.

Forgive this too long letter, and believe me,

Very truly yours,

JOHN BRIGHT.

THE FUTURE OF IRELAND.

Written to Mr. Barry O'Brien in reference to his work, " Fifty Years of Concession to Ireland," published in 1883.

One Ash, Rochdale, October 4, 1883.

DEAR SIR,—The handsome volume you have sent me reached me last evening. I occupied a portion of the evening in reading it. I am sure I shall find much valuable matter in it, and I wish it could be extensively read in England and in Ireland. Ireland needs to be informed as well and as much as England; but while

England is willing to learn, and is now well disposed, a large portion of Ireland is not willing to learn, and has put itself into the hands of men whose purpose is that it shall only learn what is hostile to England, and, as I think, must be injurious to itself.

As to the future, I do not take so gloomy a view as many writers do. I believe in just measures, and in their effect, and in time and patience, and I am ready to hope, and even to believe, that within a reasonable period we shall see a change for the better in Irish affairs. If men will read your book of the "Fifty Years," they will know more about Ireland and may make more allowance for the present unhappy state of the relations between her and the more powerful island. I thank you for your kindness in sending me your book. I hope it will be extensively read and extensively useful. I am, very truly yours,

JOHN BRIGHT.

HOME RULE.

Rochdale, January 20, 1872.

MY DEAR O'DONOGHUE,—It is said that some persons engaged in the canvass of the County of Kerry have spoken of me as an advocate of Home Rule for Ireland. I hope no one has ventured to say anything so absurd and untrue. If it has been said by any one of any authority in the county, I shall be glad if you will contradict it. To have two Legislative Assemblies in the United Kingdom would, in my opinion, be an intolerable mischief; and I think no sensible man can wish for two within the limits of the present United Kingdom who does not wish the United Kingdom to become two or more nations, entirely separate from each other.

Excuse me for troubling you with this. It is no duty of mine to interfere in your contest, but I do not wish to be misrepresented.

I am, yours very truly,
JOHN BRIGHT.

The O'Donoghue of the Glens, M.P.

HOME RULE.

Written to the Rev. Thaddeus O'Malley, Dublin.

London, Reform Club, February 25, 1875.

DEAR SIR,—I thank you for your letter and the little book on " Home Rule; or, The Basis of the Federation." I have read the book. Shall I tell you what I think of two Irish plans on this Irish question? The Mitchell plan is easy to understand, and if Ireland were unanimous and strong enough, it might be attempted, and might succeed. It is very simple, and under the conditions I have mentioned is not, or would not be impracticable; but the conditions are wanting, and therefore there is this fatal objection to it, that it is impossible, and only men partly mad or wicked will urge Irishmen to attempt it. As to your Federation plan, the Home Rule scheme of which you are evidently proud to be thought the author, is in my opinion quite as impossible as the other, and I must say that it seems to me far more absurd. To look at it only for a moment raises wonder that any man or number of men should imagine or think seriously of such a scheme. How many Home Rulers, how many men of that faith are there in Ireland? Certainly not more than a million. If I give you four millions of the disaffected Home Rulers, Repealers, Irish Republicans, or other antagonists of Great Britain—and this is more than you can fairly claim—they will give you only one million of men, and of these not one half have any knowledge of political and public affairs; and yet you propose, in order to allay the discontent of this part of your population, not only to make a revolution in Ireland, but to do the same in England, Wales, and Scotland. In Great Britain nobody wants two Parliaments of Lords and Commons. Nobody wants a third Imperial Parliament. And yet you propose, with a childish sympathy and enthusiasm, to force upon England, Wales, and Scotland these additional representative and legislative bodies, in order, apparently, to justify or balance the creation and establishment of like arrangements in Ireland. Surely so absurd and monstrous a proposition was never before heard of! You propose that twenty millions in Great Britain shall, in a manner, turn everything to which they are accustomed, and with which, in the main, they are satisfied—upside down, in the hopeless attempt thereby to allay the discontent of a portion of the people of Ireland—the said portion of your people never having been able to make a clear statement of its grievances, and being, as you must feel, totally unable to agree in any remedy for them.

I do not enter into any examination of the details of your little book, or I might point out many inaccuracies into which you have fallen. I confine myself, in this reply to your letter, to the main features of the two plans for the regeneration of Ireland. I believe them both to be impossible ; but your plan of Home Rule seems to be eminently childish and absurd. I must ask you to forgive the plain speaking or writing of this letter, but I am unwilling to leave you in any doubt of my views, after I have read the little book you have been kind enough to send me. Since I have taken my part in public life I have thought myself, and have intended to be, one of the best friends of Ireland, and I think now that I have never been more so than I am at this moment.

I am, very faithfully yours,
JOHN BRIGHT.

Rev. Thaddeus O'Malley, 1, Henrietta Street, Dublin.

THE TACTICS OF THE IRISH NATIONALIST PARTY.

The following letter was addressed during the election of 1885 to Mr. Blennerhassett, Liberal candidate for the North-Eastern Division of Manchester, whose election meetings were much disturbed by Irishmen. At the municipal elections a city councillor was unseated by the Irish vote on account of his political sympathy with Mr. Blennerhassett.

One Ash, Rochdale, November, 2, 1885.

DEAR MR. BLENNERHASSETT,—I observe that you are making a strong fight for your division of Manchester, and that your violent opponents are from your own country. They join English Tories, who have ever refused concession and justice to Ireland, against you and your friends the English Liberals, who have always been willing to remove every grievance of which Ireland has justly complained.

The English Government in past times has been cruel to Ireland. In our day, it seems to me, the great enemies of Ireland are those who profess to lead her people, and who lead them to disorder and to the destruction of their industry. I hope, notwithstanding the wild violence of a portion of your Irish population, there may be found among them some who will unite with Englishmen to send to Parliament a representative whose only object in the House of Commons will be to promote what is just to your country and to mine, and to restore the harmony which is essential to the welfare of the United Kingdom. If I were in your division, I would gladly give a vote, but it is only in my power to send you good wishes for your success.

I am, sincerely yours,
JOHN BRIGHT.

R. P. Blennerhassett, Esq., M.P.

MR. GLADSTONE'S IRISH SCHEME.

On the 26th of April, 1886, Lord Hartington addressed a meeting of his constituents at the Co-operative Hall, Rawtenstall, at which the following letter, addressed to Lord Hartington's chairman, was read :—

April, 1886.

DEAR SIR,—I cannot attend any meeting during the recess, but I feel an interest in your meeting at which Lord Hartington is to speak. There is a division in the Liberal party on the subject of the Irish Bills now before the House of Commons, to which your representative is opposed. To me, he seems to have acted in a manner at once consistent and courageous, having done in the House of Commons exactly what his constituents might have expected him to do from his speeches during the election contest. The Irish Bills are of such magnitude and importance that difference of opinion was unavoidable. Does any one imagine that such Bills can become law without the manifestation of the difference of views which they have created? It would be a calamity for this country if measures of this transcendent magnitude were to be accepted on the authority of a leader of a party or of a minister, however eminent, and that no other member of the party was to be permitted to hold or to express strong doubts or even diverse opinions of the measures proposed. For the constituencies to accept the system would be to deprive of their value the working of representative institutions. Party division has arisen from the introduction of measures of vast importance without any sufficient preparation of the public or the party mind to accept them. The measures themselves, and the time and manner of their introduction in Parliament are the causes of the division of the Liberal party, and not the opinion and criticisms of honourable men. The party may be shaken for a time, but it will revive, for consistency is not without value in the estimation of our countrymen.

I am, yours truly,
JOHN BRIGHT.

Thomas Brooks, Esq.

THE HOME RULE BILL OF 1886.

The following letter was written to Mr. Grosvenor Lee of Birmingham, during the discussion of the second reading of Mr. Gladstone's Home Rule Bill :—

Reform Club, May 31, 1886.

DEAR SIR,—Forgive me for not having replied

sooner to your letter.   The debate will soon close, and there will be time to discuss the bills after they are withdrawn.   I think the Home Rule Bill should have been withdrawn before the second reading, and but for the fear of a dissolution, which decides the votes of some scores of members, this would have been done.   I hope the course I shall take will meet with the approval of those whom I am permitted to represent.   At some not distant day I shall seek an opportunity of discussing the whole Irish Government question in your Town Hall.   My sympathy with Ireland, north and south, compels me to condemn the proposed legislation.   I believe an united Parliament can and will be more just to all classes in Ireland than any Parliament that can meet in Dublin under the provisions of Mr. Gladstone's Bill.   If Mr. Gladstone's great authority were withdrawn from these bills, I doubt if twenty persons outside the Irish party would support them.   The more I consider them the more I lament that they have been offered to Parliament and the country.

I am, yours sincerely,

JOHN BRIGHT.

INTOLERANCE AMONGST LIBERALS IN RELATION TO HOME RULE.

The following letter was received by Mr. Rylands during his candidature as a Liberal Unionist for Burnley in June, 1886 :—

June 25, 1886.

MY DEAR RYLANDS,—I see that some of your old friends are at war with you, and am sorry to see it. They make no allowance for what they think an error, even when viewed in connection with many years of honest service, and when the future may show that what to them is error will turn out to have been patriotism and wisdom.   It is grievous to see with what bitterness Liberals can treat Liberals, whose fault is that they have consistently supported principles which all Liberals accepted less than a year ago. Honesty and capacity in a member are with some of small value in comparison with the suppleness which permits and enables him to "turn his back upon himself" when a great political leader changes his mind and his course. I am surprised that any real Liberal should be induced to oppose you. He cannot excel you in discharge of Parliamentary duty, and I should think he should rather admire than blame your steadfast adherence to that policy on which you believe you were elected in November last. If I have a place in the new Parliament I hope I shall find you in your seat, which is very near the one I often occupy.

I am, yours truly,
JOHN BRIGHT.

Peter Rylands, Esq., M.P.

MR. BRIGHT AND MR. GLADSTONE, IN RELATION TO HOME RULE.

On the 1st July, 1886, Mr. Bright addressed his constituents at Birmingham on the occasion of his re-election for the Central Division of that constituency. On the following day Mr. Gladstone addressed to him the following letter:—

Hawarden, July 2, 1886.

MY DEAR BRIGHT,—I am sorry to be compelled again to address you.[1] In your speech you charge me with having successfully concealed my thoughts last November. You ought to have known that this was not the fact, for, in reply to others from whom this gross charge was more to be expected than from you, I pointed out last week that on the 9th of November, at Edinburgh, I told my constituents that if the Irish elections went as expected, the magnitude of the subject they would bring forward would throw all others into the shade, and that it "went down to the very roots

---

[1] Mr. Gladstone had written to Mr. Bright a few days before with reference to his letter to Mr. Rylands.

K

and foundations of our whole civil and political foundation "(Midlothian Speeches 1885, p. 44). Do you now adhere to your accusation? You say I have described a conspiracy now existing in Ireland as " marching through rapine to the breaking up of the United Kingdom." This also is contrary to the fact. In 1881 there was in my opinion such a conspiracy against the payment of rent and the union of the countries, and I so described it. In my opinion there is no such conspiracy now, nor anything in the least degree resembling it. You put into my mouth words which coming from me would be absolute falsehood. Third, you charge me with a want of frankness, because I had not pledged the Government to some defined line of action with regard to the Land Purchase Bill. A charge of this kind as between old colleagues and old friends is, to say the least, unusual. Evidently you have not read the Bill or my speech on its introduction, and you have never been concerned in the practical work of legislation on difficult and complicated subjects. The foundation of your charge is that on one of the most difficult and most complicated of all subjects I do not in the midst of overwhelming work formulate at once a new course or method of action without consulting the colleagues to whom I am so much bound, and from whom I receive invaluable aid. It might, I think, have occurred to you, as you have been in the Cabinet, that such a course on my part would have been indecent and disloyal, and that I should greatly prefer to hear all the charges and suspicions which you are now unexpectedly the man to thrust upon me. You state you are convinced it is my intention to thrust the Land Purchase Bill upon the House of Commons. If I am a man capable of such an intention, I wonder you ever took office with one so ignorant of the spirit of the constitution and so arbitrary in his character. This appears to be, in your opinion, held by my countrymen in general. You quote not a word in support of your charge. It is absolutely untrue. Every candidate, friendly or unfriendly, will form his own view and take his own course on the subject. We must consider to the best of our power all the facts before us, but I certainly will not forego my right to make some effort to amend the dangerous and mischievous Land Purchase law passed last year for Ireland, if such effort should promise to meet approval. I have done what I could to keep out of controversy with you, and while driven to remonstrate against your charges, I advisedly abstain from all notice of your statements, criticisms, and arguments.

Always yours sincerely,
W. E. GLADSTONE.

Mr. Bright replied to Mr. Gladstone as follows :—

Bath, July 4, 1886.

MY DEAR GLADSTONE,—I am sorry my speech has so greatly irritated you. It has been as great a grief to me to speak as I have spoken as it can have been to you to listen or to read.

You say it is a gross charge to say that you concealed your thoughts last November. Surely when you urged the constituencies to send you a Liberal majority large enough to make you independent of Mr. Parnell and his party, the Liberal party and the country understood you to ask for a majority to enable you to resist Mr. Parnell, not to make a complete surrender to him. You object to my quotations about a conspiracy " marching through rapine to the break up of the United Kingdom," and you say there is now no such conspiracy against the payment of rent and the union of the countries. I believe there is now such a conspiracy, and that it is expecting and seeking its further success through your measures.

You complain that I charge you with a want of frankness in regard to the Land Purchase Bill. You must know that a large number of your supporters are utterly opposed to that Bill ; if you tie the two Bills together, their difficulty in dealing with them will be much increased and their liberty greatly fettered. I

K 2

think your friends and your opponents and the country have a right to know your intentions on so great a matter when you are asking them to elect a Parliament in your favour. Your language seems to me rather a puzzle than an explanation, and that of your colleagues, though contradictory, is not much clearer.

" I have done what I could to keep out of controversy with you." I have not urged any man in Parliament, or out of it, to vote against you. I have abstained from speaking in public until I was in the face of my consti-tuents, who have returned me unopposed to the new Parliament, and to them I was bound to explain my opinion of, and my judgment on, your Irish Bills. I stand by what I have said, and shall be surprised if the new Parliament be more favourable to your Irish measures than the one you have thought it necessary to dissolve.

Though I thus differ from you at this time and on this question, do not imagine that I can ever cease to admire your great qualities or to value the great ser-vices you have rendered to your country.

I am, very sincerely yours,
JOHN BRIGHT.

MR. BRIGHT'S CONSISTENCY WITH REGARD TO IRELAND.

Written to a Birmingham correspondent :—

One Ash, Rochdale, July 26, 1886.

DEAR SIR,—I have your note enclosing a copy of a letter from Mr. Gladstone to Mr. Napier, late candidate for Roxburghshire, in which it is said that " I contended in the year 1866 for a Legislature in College Green." The only foundation for this statement is that I said the Irish farmers would have more direct influence on a Parliament in Dublin than one in Westminster, which is quite true. I do not give you the words I used, but I give the true sense of them, and they in no

degree express the opinion that I was then, any more
than I am now, in favour of a Parliament in Dublin.
If the farmers in Ireland can claim a Parliament in
Dublin for their especial benefit, the people of Ulster
may ask for one in Belfast, and the crofters in the
Highlands of Scotland may demand one in Edinburgh
or Inverness.   It may be admitted that the nearer a
Parliament is to those it represents, the better it is
likely to be for both Parliament and people.   This is
an argument everywhere for Home Rule and for any
number of Parliaments, but it does not settle the right
or wrong of any particular demand.   I have never
expressed or held the opinion that a Parliament in
Dublin would be an advantage to the people of Ireland.   In the speech to the Cork Farmers' Club, to
which doubtless Mr. Gladstone refers, I showed how
little force there was in the Irish representation from
the want of unity among its members, half sitting on
one side of the House of Commons and half opposing
them on the other side.   If the Irish members had
been agreed upon any policy they could have carried
any measure that was reasonable and just in the House
at Westminster.   They could have disestablished the
Irish Church, and they could have passed the Land
Acts.   In the session of 1873, they combined, at the
command of the Irish Catholic Bishops, and threw
out Mr. Gladstone's University Bill and destroyed his
Government.   There is no record of their having combined when I spoke in 1866 for anything wise and
good for their country.   What I said to the deputation from the Cork Farmers' Club was in part an
argument, that may be used in favour of Home Rule
by those who are in favour of constitutional change.
It is an argument, the weight and effect of which
must depend upon circumstances.   In the case of
Ireland it seems to me to have little weight, for surely
the concessions to, and the liberal and, I hope, wise
legislation for, Ireland by the United Parliament since
the year 1866, are enough to convince any reasonable

man that the interests of the United Kingdom may be left to the Parliament at Westminster. Our experience during the last twenty years is, to my mind, strong confirmation of the view I have always held on the Irish question. You will see from what I have written that my opinion on the question of separate Parliaments in Great Britain and Ireland has undergone no change.

I am, very truly yours,

JOHN BRIGHT.

Mr. George Sumner, 1, Richmond Road,
    Birmingham.

POLITICAL INDEPENDENCE IN RELATION TO MR. GLADSTONE'S IRISH POLICY.

The *Manchester Examiner and Times* of October 23rd, 1886, had a leading article on the subject of Frederick Douglass, the emancipated slave, who had recently visited this country. In the course of the article, the writer, alluding to the struggle which took place in America for the abolition of slavery, said :— " In the crisis of the struggle, when Abolitionists were hooted and hustled on the Exchange flags at Liverpool, and the advocates of Emancipation could scarce get a hearing even in Manchester, one brave, true note sounded from Rochdale, vibrating through the land. Frederick Douglass never wanted an honest and trusty friend, nor the Abolitionists a champion, when Mr. Bright was ready to stand alone in their cause in England. Shame should fall on a pen, held in the Liberal hand, which now writes bitter revilings against the stoutest and most chivalrous champion of freedom and justice our country boasts. If it is a disappointment to any Liberal that Mr. Bright at this day believes his party in error, and so holds his peace, let us remember, in due submission of our own judgment, that before now he has differed from his party leaders, and has borne revilings, and has proved right in the end."

A correspondent writing to Mr. Bright on the subject of this leader, stated, in illustration of the necessity of the advice given in it, the fact that a Liberal club which had formerly exhibited a bust of Mr. Bright in a conspicuous position, had removed it into obscurity at the previous General Election, on account of Mr. Bright's divergence from Mr. Gladstone's Irish policy. Mr. Bright replied to his correspondent as follows :—

October 29, 1886.

DEAR SIR,—I thank you for your very friendly letter. The incident about the bust is interesting and may teach us something. Club and political associations regard themselves as existing to support a party, and they follow their leader so long as he is the accepted and acting leader. They mainly support Mr. Gladstone on the Irish question ; a year ago they would have repudiated any candidate who was in favour of a Dublin Parliament. They now charge the independent Liberals with breaking up the Liberal party, which charge can only be sustained on the principle that, wheresoever the leader of a party may go, the whole party is bound to follow him.

This is a principle I cannot adopt. I did not follow Lord Palmerston on the Crimean war, in which half a million of lives were sacrificed. I did not follow my colleagues in the Government of 1882 in the bombardment of Alexandria and in the Soudan war. I have not been able to march with the clubs and associations which shout for measures which, little more than a year ago, they would have condemned. We have not yet had an infallible leader, and till he appears upon the scene I must preserve my own liberty of judgment.

The Liberal party will not be destroyed. It will be instructed, and may be more competent for the work before it. I hope with you that we may see better times, but reunion will not come until a change comes which I may hope for, but of which at present I can discover no signs. Smooth talk on platforms will not bridge over the chasm which has been opened in our ranks.

I am, sincerely yours,

JOHN BRIGHT.

MR. GLADSTONE AND THE IRISH PARLIAMENTARY PARTY.

Written to the Marquis of Hartington in connection with a Conference of Liberal Unionists which was held in London on the 7th of December, 1886. Lord Hartington presided over the Conference, and in opening the proceedings read the letter :—

One Ash, Rochdale, November, 1886.

MY DEAR LORD HARTINGTON,—Your letter has caused me some anxiety, and I wish I could reply to it as you wish. As you know, I am against anything like a Parliament in Dublin—more against it, I suppose, than many or some of those who are acting with you. If present at the Conference or the banquet, I might be expected to say something, and should probably find myself in some difficulty. I fear to speak or even to write. The course taken by Mr. Gladstone since the close of the session has astonished me, and has given me great trouble. His speaking and writing, and especially his reception of the Irish deputation, seem to me to have driven him so far in a wrong course that we can have no hope of any more moderate policy from him. If I had to speak, what could I say? I could only deplore and condemn, and it would be impossible to avoid opening still more widely the breach which now exists between us, and which has given me so much pain. At this moment his allies in Ireland, Dillon, O'Brien, and Co., are driving matters to an extremity, and he and Mr. Parnell say not a word to arrest or lessen the calamity which I fear is impending. Mr. Parnell is, I believe, a proprietor of the League organ, *United Ireland,* and this paper is the chief promoter of the social war into which the people are being driven. Mr.

Gladstone is leading the bulk of the Liberal party in support of the men who are the authors of the desperate struggle which is now being waged between the owners and occupiers of land in Ireland. His voice is not heard in behalf of peace and moderation.

The Government may be compelled to take measures of repression, and the Liberal speakers at conferences and on platforms are pledging themselves and their audiences to oppose every form of law or of administration which has the semblance of what is termed coercion or of giving increased strength to the Irish Executive. If I were forced to speak, I should have to say some strong things, and I fear much I might not be of any real service. I could say nothing without seeming to attack Mr. Gladstone. This I might even do if I were sure of doing good, but I am not sure of this, and I abstain from attacking him from my personal regard for him, which even his present unwisdom cannot greatly diminish.

I do not feel that I can come to the Conference or the banquet with a prospect of being useful or with comfort to myself. I hope your meeting may be large and influential, and that its effect may be good in the country, and that it may add strength to the Government so far as it may be our duty to support them. If this letter disappoint you, I trust to your forgiveness after the explanation I have thought it right to give you.

I am, sincerely yours,
JOHN BRIGHT.

The Marquis of Hartington, M.P.

IRISH INDUSTRIES.

The following letter was written to Mr. Robert Dennis, author of "Industrial Ireland":—

One Ash, Rochdale, January 28, 1887.

DEAR SIR,—I thank you for sending me your volume on "Industrial Ireland." I have read it with much interest, and wish it could be read in every household in Ireland. It is a deplorable thing that the men who are now supposed to represent Irishmen and Irish tenants are never heard to speak a word of counsel to their countrymen on behalf of industry, honesty, or temperance. They might sometimes point out that industry and temperance would do much to lessen the evils with which Ireland is afflicted ; but that might not add to their influence or to the money contributions they raise from Irishmen in Ireland or in America. The Land Act of 1881 gave a most complete security to the results of industry on the part of the tenants, but their leaders have condemned the legislation so much in their favour, and have never advised them to make an honest use of their new position. Industry has no chance in the turmoil of revolution, and so long as the Irish tenantry are influenced and misled by a conspiracy whose main objects are to plunder the landowners and excite bitter hatred of England, I see little hope of improvement in the condition of the country. I hope your volume may be widely read in Ireland ; it will excite much thought, and can do only good.

Yours very sincerely,
JOHN BRIGHT.

Mr. Robert Dennis.

THE BREAK IN THE LIBERAL PARTY IN CONSEQUENCE OF MR. GLADSTONE'S IRISH POLICY.

The following letter was addressed to a Liberal Unionist of Birmingham who had asked Mr. Bright whether he intended to address his constituents shortly, and for his views as to the negotiations relating to the project of Liberal reunion :—

Alexandra Hotel, Hyde Park Corner, London,
February 9, 1887.

DEAR SIR,—You ask questions which no one can answer. I have been accustomed to go to Birmingham at the invitation and under the arrangements of the Liberal Association. I suppose it has been thought best not to hold any meeting under the present confusion in the political world. As to my opinions I stated them very fully at the Town Hall meeting on the 1st of July last. I left no one in doubt as to my views on the Irish question, and what has happened since has only tended to confirm me in those views. The break in the Liberal party is to be attributed to the unwisdom of its leader; and the most deplorable thing in the whole of the disaster is the manner in which the bulk of the party has abandoned its position and its policy to adopt a new position and a new policy at the invitation or command of that leader. Thirty years ago the bulk of the Liberal party, pledged to peace, retrenchment, and reform, followed Lord Palmerston into the war with Russia. Now the party will condemn their course of thirty years ago. At this moment they are talking for and voting for measures which few of them understand, accepting them as good from the hands of a popular Minister. I have been associated very intimately with this popular Minister for twenty years. I have spoken for Ireland for thirty years, and have implored successive Prime Ministers to do what legislation can do for that country. My sympathy for the Irish people is as warm and as real as it ever was, and it is with this sympathy unbroken and unimpaired that I dare not hand over their interests to the conspiracy which is bent on destroying the owners of the land as one step—as they hope a successful step—towards the severance of Ireland from the United Kingdom. I think a majority of instructed and thoughtful men in Ireland will prefer the protection and the justice of the Parliament of the three kingdoms at Westminster to the rule of the conspirators, to whom so much of the present suffering and demoralization of their unhappy country is due. I have not answered your questions, but have said what occurs to me as I read your letter.

Yours very truly,
JOHN BRIGHT.

THE IRISH MEMBERS AND THEIR SUPPORTERS.

The following letter was written to the Rev. John Sherlock, a Roman Catholic clergyman of Birmingham, in reply to one he had addressed to Mr. Bright a few days before :—

Reform Club, Pall Mall, S.W.,
March 15, 1887.

DEAR SIR,—I have little to add to what I have said in my speech at Birmingham on the 1st of July last, and in letters I have since and recently written on the questions on which you have addressed me. My sympathy for Ireland is as strong as in past years, and I am as anxious to do justice to her people ; and it is this sympathy which makes it impossible for me to consent to hand over to this "rebel conspiracy" the government of five millions of the subjects of the Queen, of whom I cannot doubt two millions are loyal and content with the Union with Great Britain. You speak of the majority in Ireland and ask, "Why should they not prevail ?" that majority would probably vote to make their country a State of the American Union if it were put to them by their present leaders. But should the majority of the United Kingdom consent to it ? I am asked why I cannot trust those leaders. I do trust them most entirely. I have seen their course for seven years past, and have heard and read their speeches. I believe in those speeches, and see in them only hatred to England and disloyalty to the Crown, and I am unwilling to intrust to their tender mercies any portion of the population now under the government of the Imperial Parliament. It is believed that there are probably forty members from Ireland who sit in our Parliament, if not by votes, yet by the support of dollars contributed by the avowed enemies of England on the American continent. Am I to trust these men and to make them masters of one of the three kingdoms ? Is it not possible that my sympathy may be as warm as yours for the Irish people, and even as warm and intelligent for those who are members of your Church ? Do not imagine that I have given up the principles of my early days. I adhere to them without doubting as to their soundness, and never more firmly than now.

I am, very respectfully yours,

JOHN BRIGHT.

Rev. John Sherlock, 123, Moor Street,
Birmingham.

COERCION IN IRELAND.

In response to resolutions passed at a meeting of the members of the Borough of Greenwich Conservative Association approving the Irish policy of the Government, and thanking the Liberal Unionists for their patriotism, Mr. Bright addressed the following letter to the chairman. The Bill referred to was the Criminal Law Amendment (Ireland) Bill, which was then being discussed in the House of Commons :—

One Ash, Rochdale, April 27, 1887.

DEAR SIR,—I thank you for sending me a copy of the resolution to which your note refers. I believe it is necessary to strengthen the Executive power in Ireland, and I have, therefore, hitherto supported the Bill now before the House of Commons.

No Government, Liberal or Conservative, will promote measures of this kind except under a strong sense of their necessity.

They bring a Government into much difficulty, and, with not a few persons, make it unpopular, and they interfere greatly with the Parliamentary measures which every Administration is anxious to carry through Parliament. The present Government believes in the necessity for this Bill, or of some Bill having a like object. I believe that some measure of the kind is demanded by the condition of Ireland. In 1881 and 1882 I consented to measures of repression for the sake of law and order. I was then a member of the Government. What I thought needful then and what I think needful now, I will not condemn or oppose because it is introduced into Parliament by a Conservative and not by a Liberal Government.

I am, respectfully yours,
JOHN BRIGHT.

THE UNIONIST CAUSE AND ITS OPPONENTS.

The following letter, addressed to Mr. Chamberlain, was read at the evening meeting held at the Town Hall, Birmingham, under the auspices of the National Radical Union :—

Rochdale, May 30, 1887.

An engagement entered into two months ago, and which I cannot now break, will not allow me to take part in your meeting on Wednesday. I can only wish you the success which our cause merits, and, observing what is passing around us, I come to the conclusion that the cause is prospering. The friends of disunion become more angry and their language in regard to us who differ from them, more severe and more bitter. This is some proof that they feel that their restoration to office and to power is becoming less probable and possible so long as they adhere to the policy which was so signally defeated at the election of last July. It is impossible to believe that the constituencies can see with sympathy and approval the conduct of the Opposition which is led by the dual partnership of Mr. Gladstone and Mr. Parnell. Within the last two years, and indeed within one year of that period, we have seen three Administrations outvoted and destroyed in the House of Commons. Mr. Gladstone's Government was destroyed by the vote on Mr. Childers' Budget, on June 8, 1885. Lord Salisbury came into office; he was beaten, and his Government destroyed by the special action of Mr. Gladstone, on January 30, 1886; and on June 7, six months later, Mr. Gladstone was defeated on his Irish Government Bill, and now he is doing all in his power to overthrow the Government of Lord Salisbury. I do not know if there is any other case in our Parliamentary history in which so many changes of government have taken place in so short a time. The French Government, I suspect, does not offer an example of a fatal defeat of three Administrations within twelve months. Mr. Gladstone was beaten on his Irish Government Bill on June 7, 1886, and he instantly dissolved Parliament. His Irish Bills had been fully explained and discussed, and a majority of thirty votes decided against him. He appealed at once to the constituencies, to the masses, to the householders of the United Kingdom. The result was fatal to his Bills and to his Government. If the eighty-six disloyal Irishmen had been absent, taking the whole of the representatives of Great Britain and the loyal Irishmen from Ulster, the majority returned was as two to one against him ; and, admitting the eighty-six members of what is termed the Irish party, there is a majority of more than 100 against him. To this great majority, given on a specific question of his own raising, it might have been expected that an experienced statesman would have yielded. But instead of this, he abuses the majority, says unpleasant things of the members who have deserted him, and, having turned his own coat so suddenly, has no patience with Liberals of even longer standing than himself who refuse to turn their coats at his bidding.

But what of the partnership, and to what has it led ? I venture to say to such a humiliation of the Liberal party which still adheres to Mr. Gladstone as its history has not before exhibited. The Liberal party plunged with Lord Palmerston into war with Russia in 1854, and crowds of Nonconformists and their ministers were enthusiastic in his support. How many of them can look back upon their conduct without shame and regret ? And now crowds of Nonconformists and their ministers, it is said, march with Mr. Gladstone, it may be to a future of equal shame and regret. But the Ethiopian of 1881 and 1882 has changed his skin. Where is the proof of this? The Dublin newspaper, *United Ireland*, is said to be the property of the two leading members of the Irish party, and Mr. O'Brien is its editor. Its editor is now in Canada or the United States. He has visited Canada that he might slander the representative of the Queen, and, it may be, to excite something like insurrection against him. The last report of him is that he would not spend the Queen's birthday on territory under the British Queen, so great is his hatred of England and England's Sovereign. In Ireland an active member of the rebel conspiracy congratulates the mayor of an important corporation on his refusal to show civility or loyalty to one whom he described as a foreign Sovereign ; and *United Ireland*, the newspaper which is the property of Mr. Gladstone's most important Irish supporters in Parliament, concludes an article on the course taken by the town council of the city of Cork, in regard to the Thanksgiving Service in Westminster Abbey, by saying that the mayor caused a letter to be written setting forth why he and the town council declined to take part in a celebration which to all true Irishmen must be sickening.

It is to this conspiracy, consisting of men of this character, that the great surrender is to be made. It is to the eighty-six members, of whom it is said that at least forty of them sit in Parliament by right of dollars contributed in America by the avowed enemies of England and of the Queen's right of government, that the great English Liberal party is called on to abandon its past policy and to prostrate itself before an odious, illegal, and immoral conspiracy ; and to this conspiracy, made a Parliament in Dublin, we are to transfer the government of two millions of the Irish people who are as loyal as are the inhabitants of the county Warwick. And all this we are asked and advised to do by a statesman who has been for ten years the chief adviser of the Crown.

There are some men in the House of Commons now

following Mr. Gladstone and his Irish colleagues who do so with great doubt—some, I am persuaded, with a feeling not far removed from loathing. Their countenances express dissatisfaction and regret, and something akin to shame. How long they will march in line with the Irish eighty-six, how long they will come up day by day to the whip of the front Opposition bench, the progress of the session will show.

We, who remain true to the principles and policy of the Liberals who have gained so many victories of recent years, must grieve over the temporary ruin of the party. But we may console ourselves with the knowledge that our course has been direct, and that we stand before the country guiltless of the mischief and without shame.

I am, faithfully yours,

JOHN BRIGHT.

MR. GLADSTONE'S TREATMENT OF ULSTER.

The following letter was written by Mr. Bright in reply to one he received enclosing copies of resolutions passed at a Liberal Unionist meeting held a short time before in Belfast. The speeches to which allusion is made in the letter were delivered by Mr. Gladstone at Singleton Abbey, South Wales, on the 4th June, 1887 :—

One Ash, Rochdale, June 6, 1887.

DEAR SIR,—I thank you for your friendly letter and for the copy of the resolutions passed at your recent great meeting on the question of the Union.

I have just been reading Mr. Gladstone's speeches in South Wales. He speaks as if there were no province of Ulster, and no Protestant or loyal Catholic population in Ireland.

He seems ignorant or unconscious of the fact that the whole of Wales had a population in 1881 of only 1,360,000, which is, I think, less than that of Ulster by something more than 300,000. Ulster may be a nationality differing from the rest of Ireland at least as much

L

as Wales differs from England, but Wales is treated to
a flattery which, if not insincere, seems to me childish,
and Ulster is forgotten in the discussion of the Irish
question.

Is it not wonderful how one-sided Mr. Gladstone can
be, and how his great intellect can be subjected to
one idea, and how he can banish from his mind everything, however important, which does not suit the
purpose or object he has before him? He speaks,
too, as if it were a good thing to make Wales almost
as un-English as he assumes all Ireland to be. He
conceals the fact that there are more loyal men and
women in Ireland than the whole population of men
and women in Wales. It is sad that a great Minister
should descend to artifices so transparent and that
crowds of his countrymen should be thus imposed
upon.

Yours very sincerely,
JOHN BRIGHT.

Thomas Sinclair, Esq., Hopefield, Belfast.

In reference to the foregoing letter, Mr. Gladstone
wrote as follows to Mr. Bright :—

Dollis Hill, June 11, 1887.

MY DEAR BRIGHT,—Having my attention called by
many correspondents to your letter of the 6th inst., and
always regarding you as a good and kind friend, I write
to apprise you that you have inadvertently fallen into
an error of fact when, as you say, I spoke as if there
were no province of Ulster. In that same speech,
referring to the essentials of the Irish Government Bill,
I spoke expressly of Ulster, as you will find by reference
to any report of tolerable accuracy.

Yours sincerely,
W. E. GLADSTONE.

Mr Bright replied to Mr. Gladstone as follows :—

June 15, 1887

MY DEAR GLADSTONE,—My remark as to your

speech was not strictly accurate. I wrote from memory, and the sentence about Ulster was not sufficiently definite to have fixed itself in my memory. I regret the apparent want of accuracy, but on reading over the report of your speech I may observe that you deal with the Ulster question in a way not calculated to give any comfort or any hope to the loyal population of that province.

You say, "If there be a desire, a well-considered desire, on the part of the Protestant population in the portion of Ulster capable of being dealt with separately, we were perfectly agreed to consider any plan for the purpose." But can anything be more unsatisfactory than this sentence? You ask for a "well-considered desire" on the part of the "Protestant population." Has it not been known to all men that the desire has been "well considered," and that it has been expressed in the loudest tones by those who are entitled to speak for the Protestant inhabitants of the province?

You speak of the Protestants "in the portion of Ulster capable of being dealt with separately," and for these you are prepared "to consider any plan for the purpose;" but you must know that any plan for dealing only with the Protestants of Ulster by themselves, and not associated with the rest of the population of the province, is an impossible plan, and not worth one moment's consideration.

In dealing with this question, even in a speech to Welshmen, I think Ulster has a claim upon you for a definite expression of opinion as to your plan for the future government of the province. Your plan a year ago was to place Ulster under the rule of a Parliament in Dublin, and the people know and dread that their future fortunes would be subject to the control of a body of men about whose character and aims you and I differ very seriously. You deem them patriots, I hold them to be not patriots, but conspirators against the Crown and Government of the United Kingdom. It is not long since we agreed, or I thought we agreed, on this point.

You have changed your opinion. I can only regret that I have not been able to change mine.

The recent astounding revelations in the *Times* newspaper must have confirmed the fears and anxieties of the people of Ulster, and have increased their dread of being subjected to the rule of Mr. Parnell and of his agents and followers in Ireland and in the House of Commons.

I grieve that I cannot act with you as in years past, but my judgment and my conscience forbid it. If I have said a word that seems harsh or unfriendly, I will ask you to forgive it.

Always sincerely yours,
JOHN BRIGHT.

The Right Hon. W. E. Gladstone, M.P.

THE REFERENCE TO AN IRISH PARLIAMENT IN MR. BRIGHT'S SPEECH OF 1866.

On the 24th June, 1887, a gentleman in Edinburgh wrote to Mr. Bright asking him for an explanation of the following passage in his speech to a deputation of the Cork Farmers' Club in 1866 :—

"If you had a Parliament in College Green, clearly the tenantry of Ireland, with the present feeling in Ireland, would be able to force that Parliament to any measure of justice they desired; but as you have to deal with a great Parliament sitting in London, all the clamour you make, the demands you may urge, from this side of the Channel, come with a very feeble effect in London."

Mr. Bright replied as follows :—

18, Clifford Street, London, June 30, 1887.

DEAR SIR,—What I said to the Cork Farmers' Club was true, and I have nothing to retract. The same may be said of Scotland and Wales, and of the great counties of Lancashire and Yorkshire; but it does not follow that it would be wise to establish so many Parliaments in order to give special influence to special portions of our population. When I spoke the representation of Ireland was divided, half on one side of the House and half on the other side. No Irish member or party seemed to know what Ireland required, and until the formation of the Government of Mr. Gladstone, at the end of the year 1868, no resolute attempt was made to deal with Irish questions. Up to this period the House of Lords had constantly rejected measures, however small, which were intended to redress any Irish grievance, and that House had done much to create the mischief which has followed. Since that period—since 1868—great measures of Irish relief have passed both Houses of Parliament ; and Ireland has freely partaken of such legislation as it has been in the power of Government and Parliament to enact. Ireland is not neglected. The good measures passed since the year 1880 have been obstructed by a conspiracy which derives its funds and its inspiration to a large extent from enemies of England in the United States of America. But for the action of that conspiracy I believe the great Land Bill of 1881 would have given tranquillity to the tenantry of Ireland. I need not tell you how I have advocated economical and political changes for Ireland long before they were mentioned or thought of by men and statesmen who now pretend to a special interest in the country. I am as true a friend to Ireland now as I have ever been, and it is for this reason that I object to sever the United Kingdom and to surrender 5,000,000 of our population to the rule of a conspiracy which is represented in the House of Commons by forty or fifty members who sit there by virtue of contributions from America from men whose avowed object is to separate Ireland from Great Britain, and permanently to break up the union of the three kingdoms. I have made no change in my opinions of the Irish question. Others have changed, and to them my consistency is offensive. They follow their leader and strive to look happy in the pit of difficulty and party ruin into which his mistakes have led them. I cannot join them or help them. I can only deplore the wreck of the Liberal party power which I see around me.

Yours very truly,
JOHN BRIGHT.

THE GLASGOW CONTEST IN 1887.

The following letter was addressed to an elector of the Bridgeton Division of Glasgow during the by-election in July, 1887 :—

London, July 28, 1887.

DEAR SIR,—You ask my opinion as to the candidates who are now before the electors of your division of Glasgow. Under ordinary circumstances I would rather not interfere in your contest, but the circumstances are not ordinary, and I will answer your question with the frankness which you desire.

Your candidates are Liberals with whom I have acted and voted for many years in the House of Commons. Each of them, in ordinary terms, would have claims on the confidence of a Liberal constituency. But a great question has been forced to the front by an eminent leader of the Liberal party, and your election will turn upon that question. To me it seems that Sir George Trevelyan thinks no sacrifice too great to sustain the unity of the Liberal party ; for this he is now willing to give up the unity of the three kingdoms, having abandoned the position he occupied a year ago. Then he denounced the Irish policy of Mr. Gladstone, which he is now willing and even eager to accept.

Mr. Gladstone's disunion policy has undergone no essential change. He gives us many speeches, but there is no clear departure from his scheme of last year. Sir George Trevelyan asks you to send him to Parliament to support Mr. Gladstone, whose return to office and to power, so long as he is resolved to give up the government of Ireland to Mr. Parnell and his followers, would in my opinion be a great calamity to Ireland and to Great Britain.

Mr. Ashley, your other candidate, is a Liberal, as Sir George Trevelyan is, but with this essential difference. He doubtless values party, but for party he is unwilling and unable to sacrifice the unity and vital interests of his country. I value the Liberal party, and have worked much longer for it and with it than either Mr. Gladstone or Sir George Trevelyan has done, but I will not follow a majority of the party led by a statesman whose Irish policy little more than a year ago the whole party almost unanimously condemned.

Mr. Gladstone has led the Liberal party into difficulty and danger. The country will not let him go forward, and Mr. Parnell will not let him go back. Of the future it is difficult to speak, but to my view our duty is clear. If I were an elector in your division or city, I should give my vote to Mr. Ashley, for my country and its true interests, and not for a candidate ready to follow a leader whose Irish policy, in my judgment, tends only to confusion and danger.

I am, very respectfully yours,

JOHN BRIGHT.

Mr. John W. Mitchell, 33, Hope Street, Glasgow.

THE UNION.

The following letter was written to a gentleman in Ireland :—

London, August 8, 1887.

DEAR SIR,—I have read Mr. Dunbar Ingram's book with great interest, and hope it may be widely read. It gives a complete answer to the extravagant assertions of Mr. Gladstone as to the manner in which the Union was accomplished. I have, in years past, said some things about the Union, and what was done by the Government at the time, which I should not have said had I known the facts which Mr. Ingram has brought

before the public in his book.   There can be no doubt
that the Catholic bishops and the Catholic population
in general were in favour of the Union.   It relieved them
from the supremacy of the Protestants, and placed them
under the more just and generous control of the Imperial Parliament.   It would be well to have a cheap
edition of Mr. Ingram's work.   In 1800 the Catholics
sought relief from the intolerance of the Protestant
party.   In our day the Irish Protestants protest
against being subjected to the Catholic Parliament and
party which Mr. Gladstone's policy would place in
supreme power in Dublin.   I believe the most intelligent
of your Catholic countrymen and the possessors of property among them would prefer to intrust their future
and their fortunes to an Imperial Parliament in Westminster rather than to an Assembly in Dublin directed
by the leaders of the revolutionary schemes now pressed
forward, in alliance with the bitter hostility of the Irish
and anti-English party in the United States.   Mr.
Ingram's excellent book will be very useful with all who
can read and reason upon the great contest which is now
before us.

Believe me, sincerely yours,
JOHN BRIGHT.

COERCION IN IRELAND.

The following letter was written during the by-election
for North Hunts in August, 1887, to a voter in that
constituency, who had called Mr. Bright's attention to a
letter which was being circulated in the division by the
Liberal party, containing extracts from his speech on
Coercion, in 1866 :—

Tenby, South Wales, August 19, 1887.

DEAR SIR,—I am not surprised at anything the
Gladstonian candidate may write or say on the subject
of coercion.   He will, probably, not tell those who listen
to him that Mr. Gladstone's Government, of which I
was a member, passed two Coercion Bills in the years

1881 and 1882 far more coercive than the Crimes Bill of this year, the Bill of 1881 having seized and put in prison for many months many hundreds of men against whom no charge was preferred, who were brought before no magistrate, and no Court of Justice, on whose behalf no counsel was heard, and for whom no witnesses appeared, and whose period of imprisonment had no fixed limit, but was determined only by the will of the Irish Secretary for the time. I have been a long time in Parliament, and many Irish Bills have been passed to strengthen the Executive ; in my opinion these Bills were necessary, and I have never, so far as I remember, strongly opposed them. But I have condemned successive Governments for not attempting such legislation as I thought desirable, and indeed loudly called for, for the improvement of the Irish tenants and people. I believe the Bill of this year is a necessary measure, and I have voted for it. If Mr. Gladstone's Government had remained in office in the summer of 1885, I believe he would have been forced to continue or to introduce a measure of a like character, which I should have supported, for then and now I could not have complained that the Government was unwilling to pass useful and generous measures for the benefit of the Irish people. No Minister has done more, as Minister, for Ireland than Mr. Gladstone, and I am often almost ready to think that in despair he is willing to hand them over in future to the tender mercies of the men who have given him so much trouble during his tenure of office from 1880 to 1885. It should be remembered that no Government, Conservative or Liberal, ever brings in a Bill of coercion except under the pressure of a belief in its necessity. Such a Bill is unpopular in Parliament, and it makes a Government unpopular in the country ; and so long as a Government can avoid it, it does avoid it. I know this from my experience as a member of Mr. Gladstone's Government in the sessions of 1881 and 1882. The Opposition is generally unjust and unscrupulous ; it was never more so than now. A mixture of those who clamour for office and those who clamour for the separation of Ireland from England is one to be wondered at, and dreaded, and condemned. Pray excuse a somewhat long letter in reply to yours received this morning.

Yours, with great respect,

JOHN BRIGHT.

MR. BRIGHT'S FRIENDSHIP FOR IRELAND.

Written to a gentleman at Paisley with reference to some criticism passed upon him at a Ladies' Land League meeting in that town :—

Melrose, October 1, 1887.

SIR,—I never was more the friend of Ireland than I am now, when objecting to hand over that unfortunate country to the rule of the revolutionary and rebel conspiracy with which the Government is now contending. The justice that Ireland requires is not only that the laws should be just, but that they should be obeyed. It is my sympathy for the Irish people which forces me into strong opposition to the political views of Mr. Gladstone and Mr. Parnell. The latter, as far as I know, has not changed. The former, five years ago, condemned and denounced him ; now he comes forward as his apologist and defender. Am I wrong not to follow him ?

Yours very truly,

JOHN BRIGHT.

"FORCE NO REMEDY."

A Liberal Unionist in Derbyshire having called Mr. Bright's attention to the fact that the Gladstonians had stated that he could not support the Irish policy of the Government, especially the suppression of the National League, inasmuch as he had declared " that force is no remedy," Mr. Bright replied :—

Melrose, N.B., October 2, 1887.

DEAR SIR,—I am not surprised at what you tell me. The disunionists, whether under Mr. Gladstone in England or under Mr. Parnell in Ireland, are not careful as to the truthfulness of their statements. They quote my expressions of sympathy with the Irish people in past years as justifying the demand for a Parliament in Dublin. They quote a passage from one of my speeches —" force is no remedy "—which is quite true now as it was true when I used those words. Force is no remedy for a just discontent, but it is a remedy, and often the only remedy, for the disorder and the violence against which our laws are provided. I supported the Acts of Mr. Gladstone's Government in 1881 and in 1882 to put down the Land League and the disorder in Ireland. I now support the Government in their endeavour to suppress the rebel movement of the National League, which is the Land League under another name. My sympathy for Ireland was not born of faction and in a struggle for office, and pay, and power. It was as strong as it is now thirty years ago, before Mr. Gladstone, Sir William Harcourt, or Mr. Morley and their noisy followers had a word to say in favour of the Irish tenantry or of the sufferings of any portion of the Irish people. That sympathy is not lessened in my mind but is strengthened by recent events. We have delivered the Irish tenant from all that was unjust and oppressive in laws affecting his tenure of land. What more is needful, or most needful, is to set him free from the wicked conspiracy which is leading him to dishonesty and to crime. He is taught by the leaders of this conspiracy that his true interest is to plunder his landlord and to cherish a bitter hatred of England ; and industry, and honesty, and regard for law are not only neglected, but despised and condemned. It is this conspiracy which the bulk of the Liberal party is now asked to ally itself with. Its leaders, forgetting whatever is honourable in its past history, ask their followers to march in a path which can lead only to party disgrace and national disaster. I would save the Liberal party—with which

I have been much longer associated, and for which I have worked more than any of its present acting leaders —from the humiliation to which it is invited, and I would, with my sympathy for Ireland, save its population from the future conduct of the men who are answerable for much of its present sufferings, and for all the disorder by which it is now afflicted and disgraced. There are two millions of loyal people in Ireland ; let us be firm in our resolve, and if it be possible, as I believe it is possible, save them from expulsion from the guardianship of the Crown of the United Kingdom, and from the shelter and the justice of the Imperial Parliament. This is the answer I give to the false and malignant aspersions by which I am assailed, and to which you have called my attention.

I am, very truly yours,

JOHN BRIGHT.

SOME FEATURES OF THE HOME RULE POLICY.

On October 2nd, 1887, the Hon. A. D. Elliot, M.P. for Roxburghshire, addressing a meeting of his constituents at Kelso, read the following letter from Mr. Bright :—

Melrose, October 3, 1887.

DEAR MR. ELLIOT,—I see you are expected to address your constituents at Kelso on Wednesday of this week. I should like to be there if I could be present only as a listener, but that is scarcely possible ; but if I do not speak I may write a few lines to express my sympathy with you, and my hope that you will be able to explain clearly what are the grounds on which we are compelled to differ from great numbers, and indeed from the main portion, of the Liberal party, led they scarcely know whither by Mr. Gladstone in connection with his Irish policy. For myself I do not discuss the question of a little more or a little less of a Parliament in Dublin. A Parliament is a great weapon if once created and opened—not difficult to form, but dangerous to deal with ; and to set up a Dublin Parliament now, would make Mr. Parnell one of the Prime Ministers of the Queen, at least nominally of the Queen. At present he sulks or skulks at Avondale, and keeps silence amid the tumult he has done so much to create, while his lieutenants keep the rebellion pot boiling in three of the provinces of Ireland. His right hand clasps the hand of Mr. Gladstone on this side of the Atlantic, and with the other he maintains a fraternal greeting with the gang in New York by whom outrage and murder were and are deemed patriotism in Ireland, and who collect the funds out of which more than half the Irish party in the Parliament at Westminster receive their weekly and monthly pay to insult the Speaker and to make useful legislation impossible. Mr. Gladstone tells us that a preliminary condition as to the future Irish measure is that it must be satisfactory to Ireland—meaning Mr. Parnell. Thus his coming Bill or Bills must run on the lines of the leader of the section of the House who are paid to play at rebellion in Ireland and to discredit the Parliament of Great Britain. The Liberal party is to forget its honourable past and to adopt this hideous policy for its future, and all this is to be done at the bidding of one man, a statesman of great eminence, but no more free from liability to error than are other statesmen who have been held in some respect by the country. The two millions of loyal population in Ireland are to be forgotten and their claim to a voice in this crisis of their fate is derided and rejected. In this Jubilee year they are to be blotted out from the grand list of the subjects of the Queen, and to be passed over to what there is of truthfulness and wisdom and justice in the men in whom we have seen these qualities and virtues wholly ignored during the last seven years. The Liberal party is asked to make this great surrender, it is to forget its noble past, and to adopt a future leading to a gulf the depth of which no man can sound. Surely the Liberals of your noble county will not knowingly make a surrender which may be so fatal and must be so humiliating and ignominious. I place the question before you as it stands before me. I deal in no extravagance of language, but state the case in simplicity and, I hope, with clearness.

Believe me, sincerely yours,

JOHN BRIGHT.

The Hon. Arthur Elliot, Minto House, Hawick.

MR. COBDEN AND HOME RULE.

A Stockport correspondent having called Mr. Bright's attention to the statement of Mr. Gladstone at Northenden on the 18th October, 1887, that he had no doubt Mr. Cobden, if alive then, would have been a champion of the Home Rule cause, received the following reply :—

Melrose, October 20, 1887.

DEAR SIR,—I will say nothing as to what Mr. Cobden would have said if his valuable life had been spared to us ; but Mr. Gladstone must be hard pressed for authorities when he quotes as the probable opinion of an eminent man who died more than twenty years ago what is contradicted by all that we have of his views on the Irish question, and of his letters which remain with us.

Yours very truly,

JOHN BRIGHT.

MR. GLADSTONE'S IRISH SCHEME.

Mr. William Armstrong, of Chichester, wrote to Mr. Bright with regard to his scheme propounded before the electors of Birmingham, providing for the reference of Irish Bills to a Grand Committee of Irish members sitting at Westminster. Mr. Bright replied as follows :—

One Ash, Rochdale, November 21, 1887.

DEAR SIR,—The Irish rebel party will not look at my suggestion, because they are rebels ; and with rebel Irish members in the House, the plan would not be allowed to work. Mr. Gladstone has a hobby or plan of his own, in which the rebel leaders for the time have agreed to join him. He is committed to it, and cannot condescend to another plan which is less pretentious and more reasonable than his own.

He has offered a scheme which the country has rejected, but which has made all other schemes almost impossible. I do not think anything can be done until his Bills are entirely got rid of, and the present position entirely changed. Mr. Gladstone stops the way. He insists on an impossible legislation for Ireland, and insists upon it to the exclusion of legislation for the whole kingdom, and his followers still have faith in him, and are anxious to return him to power. They are furious because the Conservatives are in office, and blame me and others for keeping them there. They seem blind to the fact that Mr. Gladstone put them in office. He appealed to the electors on the merits of his Irish Bills, and the electors of Great Britain, by a majority of nearly two to one, condemned his Bills and destroyed his Administration.

We cannot allow Mr. Gladstone to come back to office with his Irish policy, and are willing to support a Government which the constituencies had by a great majority placed in power.

I prefer to join hands with Lord Salisbury and his colleagues than with Parnell and his friends—the leaders of the Irish rebellion.

Yours very truly,
JOHN BRIGHT.

COERCION IN IRELAND.

An Irish voter in Mr. Bright's constituency having written to the right hon. gentleman asking him how he reconciled his recent speeches and letters with a speech delivered in 1870, in which he said that it was the custom of the Tory party to meet every demand for reform in Ireland with coercion, Mr. Bright sent the following reply :—

One Ash, Rochdale, December 9, 1887.

DEAR SIR,—Surely the extract you send me answers your question ? What has Parliament been doing since 1871, but making concessions and granting reform for Ireland ? When reforms were not made I did not oppose the Acts giving strength to the Executive ; and now, when the great object of Parliament is to do full justice to Ireland, I am the less likely to see a system of terror in operation over a large portion of the country, and to refuse the legislation which the Government believe, and which I believe, to be necessary to repress it.

You speak of the drastic policy of the Government. It is much less drastic than the policy of Mr. Gladstone's Government in 1881 and 1882, and if any one denies this he is either ignorant of the Acts of those years or he is guilty of falsehood.

In 1881 many hundreds of men were put in prison for months without trial, without evidence against them, without defence of counsel, and without any proof of having broken the law. Now no man is punished or imprisoned except after trial by two magistrates in an open Court, when witnesses may be heard in his behalf, and when counsel may be heard in his defence.

The ruffians who are exciting your sympathy are the supporters of the terror which prevails, and their punish-ment, so far as I have seen any description of it, is much more mild than their offences warrant. I have written other letters in which I have explained the course I have taken. It would seem that you have not seen or read them. This short reply to your note may give the information you seek.

I am, very truly yours,
JOHN BRIGHT.

THE IRISH PARLIAMENTARY PARTY.

At a Radical Union meeting held at Handsworth, near Birmingham, on January 12, 1888, the following letter was read from Mr. Bright:—

One Ash, Rochdale, January 9, 1888.

DEAR SIR,—I cannot be present at your meeting on Wednesday, but I may be permitted to write to you a few lines on the great question which you are about to discuss.

Many of our opponents condemn us because we have not blindly followed Mr. Gladstone as they have done, and that we have not sacrificed our principles in order to maintain unity in the Liberal party. Let me remind you and them what we have done, and how far the result has justified our course. If the Unionist section of Liberals in the session of 1886 had supported the Irish bills of Mr. Gladstone, his Irish Government Bill would probably in some shape have passed. The Land Bill would not have passed, for being more easily understood it was more generally condemned. We should, I suppose, by this time have seen an Irish Parliament sitting and debating and legislating in Dublin, and we should also have seen Privy Councillors and Cabinet Ministers of the Queen in their high offices in connection with the bar in the Dublin Parliament. Where would the Queen find her Privy Councillors and the members of her Irish Cabinet, and from what section of the Irish Parliament would she select them ? Would the Dublin Parliament differ materially from the well-known 86 Irish members now sitting in Westminster? If not, how many of the men with whose faces and conduct we have been familiar during the last seven years would be installed as Ministers of the Crown ? Look over the names of some of these men. Begin with Mr. Parnell, and then go on to O'Brien and Dillon, and Healy, and O'Connor, and Harrington, and Biggar, and possibly we might add to them some of the Irish patriots who collect funds for the Irish revolution, but

M

who now prudently keep the Atlantic between them and the Irish courts of law. Out of these, and such as these, without doubt the Queen would have had to select her confidential advisers.

Look at what these men have said and done. One of them—and not the least important of them—urges his countrymen to treat as a leper the man who breaks an order of the Land League. He urges, in a public manifesto, all Irish tenants to refuse payment of rents, and in a noted speech to Irishmen in America, from whom the main portion of his funds are derived, he is reported to have said, "When we have given Ireland to the people of Ireland, we shall have laid the foundation upon which to build up our Irish nation. And let us not forget that this is the ultimate goal at which all we Irishmen aim. None of us, whether we be in America or Ireland, will be satisfied until we have destroyed the last link which keeps Ireland bound to England."

If I could speak to every thoughtful and loyal man in the United Kingdom, I would ask him to consider this matter, not in connection with Mr. Gladstone's leadership or the overthrow of Lord Salisbury's Government, but with something much higher than mere party strife. The nation has just celebrated the half century of the reign of the Queen, the people having shown their reverence for her high station and her noble life ; and they are advised when the general election takes place to force upon her a Minister whose policy in regard to Ireland would subject her to the monstrous and intolerable indignity of selecting her Irish councillors and Cabinet Ministers from the men who have given abundant proof of their disloyalty to the throne and of a bitter hostility to the people of Great Britain. What would English, and Scotch, and Welsh constituencies think and say if, after returning Mr. Gladstone to power, they find him surrounding himself with colleagues from leaders of the Irish revolutionary party ? And yet these men are now as legally qualified to be English as

Irish Ministers. We are asked to deliver the Irish people, of whom two millions out of less than five millions are horrified at the prospect, to a party whose entrance to a British Cabinet would be likely to produce an immediate insurrection.

What, then, has the Unionist section of the once honoured and powerful Liberal party done? It has saved the nation from a great peril, and it has saved the Sovereign of the three kingdoms and of a wide empire from the terrible indignity to which the passion of a statesman—aged and most eminent—and the credulity of a rash and unthinking party would have subjected her. Let us then be content with what we have done. The future will not fail us if we remain firm and true to our principles and to our faith.

Pray excuse this perhaps too long letter, and believe me, sincerely yours,

JOHN BRIGHT.

MR. BRIGHT'S CONDUCT ON THE HOME RULE QUESTION.

Written to a correspondent who had made some friendly criticisms on Mr. Bright's conduct on the Irish question.

One Ash, Rochdale, February 13, 1888.

DEAR SIR,—I thank you for your friendly letter. But you are in error. I do not go with Mr. Chamberlain, or with any other person, to meetings to speak for the Tories. I have attended no meetings since my election in 1886. You evidently think parties are everything, and that to keep the Liberal party together it is necessary to follow your leader. There are great questions on which leaders and parties may go wrong. I did not go with the Liberal party in 1854 when they plunged into the war with Russia. I was then attacked and blamed more than I am now. I was, it is said, burned in effigy in Manchester, and soon after lost my seat for that great constituency, but who now condemns me for the course I then took ? I left Mr. Gladstone's Government when they bombarded Alexandria and entered into war with the Soudan. Who blames me now for my desertion of the Liberal leader at the time for that cause ? The Russian war cost more than half a million of human lives. The bombardment of Alexandria and what followed cost most probably more than 50,000 lives, most of which were of men of whom I think Mr. Gladstone said they were rightly struggling to be free. Am I to prostrate myself before a leader in whose great career there are blunders so enormous as those to which I now refer ? I am sure your good sense will give a right answer to this question. It is said Mr. Gladstone's Irish bills are dead. Then what are we contending for ? Has he still the old bills in his pocket, or has he new ones ? If new ones, why not bring them before Parliament or the public for discussion ? Are you willing to go on blind-fold—happy to follow and in total ignorance as to where you are going ? If Mr. Gladstone has made so grievous a blunder less than two years ago in measures which are now universally condemned, how dare you trust him further in that which he studiously conceals from Parliament and the country ? I am, and always have been, against having two Parliaments in the United Kingdom ; and so long as the Liberal and Gladstone policy is in favour of two Parliaments I must follow my own judgment and conscience, and not the voice of any party leader.

Yours very sincerely,

JOHN BRIGHT.

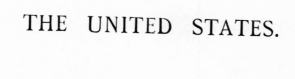

THE UNITED STATES.

THE UNITED STATES.

From the beginning of the terrible struggle between the Northern and Southern States of America, Mr. Bright was the friend and champion of the North and their cause, and many enthusiastic acknowledgments have since been made to him by the American people of the services he rendered to their country at that time. The first public recognition he received was from the Chamber of Commerce of the State of New York, the members of which, at a meeting on Thursday, the 6th of March, 1862, unanimously adopted a resolution recording their gratitude for his eloquent and fearless advocacy of " the principles of constitutional liberty and international justice for which the American people were contending."

This resolution having been forwarded to Mr. Bright, he replied as follows :—

London, April 4, 1862.

DEAR SIR,—I have received through the hands of the Hon. Mr. Adams, the Minister of the United States, your letter of the 8th of March, and the resolution unanimously adopted by the Chamber of Commerce of the State of New York on the 6th of March.

I wish you to convey to the eminent body of gentlemen over whom you preside the expression of my sense of the honour they have conferred upon me, and of the pleasure which it gives me to know that the course I have taken in reference to the events which are now passing in your country has met with the warm approval of those whom they represent. I accept their most kind resolution, not only as honourable to myself, but as a manifestation of friendly feeling to the great majority of my countrymen, whose true sentiments I believe I have not mistaken or misrepresented, when I have spoken on the side of your government and people.

I believe there is no other country in which men have been so free and so prosperous as in yours, and that there is no other political constitution now in existence, in the preservation of which the human race is so deeply interested, as in that under which you live. This is true, beyond all doubt, when applied to the Free States of your Union; I trust the time is not distant when it will be true all over your vast territory, from the St. Lawrence to the Gulf of Mexico.

Notwithstanding much misapprehension and some recent excitement, I am sure that an overwhelming majority of the people of the United Kingdom will rejoice at the success of your government, and at the complete restoration of your Union.

While asking you to convey the expression of my grateful feelings to the members of your Chamber, I desire to tender to you my thanks for the very kind letter from yourself which accompanied the resolution.

I am, with great respect, very truly yours,
JOHN BRIGHT.

To P. Perit, Esq., President of the Chamber of Commerce of the State of New York.

THE UNITED STATES AND CANADA.

Read at the sitting of a commercial convention held at Detroit on the 12th of July, 1865.

London, June 10, 1865.

DEAR SIR,—I am much obliged to you for the invitation to your approaching commercial convention, to be held in the month of July. If I were on your continent I should avail myself of your friendly offer to be present at your deliberations, and if I could not add much to their usefulness, I could learn much from them; but to me Detroit seems a long way from England, and, unfortunately for me, I seem never to be able to steal three months from my many engagements here, to enable me to pay a long-hoped-for visit to the United States, and now I find it quite out of my power to avail myself of your tempting invitation.   The project of your convention gives me great pleasure.   I hope it will lead to a renewal of commercial intercourse with the British North-American provinces, for it will be a miserable thing if, because they are in connection with the British crown, and you acknowledge as your chief magistrate your President at Washington, there should not be a commercial intercourse between them and you, as free as if you were one people, and living under one government.   I have faith that when your people, so free and so instructed, apply their minds to any question of commerce, they will soon discern what is true and adopt it, and in this faith I shall look with confidence for the most beneficial results from the discussions into which you are about to enter.   Whatever tends to promote harmony and commercial dealings between the United States and the Canadas will be favourably regarded by every intelligent statesman in this country.

Wishing you the happiest results from the convention, and thanking you for your letter,

I am, with great respect,

Very sincerely yours,

JOHN BRIGHT.

Joseph Aspinall, Esq.

SLAVERY IN THE UNITED STATES.

Written to Mr. John Lobb, the editor of the " Life and Times of Frederick Douglass," a history of an American slave's experience, and prefixed to the work.

132, Piccadilly, London, March 8, 1882.

DEAR SIR,—I am glad to hear that you are about to

publish an English edition of the "Life and Times of Frederick Douglass," in his youth a slave in the State of Maryland, now holding an honourable office in the district of Columbia, in the United States of America. I have read the book with great interest. It shows what may be done and has been done by a man born under the most adverse circumstances—done not for himself alone, but for his race and for his country. It shows also how a great nation persisting in a great crime cannot escape the penalty inseparable from crime. History has probably no more striking example of the manner in which an offence of the highest guilt may be followed by the most terrible punishment than is to be found in the events which make the history of the United States from the year 1860 to the year 1865. The book which you are about to offer to English readers is one which will stimulate the individual to noble effort and to virtue, whilst it will act as a lesson and a warning to every nation whose policy is based upon injustice and wrong.

I hope it may find its way into many thousands of English homes.

I am, with great respect, yours sincerely,
JOHN BRIGHT.
To Mr. John Lobb.

THE UNITED STATES AND PEACE.

Written to Augustin Jones, of the Friends' Boarding School, Providence, in reply to a letter announcing that a marble bust of Mr. Bright was to be erected there.

London, March 10, 1884.

DEAR FRIEND,—I regret that I have so long delayed an answer to your most kind letter, which reached me some weeks ago. It informed me of the singular and great compliment you were about to pay me by placing a marble bust of me in the lecture-hall of your noble school. I was surprised to hear of the project; but I cannot but be much gratified at the friendly feeling manifested to me by yourself and the authorities connected with your institution. You say that I was a friend to your country in the day of need. I did what I could to prevent discord between the two English nations, and to teach our people the nature of the great issue which depended on the conflict in which twenty years ago your people were engaged. I lamented the conflict ; but I wished that England should offer her sympathy on the side of freedom to the slave, and in favour of the perpetual union of your great Republic. I look back on the part I took with unalloyed satisfaction, and would withdraw no word I uttered in connection with a contest on which England and the civilized world looked with a profound interest.

The question of peace, to which you refer, claims the sympathy of all Christian nations. On your continent we may hope your growing millions may henceforth know nothing of war. None can assail you ; and you are anxious to abstain from mingling in the quarrels of other nations. Europe, unhappily, is a great camp. All its nations are armed, as if each expected an invasion from its neighbour, unconscious, apparently, that great armies tempt to war the moment any cause of dispute arises. The potentates and Governments of Europe, I doubt not, dread war. They seek to guard themselves against it by enormous armaments.

We, in England, are not free from blame ; but with us the love of peace is increasing, and no Government can engage in war without risking, and even losing, the support of our people. We are so involved with territory and populations over half the globe that difficulties are almost constantly arising, and our danger of war is greater than that of any other nation. I am, however, confident that our feeling against war is sensibly increasing, and I trust and believe the moral sense of our people will more and more condemn it.

I have read with much interest the report of your great school which you sent me. I hope your efforts in behalf of a sound, liberal education may prosper, and that your students, as they enter and pass through the world, may strengthen the moral sentiment which pervades so large a portion of your population. I can only wish you success in your great work, and thank you and all connected with your institution for the kindness you have shown me.

England and your United States are two nations, but I always like to regard them as one people. On them the growth of all that is good in the world greatly depends.

Believe me, your sincere and grateful friend,

JOHN BRIGHT.

THE FUTURE OF THE UNITED STATES.

Mr. Bright addressed to the Committee of the Centennial Commemoration, held in September, 1887, in Philadelphia, the following reply to an invitation to him to attend the celebration :—

September 9, 1887, One Ash, Rochdale.

DEAR SIR,—I am much indebted to you and your colleagues for the invitation with which you have favoured me to be present at the first Centennial Anniversary of the framing of the Constitution of the United States, to be celebrated during the present month in the city of Philadelphia.

It is not a pleasant thing to have to decline such an invitation, and yet I must ask you to excuse me if I am unable to accept it. I do not look upon two voyages with pleasure, and I have always been disposed to avoid great assemblies and great ceremonies.

I need not say how much sympathy I feel with the gathering to which you are looking forward with so great interest. All the civilized world, and all who love freedom in it, must regard the event which you are about to commemorate as one of the most important in the annals of men.

In the great struggle of twenty-five years ago the strength of your country was shown, and its unity was secured. My voice was raised at that time in favour of that unity, which I hope may never again be endangered or impaired. And now I would look forward with hope and faith. As you advance in the second century of your national life may we not ask that your country and mine may march in line in the direction of freedom and the policy which the moral law will sustain ?

May we not comfort ourselves with the belief that your country, under a succession of noble Presidents, with their Ministers and your Congress, and my country under a succession of patriot Sovereigns, with their Ministers and Parliaments, may assist and guide the growing millions for whom they act, to nobler ends than have hitherto been reached ? May we not ask that our two nations may be one people, and that in years to come—and years not very remote—the millions with you and the millions with us, whilst growing in numbers and in strength, may grow in wisdom, and may enter more fully into the enjoyment of the boundless blessings which are offered to the nations in the perfect freedom of human industry, and in the establishment of a perpetual peace ?

I am grateful to you and to those associated with you for your most kind invitation, and subscribe myself with every sentiment of respect,

Yours very sincerely,

JOHN BRIGHT.

To John A. Kasson, Esq., Philadelphia, U.S.A.

INDIA.

THE GOVERNMENT OF INDIA.

Written to Mr. Alderman Lloyd, of Birmingham, the day before the opening of Parliament in December, 1857. The terrible struggle for the suppression of the mutiny in India was at that time taking place.

Rochdale, December 2, 1857.

My dear Sir,—As Parliament, contrary to expectation, is about to meet before the usual time, I fear the electors of Birmingham will feel some disappointment if I do not make my appearance in the House during the present week, and the more so, from the circumstance that my colleague, Mr. Scholefield, will also be absent.

It is not necessary for me to explain to you, or to the gentleman who communicated with me at the time of the election, why I am not likely to begin my parliamentary duties before Christmas. It was then understood that, for six months, that is, until the time when Parliament usually assembles, I was not to be expected to undertake any labour connected with the position in which I was then placed by the good opinion of the electors of Birmingham. My own judgment, and the urgent advice of my friends and medical advisers, compelled me to make a resolution to that effect, and those of my Birmingham friends with whom I had any communication granted me a dispensation for that period. I do not suppose that any real business will be transacted before February, and therefore I hope that nothing which is entrusted to me will suffer from my temporary absence from the House.

It is because I wish to abstain as much as possible from public affairs, that I have not troubled my consti-

N

tuents with any views I may entertain on the great subjects which have been so much discussed during the past three months. On the question of India, indeed, I feel that it is almost rashness to utter a decided opinion, and I know not whether one ought to regard with admiration or with pity many of those who have written and spoken so confidentially upon it since the occurrence of the insurrection. Judging from the writings of the newspapers, and from the speeches of public men, I fear the country is by no means sufficiently aware of the crisis which has arisen, whether we regard the difficulty of restoring order in India, or the obstacles which oppose themselves to the future government of that country. Five years ago, when the India Bill was about to come under discussion, I thought I knew something of India, and felt that I could give advice on the subject. But the scene has totally changed, and that which was easy to be done in fair weather, may be impossible, or of little avail, when the storm rages. I presume, however, that the days of the Leadenhall Street rulers of India are numbered. Without character and without power, it requires but a vote of Parliament to give legal effect to that which, I believe, the public opinion of England has already decreed.

If the coming session shall establish the Government of India on a secure and wide basis, so far as that is possible in the unnatural position in which we stand to that country, I shall feel that Parliament has not laboured in vain ; and if the threatened postponement of a Reform Bill be a disappointment to me and to many others, I shall endeavour to console myself with the hope that the improvement of our representation will hereafter be entrusted to more friendly hands than those which now administer the affairs of the country.

Excuse me for troubling you with this letter, and believe me very sincerely yours,

JOHN BRIGHT.

Thomas Lloyd, Esq., Birmingham.

THE GOVERNMENT OF INDIA.

WRITTEN TO A GENTLEMAN IN INDIA.

Rochdale, January 14, 1860.

DEAR SIR,—I have received your letter on the subject of your next meeting, and informing me of the petitions which have been forwarded to my friend, Mr. John Dickenson, jun. I shall have great pleasure in presenting the petitions to the House of Commons, and in giving such help as may be in my power to your views. I am not sanguine that we shall easily produce any change in the Indian government. The whole concern is one of patronage—and those who now hold the good things will not willingly give them up. The English people, too, are very slow, and very careless about everything that does not immediately affect them. They cannot be excited to any effort for India except under the pressure of some great calamity, and when that pressure is removed they fall back into their usual state of apathy.

The English Government has always too much on its hands. To keep itself in power is considered its first duty, and there is little force and leisure to do anything else. It hands over India to Sir John Hobhouse, or Mr. Herries, or Sir C. Wood, or Lord Stanley, and takes no further interest in it until an insurrection is announced, or a loan in England is necessary ; and the Indian minister is expected never to trouble his colleagues except in the last extremity. Parliament cares about India little more than the Cabinet ; and thus the interests of your vast population are left to the tender mercies of an exclusive service whose main object of adoration is patronage. I almost despair of anything being done here, but you may rely on my honest assistance whenever there seems a chance of doing anything.

I am much obliged to Mr. Norton and to others of

N 2

your friends for their kind mention of me at the meetings, the report of which you have sent me.

I am, with great respect,

Yours sincerely,

JOHN BRIGHT.

H. Nelson, Esq.

THE INDIAN IMPORT AND EXCISE DUTIES.

London, February 7, 1878.

MY DEAR ARMITAGE,—I am surprised at the line taken by some of our friends of the Chamber of Commerce in the matter of the Indian import duties.

It seems dictated by passion and disappointment, rather than by reason and a sound judgment.

India has an interest in the question as well as England. If the people of India could speak and act as we can in England, they would oppose to the last degree of resistance any attempt to impose an excise duty of five per cent., or any amount, on the produce of their factories. If they were in theory Free Traders, and wished to be so in practice, they would oppose any such tax, and in my opinion, most rightly. They would say, as we ought to say, an excise duty on the produce of the mills is odious on every ground and cannot be permitted. They would look for the power to remove the import duties to greater economy in the public expenditure, or the regular growth of the public revenue, or the imposition of some new tax which might raise the needful 800,000*l.* a year. The grievance complained of in the Chamber can only be remedied in one of these three ways, for I feel very confident the House of Commons will never compel the Indian Government to adopt the odious and intolerable proposition which seems strangely to have found favour with some of the members of your Chamber.

I see in the same discussion in the Chamber objection is made to anything being done there which may be termed political. What is more political than a question of revenue and taxation? This dread of all serious questions is the cause of the feebleness and general uselessness of Chambers of Commerce.

I suppose the excise proposition is merely a weapon to use against the Government, and to compel it to act against the import duties. It must fail, for it is impossible to defend it. It would be much more wise to put pressure on the Indian Government to lessen its expenses, to reduce its English and native forces by the amount required, which surely may be safely done, if our Indian Government is so intelligent and so just as it constantly declares itself to be.

I write this rather hastily, after reading the report of the proceedings of the Chamber. I am not a member of the Chamber, but I shall be very sorry to see it take a course which must lessen its character for wisdom, and therefore lessen its influence.

If you think anyone will care about my opinion, you need not conceal it. I am sorry to be compelled to differ from any of our friends on this question.

Believe me, always sincerely yours,

JOHN BRIGHT.

Benjamin Armitage, Esq.,
48, Mosley Street, Manchester.

THE GOVERNMENT OF INDIA.

Written to Major Evans Bell, who was about to proceed to the United States on a lecturing tour.

One Ash, Rochdale, August 25, 1883.

DEAR MAJOR BELL,—I am always glad to hear that Englishmen are going to the States, and that Americans are coming here. The more we know of each other the better for both. I doubt if India is a subject which Americans will find or think interesting; but if you can make it so, they will learn something on a great question, which, as it concerns 250,000,000 of the world's population, must now and in future, for an intelligent people like our American brethren, have a great and growing interest.   You are supposed to judge somewhat harshly of our Indian Government.   In describing its course I do not doubt you will give it credit where credit is due, and that you will point out how much the people of England are disposed, so far as they are concerned, to govern wisely the vast population conquered by their fathers.   The task of the wise government of so vast an empire may be an impossible one—I often fear it is so— we may fail in our efforts, but, whether we fail or succeed, let us do our best to compensate for the wrongs of the past and the present by conferring on the Indian people whatever good it is in our power to give them. Perhaps when the United States are wise enough to abolish what they call protection—that is, protection of a class or classes at the expense of the nation—they may find a market in India, from which now their costly system shuts them out.   I hope you may have a pleasant voyage out and home, and that your excursion to the States may be in every way satisfactory to you.

I am, very truly yours,
JOHN BRIGHT.

THE GOVERNMENT OF INDIA.

Written on the receipt of a work which had been sent to Mr. Bright by its Bengali author.

London, November, 1884.

DEAR SIR,—You speak of my services to your country.   I wish I could have done more for your vast population now connected and subject to the rule of my country.   It is to me a great mystery that England should be in the position she now is in relation to India. I hope it may be within the ordering of Providence that ultimately good may arise from it.   I am convinced that this can only come from the most just government which we are able to confer upon your countless millions, and it will always be a duty and a pleasure to me to help forward any measure that may tend to the well-being of your people. I think I perceive an increased interest here in your welfare, and a growing intelligence and influence among the natives of India in anything that is calculated to promote their wise and just government. The principles which have distinguished the administration of Lord Ripon seem to me to be those which promise to be beneficial to you and creditable to us. I hope every future Governor-General may merit the confidence of our Government at home and of the vast population whose interests may be committed to his charge. I thank you for the gift of your volumes. I shall value them as you desire, and as a proof that in the little I have been able to do my small services have been appreciated by those for whom my sympathy and good intentions have been so strongly excited. So far as I know how to do so, I would be as much a friend of India as of England.

I am, yours, &c.,
JOHN BRIGHT.

THE LAND QUESTION.

FREE LAND.

Written to Mr. G. W. Sanders, of Stockton-on-Tees, in reply to an inquiry from that gentleman as to the meaning of the term "free land."

Rochdale, November 2, 1873.

DEAR SIR,—I have often explained in my speeches what is intended by the term "free land." It means the abolition of the law of primogeniture, and the limitation of the systems of entails and settlements, so that "life interests" may be for the most part got rid of, and a real ownership substituted for them. It means also that it shall be as easy to buy or sell land as to buy or sell a ship, or, at least, as easy as it is in Australia and in many or in all the states of the American Union. It means that no legal encouragement shall be given to great estates and great farms, and that the natural forces of accumulation and dispersion shall have free play, as they have with regard to ships, and shares, and machinery, and stock-in-trade, and money. It means, too, that while the lawyer shall be well paid for his work, unnecessary work shall not be made for him, involving an enormous tax on all transactions in connection with the purchase and sale of lands and houses.

A thorough reform in this matter would complete, with regard to land, the great work accomplished by the Anti-Corn-Law League in 1846. It would give an endless renown to the Minister who made it, and would bless to an incalculable extent all classes connected with and dependent on honest industry.

I am, respectfully yours,

JOHN BRIGHT.

Mr. G. W. Sanders, Stockton-on-Tees.

THE LAND LAWS.

Written to Mr. Hope Hume, of Torquay.

132, Piccadilly, February 27, 1884.

DEAR SIR,—The time is near when our land laws will be revised, some of them abolished. The law of primogeniture will vanish, and entails and settlements will be got rid of, or will be so far limited as to be deprived of their pernicious influence on the public welfare. I believe that opinion has so far advanced on these questions that Parliament will consent to changes which a few years ago men thought almost impossible. The ease with which the Settled Estates Bill, brought in by Lord Cairns, passed both Houses is a proof that opinion has changed, and that landowners have been instructed by the ʳadverse times through which they have recently passed. I need not tell you that I have no sympathy with some wild propositions which have been brought before the public. The path of justice and honesty in regard to land and the owners of land is one from which I would not depart, and I believe all our people of every class have no real or permanent interest in schemes of confiscation which have recently been offered for public acceptance. When the measures of parliamentary reform now contemplated have become law, I think the changes which are required in our land system will not be difficult to accomplish, if undertaken in an honest spirit and on honest principles. I am satisfied that in the main the owners of the soil will profit by the change not less than other classes of our population. Our reforms hitherto have been good for the whole nation. Acting on the same lines we shall meet with a like result. Some may be timid, some may doubt, but future years will prove the wisdom of the changes we have suggested, and which cannot now be long delayed.

I am, &c.,

JOHN BRIGHT.

LAND AND ITS RENT.

Some extracts of a paper on agricultural depression, which was read by Mr. Lywood at the Warminster meeting of the South Wilts Chamber of Agriculture in December, 1884, having been sent to Mr. Bright, he wrote the following reply :—

Rochdale, December 19, 1884.

DEAR SIR,—I know nothing of Mr. Lywood, but, judging from the extract of his speech, his mind, I fear, cannot be of a very clear or logical order. I do not know if he quotes me accurately, but I assume that he does so. Surely if the losses of the land in 1879-80 were as great as my authority estimated them to be, and if the harvests have been unfavourable for so many years, as farmers tell me is the case, we can hardly expect all this mischief to be repaired by the occurrence of one good harvest, such as that of the present year.

The present year is remarkable in this—the yield of wheat in almost every country has been good. In America the price of wheat must be lower than with us. Everywhere there is a surplus seeking a market, and a portion of that surplus comes to us, hence the unusually low price of wheat. Why wheat is cheap everybody knows ; even Mr. Lywood knows, and yet he would "ask the Government to take immediate steps to find out." The Government knows, the Parliament knows, why wheat is cheap, and we all know that wholly or partially to shut out foreign wheat would immediately stir the markets and raise the prices ; how much, would depend on the amount of the duty, and the height of the barrier raised against the import of foreign wheat.

What Mr. Lywood wants is that Parliament should create this barrier, and thus raise the price of wheat in the markets and the price of bread in the home of every English family, and this to give prosperity to the farmer, and, through him, to the general trade of the country. To do this, or to attempt to do it, would be as reasonable as to expect to improve trade by greatly raising the poor-rate to enable paupers to become better customers of our manufacturers and tradesmen.   On this system farmers are to be restored to prosperity by the levying of a "rate in aid" on all the consumers of bread throughout the country.

May I suggest to Mr. Lywood that his remedy would at once tend to give steadiness to rents, and would raise the letting value of farms, and that all this would come from the tax levied on the tables and the bread of the millions of our population ; whether it would be of permanent service to tenants may be more doubtful.   May I suggest, further, to Mr. Lywood, that if the present or future price of wheat will not yield the present rents of wheat-growing land, would it not be better to adjust the rent to the quality and produce of the soil rather than to attempt to tax all the bread consumers of the kingdom to sustain rents which the land will not yield ? If land is not worth rent, it should be, and will be rent-free.   If land is paying rent which it will not yield, then the question is one between the tenant and the owner, and the taxpayer cannot be called upon to make up the difference between them.   So long as rent is charged for a farm the tenant can only look to the owner for redress if the rent is excessive.

Mr. Lywood says the depression in agriculture is greater now than when I referred to its great losses. Bad harvests in successive years cause increasing distress, as capital is wasted and tenants are less able to meet the difficulties which assail them.   But this is found only with the occupants of wheat-growing soils ; in other departments of farming there is no special distress or complaint.   There are districts where rents are not only not reduced, but within two years from this time have been raised, and where farms are eagerly sought after by tenants.   The present price of wheat is not the permanent price.   When wheat was 80s. the quarter, or more, farmers accepted the situation, even though people were starving.   Now the price is very low ; but fluctuations are inevitable, and probably a change for the better, from a farmer's point of view, is not far off. Mr. Lywood asks for an inquiry. Has he never heard of inquiries in former years? During the protection period there were frequent inquiries. We had dismal stories from tenant-farmers, as dismal as we have now, but Parliament could discover no remedy. We had a great Commission which reported only three years ago, but it offered no remedy to the farmer in whose behalf it was appointed.

What the land wants is sunshine such as it has had during this year; it wants, further, tenants of energy and intelligence and capital, and it should be held on rational conditions, and at rents which are fair and just, depending on the quality of the soil and the nature and value of its produce. It does not want, and cannot have, a "rate in aid" raised on the tables and the bread of the laborious millions of our people. I have written you a long letter, but the question you put to me is one of much interest.

I am, very respectfully,

JOHN BRIGHT.

Mr. George Heap, the hon. treasurer of the National Industrial Association, having written to Mr. Bright to ask for an explanation of the sentence, "If land is not worth rent, it should be, and will be, rent free," contained in the foregoing letter, Mr. Bright replied as follows:—

Rochdale, December 23, 1884.

DEAR SIR,—Surely what I have written is clear enough. If land will not produce anything that will afford a rent, no one will take it on the condition of paying rent for it. There are millions of acres in the United Kingdom that pay no agricultural rent. I do not say this is the condition of wheat-growing land in England, but surely rent must be determined by the nature of the soil and its capacity to produce what the markets require. If it be a question whether rent shall fall, or shall in some cases cease to be paid, or whether the food of our people shall be limited and raised in price by the action of law and by the imposition of a tax, there can be only one answer to the question. In this country there are many mills—probably some scores of mills—which are closed owing to the competition of modern mills of better construction. It is certain that many of them will not work again ; but the owners of them do not ask for a contribution from the purchasers of our cotton manufactures, or for a tax collected by the Government, to enable them to reopen their mills and to work them to a profit. How does the profit or rent of a mill differ from the rent or profit of a farm ? If the friends of the farmers would tell them that capital and intelligence and industry are necessary for their trade, and that if these fail there is no other resource than a sufficient fall of rent, they would give them the only counsel that can be of use to them. If, as I doubt not is the case in many instances, the farmers' capital is much wasted in your county, it shows that they have paid more rent than the land was worth ; but it does not show that a higher price of food should be brought about by law to enable them to recover the excess which they have paid to the owners of their farms. If men suffer, if farmers now suffer, we may all feel much sympathy with and for them ; but we cannot depart from sound principles of legislation, and levy a general contribution to restore them to a condition of prosperity. They must be dealt with as mill-owners or renters of mills are dealt with. They must adjust their relations with their landlords, and not ask Parliament to tax the whole people for their benefit.

I am, respectfully yours,
JOHN BRIGHT.

Mr. George Heap.

LAND LAW REFORM.

Written in reply to a letter from Mr. Arthur Arnold, M.P., calling attention to the urgency of the above question.

132, Piccadilly, W., July 9, 1885.

DEAR MR. ARNOLD,—I have received with much pleasure your letter of the 6th inst., and have read with much interest your suggestions on the reform of our land laws—the great question which will demand, and I hope receive, the attention of the Parliament which will be elected in November next.

I look back with intense satisfaction on the reform of our tariff, begun by Sir Robert Peel in the year 1842, carried forward by him to the year 1846, when the odious Corn Law was condemned and abolished, and completed in after years by the great measures, carried through Parliament by Mr. Gladstone. In connection with the changes in our commercial policy, the names of Sir Robert Peel and Mr. Gladstone will for ever stand foremost and highest in the list of the Ministers and statesmen of our country. They have lifted to a higher scale of independence and comfort the industrious millions of our people.

My lamented friend Mr. Cobden, who did not under-rate the result of the struggle in which he had taken so eminent a part, on more than one occasion expressed the belief that the men or the Minister who should here-after free the land of the United Kingdom from the fetters which have hitherto bound it would confer as great a blessing on our people as that bestowed upon them by the freedom of the produce of the soil.

The time has now come when this great land ques-tion must be discussed and settled. It is well that some plans, just to the nation, and not less just to the possessors of the land, should be brought before the attention of our people. In the suggestions which you have submitted to me you offer such a plan, and I cannot but hope that it will receive, as I believe it will deserve, a very large measure of support throughout the country.

There have been wild schemes brought before some portions of our people, schemes not based on any just

O

principles ; your suggestions seemed to me just and calculated to do good to landowner, to tenant farmer, to
the industrious labourer on the soil, and to the millions
whose families subsist upon its produce.

I cannot enter into anything like a great movement
in connection with this question, but I hope we may
soon see a movement in the constituencies and in Parliament, and that another great measure of reform may
soon be added to those by which our time and our
generation are already distinguished.

Believe me, very sincerely yours,
JOHN BRIGHT.

Arthur Arnold, Esq., M.P., 45, Kensington Park Gardens.

THE LAND QUESTION.

The following letter was addressed to Mr. R. A. Jones,
of Liverpool, author of the " Land Question and a Land
Bill, with special reference to Wales," published by the
North Wales Liberal Federation :—

November, 1887.

DEAR SIR,—I thank you for sending me your essay
on the Welsh land question. I have read it through
carefully. I will not attempt a criticism of it, for I am
burdened with letters by almost every post. I may say,
however, that I can give no support to your views. If
competition is to be got rid of in respect of property in
land, why not as regards other kinds of property ? Is
not a farmer as competent to guard his own interests as
a mill-owner or other tradesman ? I would have freedom in land as in other property, get rid of primogeniture, entail, and settlements—or the last greatly limited ;
make transfer easy and cheap ; encourage by these reforms the greater diffusion of the soil among the population, and then leave the rest to the intelligence and
self-interest of those who sell, or buy, or who let or take
land.

This plan would be simple and self-acting. It requires none of the alarming complications of your

scheme, which, to my mind, would render it almost a curse to farmer and landlord alike, and would, in my opinion, break it down.

You mention the disadvantage of difference of language. That must be disappearing. At school all your children are, or now ought to be, learning English.

You would treat your farming population as children. I would treat them as men, and induce them to act as men. They buy and sell everything without the help of Commissioners, and I would trust them to take or give up farms. They can judge of the quality of land, and they know what is their capital, and what are the chances of their success; and I would leave their present and future in their hands, and to be determined by their intelligence and their industry.

As to Ireland, I am not sure too much has not been done. I am not in favour of doing more. The Irish were strong for free sale, which you condemn with arguments of much force. I am disposed to stand by old and well-recognized principles. Law may ensure justice, but there have been, and there are yet, and there may be, new laws, which tend to enfeeble, and even to destroy.

Forgive this reply to your letter, and this comment on your land reform scheme.

Yours very respectfully,
JOHN BRIGHT.

R. A. Jones, Esq.,
4, Harrington Street, Liverpool.

THE GAME LAWS.

Read at a meeting of the Midland Farmers' Club held in Birmingham on Thursday, the 5th October, 1865.

Rochdale, September 30, 1865.

DEAR SIR,—I am glad to hear that you are about to read a paper on the subject of the Game Laws. I do not think much good would be done by holding a meeting in Birmingham. The towns are known to be against the Game Laws, but so long as the county constituencies send game preservers to Parliament, the members for the towns can do nothing for the farmers.

It is about twenty years since I gave much time and labour with a view to relieve the farmers from the evil of the Game Laws ; and I spent at least 300*l.* in bringing before them and the public some of the facts of this great grievance. Up to this time nothing has been done in the way of relief, but, on the contrary, the laws which favour the preservation of game have been made more strict. I fear the evil has become, not less, but greater, and I see only one way in which any real improvement can be made. It can only be done by having in Parliament a larger number of representatives of the people, and fewer representatives of a class and of the prejudices and usurpations of a class. How can this be brought about and secured ? By the admission of another million of the people to the elective franchise, so that the House of Commons may become truly representative of the true interests and wishes of the nation.

But there is one thing which the farmers may do for themselves whenever an election for a county takes place. At present *they* are not asked who shall pretend to represent them, but the lords and squires of the county name the candidate, and, as a rule, the tenant farmers vote for him, and he enters the House to do the work of the lords and squires who selected him. A main part of that work is to keep guard over the laws which favour the preservation of game. I know how many reasons there are why a tenant should be disposed to support the nominee of his landlord. He feels in many ways his landlord or his landlord's agents can annoy and injure him, and he submits to a power which he has not learned to resist. But the time is coming when tenants will dare to believe and act for themselves in the performance of their political duties. They can combine with great ease, and, when combined, their power is irresistible. I hope the day may soon come when they will take the elections of members for the counties in some degree into their own hands ; and when this is done, their political and social deliverance will be secured.

You will see at once how easy it is for you to combine. Every farmer has a horse and gig, or dog-cart, or conveyance of some kind, so that he can go to the poll without any cost to himself. Farmers meet almost every week at their market town, and they can know the feelings of their class without difficulty. In every county they should select a " farmers' candidate." If a good tenant farmer can be selected, bring him forward ; if not, then some other respectable and intelligent man. If you can find a landlord who is willing to be just to the tenant farmers, both in his private conduct and in respect of legislation which affects them, take him as your candidate, and give him a zealous support. You can contest a county almost at no expense. A subscription of one pound from each tenant will raise a sum large enough to pay for all the printing you require ; and you can take yourselves and your neighbours to the poll at a trifling expense. The farmers' candidate will be the popular candidate. The Liberals in the towns will give him their support, and you will carry him into Parliament to do the work of the farmers and of the people, instead of that of the lords and of the squires.

Some will say I am advising you to work a revolution ; and so I am. It will be a revolution that will transfer the county representation from a dozen rich men or families to the real people of the counties. It will send men to Parliament who will care more for the rights and interests of the population than for the semi-barbarous sports of a class. When the tenant farmers see their power, and arouse themselves to exert it, the days of the Game Laws are ended, and there will not be wanting just and good men among the landlords themselves who will give them a hearty co-operation in the good work.

As to changes in the Game Laws, I see no great good in them. What you want is the repeal of all laws which are made with the object of favouring the preservation of game. The fundamental principle of the tenant farmers should be this : That they shall have absolute and undisputed ownership of, and control over, all animals which live upon the produce of the land. They occupy land, and pay rent for it ; they risk all they have—their money, their time, their labour, their hopes, their present and their future—in the cultivation of their farms ; the horses, cows, sheep, and swine are theirs ; and the hares and rabbits, and game of every kind living upon their farms should also be theirs. Till this is the settled law, and also the practice of the country, the tenant farmers will never hold the position to which they have a just claim, and the evils of game laws and game preservation will never be wholly removed.

At present it is impossible for your friends in Parliament to do anything for you. You can do much—I think you can do everything for yourselves. Let it be a rule that no tenant farmer will support a candidate who is not in favour of full justice to tenant farmers, and the whole character of county representatives will be changed.

I would advise your committee to correspond with farmers in every county in the kingdom, and to exhort them everywhere seriously to consider this great question, and to prepare to act when another general election shall take place. Your deliverance from the insulting grievance of which you complain rests mainly with yourselves.

I am, very respectfully yours,

JOHN BRIGHT.

Mr. A. Robotham, The Oak Farm,
    Drayton Basset, near Tamworth.

THE GAME LAWS.

Written in reply to a letter from Mr. W. A. Sothern, of Lowestoft, who had called Mr. Bright's attention to some remarks made upon his conduct as to the Game Laws and Malt Tax by Mr. J. S. Gardiner at a late meeting of the Farmers' Alliance at Ipswich.

One Ash, Rochdale, November 16, 1879.

DEAR SIR,—Mr. Gardiner, who spoke at the Farmers' Alliance meeting, is very ignorant or very unjust in what he said about my conduct on the Game Law question. I never promised the repeal of the Malt Tax or the Game Laws. I undertook to bring the subject of the Game Laws before Parliament, and in the session of 1845 I moved for and obtained a committee to inquire into it. The evidence was laid before Parliament and the public, and I went to the expense of 300l. in publishing an abstract of the evidence, in the hope that farmers especially might be made acquainted with it. I am sorry to say that I discovered that farmers did not buy books, and my digest of the evidence did not, I fear, circulate largely among them. It was prepared by my late friend, Mr. Welford, who was a good farmer and a good lawyer, and the case made out in it against the Game Laws was unanswerable. After this I submitted a Bill for the removal of the same nuisance to the House of Commons, but it received no support from the large party in the House who call themselves farmers' friends. On other occasions I have spoken against the Game Laws, and ten years ago, when I was a member of the late Government, I spoke strongly against them, and declared my opinion that farmers would never have their rights in this question until they were in absolute possession of all the animals which fed on their farms.

I may tell Mr. Gardiner that I unfortunately found that farmers dared not or would not make any combined effort to do themselves justice; that they still voted for "farmers' friends," who in Parliament do nothing for farmers, but watch keenly after the interests of landlords; and I was therefore compelled to abandon a question and a cause in which I found that I could do no good. I turned my attention to other questions, leaving Game Law reform, which means Game Law abolition, to some time of calamity, when farmers' rights and the public interest would force themselves on the notice of Parliament. If that time has now come, I shall be as willing as I was thirty-four years ago to offer to Mr. Gardiner and his friends any help it may be in my power to render them.

I would now advise speakers at meetings of the Farmers' Alliance not to attack their friends, and Mr. Gardiner will do well to inform himself more accurately before he again speaks to a meeting of farmers on the subject of the Game Laws.

I am, very truly yours,
JOHN BRIGHT.

Mr. William Alexander Sothern, Lowestoft.

THE DRINK QUESTION.

THE LICENSING SYSTEM.

Written in reply to an inquiry respecting Mr. Bright's speech in a recent debate on Mr. Lawson's (now Sir Wilfred Lawson) Bill, as to whether he had advocated the investing of Town Councils with the power to suppress licensing.

London, June 13, 1864.

DEAR SIR,—If it is desired to put the licensing power into the hands of the residents of any town or district, I think the municipal corporations are the proper channels for exercising that power, and they would give licences freely or not, as public opinion directed them. I did not propose to give them the power to shut up all the public-houses and beershops, but only for the future to restrict the granting of licences ; they would also have the power to suspend or withdraw licences in cases where there were just grounds of complaint against those to whom they have already been granted. I do not urge this proposition with much confidence—there is something to be said against it ; but I think it better than the schemes of the friends of the Permissive Bill. I cannot consent to the rough-and-ready way of dealing with the question which many friends of temperance in their zeal seem disposed to advocate. I think they would inflict a great injustice in many cases, and might create a strong reactionary feeling against their own principles. The case is full of difficulty, and I speak with hesitation upon it.

I am, very respectfully yours,

JOHN BRIGHT.

Robert Martin, Esq., Warrington.

THE LICENSING SYSTEM.

A Liverpool working man wrote in November, 1873, to Mr. Bright, describing the deplorable poverty, degradation, vice, and drunkenness which characterized the condition of vast numbers in that town, and asked the right hon. gentleman "to lend his powerful aid in obtaining for every householder a direct personal voice or vote on spirit-vaults and beer-shops."

Mr. Bright replied as follows :—

London, November 27, 1873.

DEAR SIR,—Your letter is interesting, but it has made me sad to read it. The evils you describe seem too vast for any known remedy, and I know not who has courage to attempt to deal with them. To your concluding paragraph I must offer one remark by way of explanation. I cannot support the Permissive Bill, for reasons which I have given in the House of Commons, and to those who have sent me there. I do not approve of our present licensing system, for I think the magistrates are not the best authority to determine the number of houses that should be licensed, or to what houses licences should be granted or refused.

I am in favour of municipal control even in this matter—that is, of the ratepayers, through the local parliament which they elect. This, to my mind, would be much better than to invite the vote of the whole town ; and I am satisfied that it would work better and more justly. The town council represents the town, and to its wisdom I would entrust the power to grant or refuse licences, subject, it may be, to such limits as Parliament might properly determine.

I think a licensing committee of the town council would be a better authority than the magistrates, and through it the opinion of the ratepayers would be expressed and enforced. I am in favour of adding to the authority and dignity of our municipal government, and with that view I should have been glad to see the management of our elementary schools placed in their hands, and partly for the same reason, I would give them control over the licensing system, as closely connected with the good order of our towns and cities.

As we are moving now, we shall soon have little to do but to fight elections, which at best are but necessary evils. Parliamentary elections, municipal elections, school-board elections are surely enough ; do not ask us to add to them Permissive Bill contests as often as a fluctuating public opinion may demand them. I have no objection to give opinion fair play, but I wish it to act through a recognized and constitutional channel.

I am, yours, &c.,
JOHN BRIGHT.

THE LIQUOR TRAFFIC AND THE TORY PARTY.

Written to Mr. T. S. Leedle, of York.

Rochdale, September 4, 1878.

DEAR SIR,—I have read your interesting letter, and wish something could be done in the direction to which you point ; but I despair of anything being done at present and for a long time to come. The " drink question " has become a political question, and the unscrupulous political party will take care that it shall remain so, and the alliance between drink and the Tories will continue, and the question will still be one which many will talk about, but which none can deal with. I have had some plan of reform on this subject in my mind, but there seems yet no suitable time for saying anything in public about it. Foreign policy has filled men's minds, to the exclusion of all matters of home and social interest, and while the present party is in power there is small hope of any improvement. You will have observed the manner in which the Tory party in Parliament hold together. It is difficult to say what it will not vote for, or what it will not resist, to maintain its supremacy and its power ; but certainly it will not break up its alliance with the great publican combination.

The Permissive Bill seems to me a great error. It is not a good Bill, and men anxious for something to be done are forced to vote against it, while almost all who vote for it condemn it in private conversation. It blocks the way, and the most eager foes of the drink curse, by their pertinacity in supporting a bad Bill, are thus a great difficulty in the way of any considerable and effective remedy being applied.

I suppose we must wait; perhaps by-and-by opinion will rise to the point of action; but advance is slow, and we may almost despair. I think your letter must be useful in its appeal to thoughful minds, and I wish all men and women could read it.

I am, very respectfully yours,
JOHN BRIGHT.
Mr. T. S. Leedle, York.

LEGISLATION IN RELATION TO THE DRINK TRAFFIC.

Written to Mr. Joseph Leicester, President of the Workmen's Political League for the Annihilation of the Liquor Traffic, in reply to a resolution passed at a meeting of working men held on the 28th of September, 1878, at Clerkenwell, calling upon Mr. Bright to frame a Bill for the purpose of controlling the liquor traffic.

Rochdale, October 7, 1878.

DEAR SIR,—I thank you for your letter, and for the copy of the resolution which you forwarded me. I cannot undertake to frame a Bill on the subject of the drink traffic, or to take the part you and your friends invite me to assume. I watch the discussion which is now in progress, and I hope it may yield some fruit, some plan of procedure which may prove useful to the cause of temperance. The subject is one of great difficulty—the inveterate custom of our people, their belief that stimulants are wholesome and necessary, their habitual and almost universal self-indulgence in them, are obstacles which seem insurmountable. While these opinions and habits prevail, it is difficult to alter the law ; a change of law, though not absolutely useless, will do much less for temperance than many sanguine people expect. I hope, however, that what change of law can do may be done, and that a more intelligent public opinion may gradually be created to do more than even the wisest legislation can do. I hope the extension of education may give our people more self-respect, and thus save them from the miserable degradation to which multitudes of them are now subjected by a pernicious indulgence in intoxicating drinks. I am sorry I do not see my way to say or do more in connection with this great and difficult question. If an opportunity offers in which I can be of service I hope I shall not neglect it.

I am, very respectfully yours,

JOHN BRIGHT.

THE PROPER METHODS OF PROMOTING TEMPERANCE.

Addressed to a gentleman at Bedford.

London, June 5, 1874.

DEAR SIR,—I cannot write you a long letter on the temperance question and my views upon it. I am sorely troubled with letters, and am obliged to omit answers to very many of them. I may say, however, that in my opinion appeals should be made to all members of Christian Churches, in the hope of creating a great public opinion among the thoughtful and religious classes in favour of temperance, and of offering through them to the view of the nation a grand example of abstinence from the use of articles which are so seldom useful and so often pernicious. If the professing Christian people would take this matter in hand, the great work would go on prosperously. Their example would tell rapidly upon public opinion and upon the customs of the nation, and a great reform would be in process of certain achievement ; and as this more rational opinion was created, it would enable the Legislature to assist in it by such reasonable restrictions as the case may require, and as the constituencies would be able to sustain.

At present a few persons clamour for legislation which the country is not prepared for, and which it will not bear. The consequence of this is failure—there being much contention and no result.

The friends of temperance should leave Parliament, and form *opinion*, trusting that when opinion is formed whatsoever is judicious in legislation will naturally and easily follow. In a great reform of this kind Parliament can do little—but that portion of our people which cares for religion can do much—it can, indeed, do all. The ministers of religion and the multitudes of good men and women who listen to them from week to week can make the reform you seek. Without their zeal and co-operation it is impossible, and a dream. If I had time and opportunity I could say much more, but this may be sufficient for the moment as a reply to your note.

I am, very truly yours,
JOHN BRIGHT.

Mr. W. H. Gregory, Bradford, Yorkshire.

THE PROMOTION OF TEMPERANCE.

Written in answer to a question as to what Mr. Bright had said with reference to his having had no intoxicating drinks in his house since he commenced housekeeping.

40, Clarges Street, London, June 6, 1874.

DEAR SIR,—I have seen no report of what I said, but I have seen some extracts from newspapers, but all more or less inaccurate. There may have been times when I have doubted if I should have adopted the same course—not that I now doubt, or that I regret what was done thirty-five years ago. There is a great movement just now on the temperance question. The public conscience, even the Parliamentary conscience, seems shocked at what was done at the late election. There is a sense of humiliation at the thought that the publicans and beer-sellers destroyed a Government and installed another in its place, and that distillers and brewers were the best candidates for the Church and Conservative party, as most likely to secure the votes of publicans and beer-sellers. If the Christian Churches would move and speak, a great reform might be effected; but without a revival among them, I fear not much can be done. The Scottish Churches might banish whisky; Christian zeal and self-denial can work wonders.

Yours truly,

JOHN BRIGHT.

PUBLIC OPINION AND TEMPERANCE.

A general Temperance Convention for Birmingham and district was held on May 10th, 1887, at which the following letter was read from Mr. Bright :—

House of Commons, May 4, 1887.

DEAR SIR,—I must ask you to excuse me if I do not attend your meeting on the 10th inst., and if I do not write anything that will deserve to be read to your assembled friends. I have spoken so often, and have written so many letters dealing with the temperance question, that I feel as if I am unable to say anything that will be of service to the great work in which you are engaged. What the temperance societies are moving for in the most part is such a change in our legislation as will compel our people to greater sobriety. Something may be done by the proposed legislation, but to force the changes which are asked for will require a more combined public opinion than has yet been brought to bear upon the question. When the public opinion is secured, and not till then, may we expect such legislative changes as will remove or lessen the many temptations to which our population are incessantly exposed. I think much requires to be done to bring over public opinion and practice to the side of temperance before

P

even such changes of the law as may be useful can be effected, and when that public opinion is formed and secured great changes in the law may not be necessary, or, being deemed necessary, they may be more easily made, and by a general consent more willingly obeyed. I believe some useful changes in the laws may be made, but I am more disposed to rely on public teaching, upon the results of extended education, and of good example, than upon anything that Parliament can do. I wish your meeting may be as successful as you will desire.

Yours, &c.,

JOHN BRIGHT.

FINANCE.

THE INCOME-TAX.

Written to the chairman of an anti-income-tax meeting at Birmingham.

4, Hanover Street, London, March 11, 1862.

DEAR SIR,—I have received your letter and a copy of the resolution on the subject of the income-tax, and thank you for them. I am not surprised at the hostility which you describe as existing in the minds of many persons in Birmingham against this tax, in truth, I am only surprised at the patience—I think I may say the culpable patience—with which it has been so long endured. At the same time I regret to say that I cannot see the wisdom of the course you recommend with a view to secure the repeal or alteration of the tax, and it does not appear to me to offer any prospect of success. I cannot, therefore, pledge myself to act as you wish; that is, to undertake to "divide the House against the present income-tax laws on every possible occasion."

The evil of which you complain is not to be got rid of through the direct action of Parliament, and the course you recommend to my colleague and to myself would, I fear, only subject you to disappointment and us to ridicule. The House of Commons, and, I may say, Parliament as a whole, including both Houses, finds no special grievance in heavy expenditure and heavy taxation; and the inequalities of which you justly complain tell in favour of the rich, and especially in favour of the owners of what is called real property. It is not from Parliament, therefore, in the first instance that you are to look for redress.

The income-tax was imposed in the year 1842, to enable Sir Robert Peel to begin the reform of the tariff. The tariff has been to a great extent reformed ; and, although the custom duties produce more now than they did in 1842, the income-tax remains with a heavier pressure and a wider field. The cause is on the surface. Parliament consents now to an annual expenditure about twenty millions in excess of that of 1842, and the income-tax raises one-half of the increased taxation required by this increased expenditure. If I complain to the Government or to Parliament that this expenditure is unnecessary, and this taxation burdensome, Government and Parliament tell me that the nation is not of my opinion, and that the people do not blame the one, or suffer sensibly under the other.

I believe a very heavy taxation can rarely, perhaps never, be levied with much regard to justice. In this country, where the rich only govern, equality and fairness in taxation are impossible. The rich may spend the public revenues with a careless prodigality, but they will fight with a desperate unity of purpose to place the burden on the whole people, with little regard to the means of those who are to bear it. In the United Kingdom there are seven millions of men who pay taxes, and of these about six millions are never consulted as to the amount which shall be spent, or the mode in which it shall be raised. Of the one million who are apparently consulted, it may be said that political power is so unequally apportioned among them, that less than one-fourth of them nominally elect a majority of the members of the House of Commons, by which seventy millions of taxes are annually collected from seven millions of men, which determines the mode in which this vast sum of money shall be raised, and how it shall be expended.

I have now had an experience of nearly twenty years in the House of Commons, and during that time I have given such assistance as I could to every attempt to keep down expenditure, and to make taxation more equal and more just. The expenditure is now twenty millions more than it was when I entered Parliament. Since 1853-4, when Lord Palmerston and Lord John Russell led the nation into war with Russia, the public exchequer has been open to the rapacity of the military services, and they have revelled, without check, in the wealth which industry has created. These old states-men, steeped in the traditions of the last generation, conceive the grandeur of a country to consist in the vastness of its taxation and the extent of its military preparations, and they have succeeded in so exciting the fears and imposing upon the understanding of the middle classes of the people, as to induce them to tolerate a constantly-growing extravagance in the executive government, and a burden of taxation which in a time of peace would have driven their forefathers into revolt.

The English middle class believes itself to be repre-sented, while its representation is mainly a fraud. The great mass of the people are purposely excluded from all representation. Force is no longer used as the in-strument of tyranny amongst us ; but fraud, and delusion, and alarm, and panic are found in our day more profitable than force. I write to you, who, in respect to the subject of our correspondence, are a representative of the middle class ; and I say until that great class, in many things so intelligent, so moral, and, when it rises to any great duty, so powerful, shall examine public affairs for itself, and shall shake itself free from the impositions which are so impudently practised upon it, I see no hope of any sensible diminu-tion of the burden of taxation, or of any more just apportionment of that taxation, from which it is im-possible to escape. If the middle class prefer an alli-ance with the aristocratic or ruling party, to the cordial co-operation and help of the great nation now ex-cluded from the franchise and from all political power, they must be content with a profligate government expenditure, and a taxation burdensome from its amount, and insulting from its inequality and injustice.

I hope I need not tell you how glad I shall be to witness an expression of public opinion in favour of economy. The old watchwords of the Liberal party were "Peace, Retrenchment, and Reform." Of late years, under the leadership of statesmen who care for none of these things, the party has become feeble, debauched, and humiliated, and has trampled in the dust the only principles on which it had any pretence to become a party.

I cannot give you any hope of diminished or more equal taxation from the House of Commons. I should only add another to the many delusions practised on the people, if I were to tell them, after nearly twenty years' experience, that anything can be done there, in your direction, except under a pressure which cannot be resisted, and which can only come from without. I shall rejoice if that pressure be created, and it will give me infinite satisfaction to assist it and to obey it.

I am, with great respect, yours sincerely,
JOHN BRIGHT.

To J. S. Manton, Esq.,
  Regent Works, Birmingham.

THE INCOME-TAX.

In a further letter on the subject Mr. Bright wrote :—

Rochdale, March 21, 1862.

DEAR SIR,—I have to thank you for your second letter. I do not know that I can add much to what I have already written to you.

If Birmingham is in earnest in a movement against the income-tax, and if other towns will join in the movement, the tax can be overthrown ; and I am not sure that it will not be overthrown more easily than made more equal and just. I can vote against the income-tax with a clear conscience, because I believe the whole sum annually raised by it might be saved by a Government anxious to do its duty to the people. But I must tell you plainly, that so long as there is an apparent popular acquiescence in the present expenditure, and particularly in that branch of it which is connected with the military services, I do not believe that the tax will either be overthrown, or its pressure sensibly mitigated.

I am prepared to vote for any honest attempt to make the tax more equal, as I am prepared to vote for its abolition. With regard to the precise course to be taken in the House of Commons in dealing with the subject, I must be left at liberty to do that which at the time may seem most judicious.

I think you should correspond with all the principal towns in the kingdom, if you wish your views on the income-tax to prevail.

I am, very truly yours,

JOHN BRIGHT.

J. S. Manton, Esq.,
Regent Works, Birmingham.

THE INCOME-TAX.

Written in reply to an invitation sent him to join a deputation from the Birmingham Anti-Income-Tax Association to the Chancellor of the Exchequer on the 6th of March, 1872.

Rochdale, March 4, 1872.

DEAR SIR,—I regret to say that I shall not be able to be in town on Wednesday, and therefore cannot take part in the proposed deputation to the Chancellor of the Exchequer.

There is little difference of opinion as to the odious and unfair character of the income-tax; but it is not easy to see where the money is to be obtained which now comes from that tax. I see no chance of its abolition, except in a lessened expenditure, and at present there seems no probability of the creation of a political party resolved to lessen the public expenditure, and adopting that policy as the one great article of its creed. I do not believe in governments that cannot govern without taking seventy millions every year from the industry of the nation, and I hope the time will come when no such government will be permitted to exist.

For myself I should be ready to vote for such reduction of the expenditure as would enable the Chancellor of the Exchequer to remove the income-tax, or to abolish the taxes which add so greatly to the price of tea, coffee, and sugar.

I am, truly yours,
JOHN BRIGHT.

G. W. Plant, Esq., Birmingham.

THE MALT-TAX.

Read at a public meeting held in the Town Hall, Birmingham, on Thursday evening, the 14th of April, 1864, to discuss the question of the total repeal of the tax.

London, April 11, 1864.

DEAR SIR,—I must ask your committee to excuse me, if I am unable to be present and to take part in the meeting to be held on Thursday next. I cannot, without the greatest inconvenience, leave town during this week. I may say, however, that I could not, if present at the meeting, undertake the part you wish to assign to me, for I am not sufficiently informed on the matter to be able to assert what is contained in the resolution you wish me to move. In taking off taxes, as in putting them on, it is the duty of Parliament to consult the interests of the people. With my present information I would prefer to return to the people the six millions raised from tea or sugar, rather than that sum raised from malt. If I joined in a vote against the malt-tax, it would be with a view to force a reduction of expenditure, and not because I thought the malt-tax so bad as the tea or the sugar tax. For the present session, however, there will be no reductions of taxation beyond those already proposed by the Chancellor of the Exchequer, and there will be time enough for tea, sugar,

and beer to fight their battle in public discussion before
any one of them is likely to be further interfered with.
I think a moderate attention to economy would enable
Parliament to repeal any one of the four great taxes—
on income, tea, sugar, or beer—and the diminution of
the public expenditure by the amount of one of these
taxes would be felt to be a great relief to the public. I
shall read the report of your proceedings with much
interest.

I am, very respectfully yours,

JOHN BRIGHT.

NATIONAL EXPENDITURE.

In response to a request made by the Secretary of the
London Junior Liberal Association that Mr. Bright
would address a few words of advice to the young
members of the Liberal party, the following letter was
written :—

Llandudno, May 17, 1885.

DEAR SIR,—I thank you for sending me the copies
of your *Junior Liberal Review*. I will not criticize what
you have noted of my public life, only to say that I
wish I were worthy of a small part of the kind things
which your contributor has written of me. In endeavouring to serve the Liberal cause, I hope you will
bear in mind that the great danger of that cause is to be
found in an unwise foreign policy, such as all our Governments are too prone to adopt. The late Government
fell from this cause, and the present Government en-
dangers itself, and the cause it was created to support,
by following too nearly the footsteps of its predecessors.
The growth of army, navy, and military expenditure is
dangerous if not fatal to a Liberal Government—and I
hope this may always be the case. At home, and in
domestic affairs, we learn much ; in foreign affairs we
seem to learn nothing, and one Government is very like
another in the ease with which it plunges into blunders
which disgrace our history and impoverish our people.

Unless the Liberal party can bring about a reform in the matter of foreign policy and in the madness of military expenditure I see no hope of good in the future; there is before us some great catastrophe as the punishment of our blindness and folly.   Nations, it is said, are taught by calamity—perhaps we may be thus taught.

Very truly yours,
JOHN BRIGHT.

Mr. William A. Proktor,
   11, Warwick Road, Stoke Newington.

CONSTITUTIONAL QUESTIONS.

THE HOUSE OF LORDS.

Read at a meeting in Birmingham on the 14th of June, 1869. The peers were at that time threatening the Bill for the Disestablishment of the Irish Church, which had just passed the House of Commons; they, however, subsequently passed it. The expression, "a little childish tinkering about life peerages," in the letter, was an allusion to a Bill which was being considered by the House of Lords, on the introduction of Earl Russell, for the creation of life peerages.

This letter, coming from a member of the Government, gave great offence to some of the peers, and it was the subject of question and comment in the House of Lords.

London, June 9, 1869.

DEAR SIR,—I must ask my friends to excuse me if I am unable to accept their invitation for their meeting on Monday next.

The Lords are not very wise, but there is sometimes profit to the people even in their unwisdom. If they should delay the passing of the Irish Church Bill for three months, they will stimulate discussion on important questions, which, but for their infatuation, might have slumbered for many years. It is possible that a good many people may ask what is the special value of a Constitution which gives a majority of 100 in one House for a given policy, and a majority of 100 in another House against it. It may be asked also why the Crown, through its Ministers in the House of Commons, should be found in harmony with the nation, whilst the Lords are generally in direct opposition to it.

Instead of doing a little childish tinkering about life peerages, it would be well if the peers could bring themselves on a line with the opinions and necessities of our day. In harmony with the nation they may go on for a long time, but throwing themselves athwart its course, they may meet with accidents not pleasant for them to think of.

But there are not a few good and wise men among the peers, and we will hope their counsels may prevail.

I am sure you will forgive me if I cannot come to your meeting.

Believe me always, very truly yours,
JOHN BRIGHT.

Mr. H. B. S. Thompson,
Secretary Birmingham Liberal Association.

THE HOUSE OF LORDS.

Read at a great reform demonstration at Accrington on the 19th of July, 1884. The meeting was held shortly after the rejection by the House of Lords of the Bill for extending household suffrage to the counties.

132, Piccadilly, July 18, 1884.

DEAR SIR,—I am glad to hear of the arrangements for your great meeting to-morrow. Accrington and the surrounding district will not fail in its duty at this crisis. The question is not one of the Franchise Bill only—that Bill will *not* be defeated, or long delayed. There has arisen another and a greater question. Shall the House of Lords subject to its will the Ministry, which represents the Crown, and the House of Commons, which represents the nation? Shall the policy of a great and free country be thwarted by men sitting in their hereditary chamber, who are there by no right of votes given them, and through whom the voice of the millions of the

United Kingdom is not heard? Their veto is a constant insult to the House of Commons, and if the freedom of our people is not a pretence and a sham, some limit must be placed upon a power which is chiefly manifested in, or by, its hostility to the true interests of the nation. A parliament controlled by hereditary peers is no better, perhaps it is worse, than a parliament influenced by and controlled by a despotic monarch. Ask your friends to consider this question seriously. Let them join with their countrymen in demanding a change which shall free the House of Commons from fetters as humiliating to it as they are injurious to the country.

Believe me, sincerely yours,
JOHN BRIGHT.

Mr. John P. Hartley, Accrington.

REPUBLICANISM.

Written to a gentleman who had been told that the English Republicans would select Mr. Bright as their first President, and who wrote to ask the right hon. gentleman if he would accept the post.

Rochdale, April 7, 1872.

DEAR SIR,—Your Republican friend must not be a very desperate character if he proposes to make me his first President, though I doubt if he can be a friend of mine. As to *opinions* on the question of Monarchy or Republicanism, I hope and believe it will be a long time before we are asked to give our opinion; our ancestors decided the matter a long time since, and I would suggest that you and I should leave any further decision to our posterity. Now, from your letter, I conclude you are willing to do this, and I can assure you I am not less willing.

I am, truly yours,
JOHN BRIGHT.

Q

IMPERIAL FEDERATION.

Written to the President of the Manchester Statistical Society in reply to an invitation to attend to hear a paper by Mr. Howard Vincent, M.P., on Imperial Federation.

One Ash, Rochdale, January 12, 1887.

DEAR SIR,—I have to thank you for your invitation to the "federation" meeting fixed for the 21st of this month. I cannot attend the meeting, and regret to have to say that I have no sympathy with its object and purpose. I am as anxious as you and your friends can be that the Colonies should remain attached to and in perfect friendship with the mother country, but I am of opinion that any attempt to unite them by political bonds more closely than they are now connected will tend not so much to permanent union as to discord and separation. England will not be governed or in any degree influenced in her foreign policy by Canada, or Australia, or the Cape. The Colonies will allow of no interference by England with them, with their laws or their tariffs. England's blind foreign policy may involve us in wars with some one or with several of the European Powers—wars in which the Colonies have no interest, but by and through which they may be subjected to serious injury. In such a case what will happen? The federation cord will be strengthened to the uttermost, it will probably break ; the Colonies will prefer separation and freedom to the burdens and sufferings which their connection with a European nation through their mother country will impose upon them.

How would your federation deal with the fisheries dispute between Canada and the United States? If Canada were an independent State the dispute would soon be settled, for she would yield to the arguments of her powerful neighbour, and if there were no "Dominion" of Canada, the dispute would soon be settled by English concession of the reasonable claims of the Government at Washington.

How would a federation composed of delegates or representatives from the Colonies of Australia, from South Africa, from Canada, and perhaps from India, meeting and acting with some representative body in England, deal with this fisheries question, and with other questions which might and would arise within the wide boundaries of our ever growing Empire?

I commend a consideration of these problems to any thoughtful men—men who are active in promoting a federation league. The federation project seems to me to be founded on ignorance alike of history and geography. It is partly or mainly the offspring of the jingo spirit which clamours for a vast and continually widening empire, and seems almost ready to boast that it fights the world outside its own limits.

I would recommend all sensible men to let the question rest. If we are conciliatory and just to the Colonies, and if our foreign policy is less mad than it has been during much of the present century, we may hope that the friendship between Britain and her daughter States may long continue and may strengthen. If changes come which we cannot now foresee, but from which nations cannot escape, and if separation becomes necessary, let us hope that what will be done will be done in peace and with a general concurrence, and that the lustre of the English name and fame will not be tarnished, but will receive an added glory from the greatness and the prosperity and the wisdom of the States which England has founded.

I am, very respectfully yours,

JOHN BRIGHT.

IMPERIAL FEDERATION.

Written in reply to a New South Wales delegate, who had written to Mr. Bright, thanking him, on behalf of the Australian working classes, for the condemnation of Imperial Federation which he had given in the preceding letter.

Rochdale, February 7, 1887.

DEAR SIR,—I thank you for your interesting letter. I believe with you that the ideas of the Federation people are impracticable and absurd. How can the colonies embark in the wild political ventures of the mother country? What would the American colonies have done as partners with England in her wars during the last hundred years?

New South Wales has again a Free-trade and Liberal Minister, who condemned the Soudan expedition. I hope that is the first and last expedition which Australia will take part in—any contest in which she has no interest.

I am, very truly yours,
JOHN BRIGHT.

Mr. John Morton.

ELECTION "FADS."

A member of Parliament, in an address to his constituents in 1883, said that he desired to see in connection with the County Franchise Bill, a plan whereby a moderate proportion of members of the House—say, 60 out of 600—should be chosen, not by the constituents, but by the members already elected in the usual way. Thus, every ten members of any party could, as it were, appoint a member, the object of this plan being to secure the admission to the House of able men, who, through weakness of voice or any other personal reason, cannot make the customary appeal to a constituency. This project was brought under the notice of Mr. John Bright, who wrote as follows :—

One Ash, Rochdale, October 8, 1883.

SIR,—I can give you no favourable opinion of the plan you refer to. It is wholly opposed to the spirit and principles of our Constitution, and offers no advantage to compensate for this. As to admitting men into Parliament, whom electors will not elect, or whose condition of health or voice will not allow them to undertake an appeal to a constituency—the proposition seems to me not a little ludicrous. Men feeble in health and men not able or willing to go through the ordeal of an appeal to a constituency, may take other means of serving the public—the Parliamentary path is not their path—and to open a new gate for those incapable of making use of the ancient and constitutional road, is a proposition not seriously to be regarded. Parliament has already an abundant supply of clever men—men who can both think and talk. We need no new plan of admitting feeble folk—feeble in body and in voice, and in the powers and qualities which recommend men to the notice and confidence of electors. I advise you to keep to the old ways—for the "fads," minority clauses, and new modes of making a Parliament, all tend to mischief; they show mistrust of the people, and they are mainly intended to weaken the popular voice. I am for none of these things.

I am, respectfully yours,

JOHN BRIGHT.

MR. HARE'S SCHEME OF PROPORTIONAL REPRESENTATION.

The remarks made by Mr. Bright in the previous letter induced an inquiry as to whether he included Mr. Hare's scheme in his general condemnation of " 'fads,' minority clauses, and new modes of making a Parliament." To this inquiry Mr. Bright replied as follows :—

One Ash, Rochdale, October 16, 1883.

DEAR SIR,—I think Mr. Hare's plan more of a " fad " than any other yet submitted to the public, and it has this disadvantage—that scarcely any one can understand it. It aims at making Parliament an exact photograph of every phase of public opinion, and under it there is no fancy or folly which might not, and probably would not, have its representative in the House. Parliament would be broken up into busy cliques, led by the political lunatics who would have entrance within its walls. My advice is, keep to the old ways—they are the safest, and the "wayfaring man, though a fool" (in some sense) "shall not err therein." I have known several or a few of Mr. Hare's supporters; but not one of them has seemed to me to possess the common sense which is as useful and necessary for legislation and government as in the ordinary pursuits of life. I am in favour of the Constitution which has come down from our forefathers, with such amendments as circumstances and our experience seem to warrant. I think they would have looked on Mr. Hare's scheme with mingled amazement and ridicule. You have asked my opinion, and I have given it. I do not seek the protection which its friends claim for the patent constitution of Mr. Hare.

I am, very respectfully yours,
JOHN BRIGHT.

THE SECOND BALLOT.

Replying to a correspondent who had urged the adoption of a second ballot in all Parliamentary elections in which no candidate receives an absolute majority of the votes polled, Mr. Bright wrote as follows :—

March 11, 1886.

DEAR SIR,—There is apparently a good deal to be said for your view, but I think the evil you wish to remedy is rather temporary than permanent, and that the experience of the late election will do much to prevent a repetition of the folly and blunders which we all regret and condemn.

I am afraid that if a second ballot were possible, as in France, we should have, as in France, far more cases of too many candidates, and that we should have more vain and foolish and sensible men offering themselves to constituencies than we have now or are likely to have if our present system is continued. I am rather inclined to rely on the good sense of electors and the lessons they learn from the experience of the failures which now and then occur. At present we have some blunders and some misfortunes ; with the change you suggest no man would have any great pressure put upon him to make him retire, and many fresh elections would have to take place, involving the great trouble of a new contest and the evil of a great increase of expense.

The mischief in London comes from the new divisions and from the novelty of the new conditions, and I am somewhat confident that this will not occur when another general election takes place. I admit the evil, but I think it will die out of itself to a large extent, and that your remedy would produce an evil perhaps even greater than that you wish to remove.

In France the number of second elections is very large. Moreover, it is not certain that the defeated minority with us would always support at a second contest the candidate who defeated them in the first.

I make these suggestions in reply to your letter. I cannot discuss the question further. You will see that the argument is not all on one side. Perhaps under either plan our representation is sufficiently complete.

I am, very truly yours,
JOHN BRIGHT.

CANVASSING AT ELECTIONS.

Written to Mr. James Eddy, of Stockton, who had asked Mr. Bright's opinion on the subject, and read at a meeting in the Temperance Hall of that town on the 28th of October, 1874.

Rochdale, October 26, 1874.

DEAR SIR,—I can give no opinion of much value on the subject on which you have written me. I suppose that so long as many electors are careless and ignorant it will be impossible to put an end to canvassing. I think the proposal to make it illegal is absurd. To canvass in an honourable manner is an innocent act, and in many cases it is useful, and any attempt to make it unlawful would fail. I speak of canvassing by friends of candidates ; for candidates in person to solicit votes is, in my view, humiliating, and the best constituencies have abolished it, though it still prevails in many boroughs.

Yours respectfully,
JOHN BRIGHT.

WORKING-MEN CANDIDATES.

In a speech delivered at Birmingham on the 28th of January, 1875, Mr. Bright deprecated the selection of working men to represent constituencies on the mere ground of their being working men. He contended that a man's fitness to discharge the duties of a Member of Parliament ought to be the consideration which should induce the electors to send him there, and that to choose men because they belonged to the working class was a mistake. " If," he said, "we are to have a Parliament composed of two classes—one working-men representatives, and one that are not representatives of working men, it appears to me it would be one of the greatest calamities that could happen in our representative system. If you can find a man, let him be a first or second-class or third-class passenger, if you can find a man with intelligence, and honesty, and firmness, and the kind of capacity which you understand for Parliamentary duty, then I say lay hold of him at once and make him a Member of Parliament."

In reference to these remarks Mr. Bright received a letter from Stoke-on-Trent, in which the writer expressed his surprise that such observations should have been made. Mr. Bright thereupon replied as follows :—

Rochdale, February 13, 1875.

DEAR SIR,—It seems impossible to say anything in public which will not be misunderstood and misrepresented.

I have no objection to working men as candidates. What I object to is that a candidate should be chosen only or mainly because he is a working man, and that I should be expected to vote for him for the same reason. I do not vote for a candidate because he is a middle-class man, or a man of high family connection; and I refuse to be under any obligation to vote for one who is chosen as a candidate because he belongs to some other class or section of the community.

If the Liberal party in a constituency, speaking and acting through its recognized organization, selected a working man as its candidate, I hope I should give him my hearty support; but I object to have him thrust upon the party merely because he is a working man. The policy now recommended to working men in regard to this matter is, in my judgment, fatal to unity, as it is to an honest representation of all classes and interests.

I hope I need not say that, if I were one of your constituency, I should have no difficulty in giving my vote to Mr. Walton.

I am sorry you should have misunderstood me. Your letter has only just reached me, and I send you this hasty reply.

I thank you for the kind expressions in your letter, and am,

Very truly yours,
JOHN BRIGHT.

Mr. Joseph Hulme, Burslem.

LABOUR REPRESENTATIVES IN PARLIAMENT.

The attention of Mr. Bright having been drawn to the result of the voting of the Northumberland miners with respect to their representation in Parliament, and his opinion asked as to the important question it raised, he replied as follows :—

Newington House, Edinburgh, September 23, 1887.

SIR,—I am not in favour of the payment of members of Parliament. I do not wish to make Parliamentary life a trade. It is quite enough so already.

As to the miners' case, I should regret to lose Mr. Burt from the House of Commons, but I doubt the wisdom of trades unions being made associations for political objects.

I am not in favour of what is called a Labour Party in Parliament. The best representatives of industry in past times have not been labourers in your sense. Mr. Hume was not a labourer, nor was Mr. Cobden, nor was Mr. Charles Villiers, nor am I one ; yet how much have we and many others done on behalf of the bulk of our labouring population.

A Parliamentary representative should strive to further the interests of all classes of our people, and to do justice to all. A Parliament divided into sections is less likely to be wise and just than one not so divided, and leads rather to confusion than to union and a powerful instrument of legislation and government.

In years past we have had too much of legislation of classes. Landowners and farmers for a generation— from 1815 to 1846—ruled both Houses of Parliament, to the great injury of the nation. Let us not return to this system, or to anything like it, under the idea that we shall advance the interests of the classes who live by and from their labour.

I write this in the interest of our whole people, so far as I am able to comprehend it.

I am, respectfully yours,
JOHN BRIGHT.

WOMEN'S SUFFRAGE.

Addressed to Mr. Theodore Stanton, and published in his book entitled " The Woman Question in Europe."

One Ash, Rochdale, October 21, 1882.

DEAR SIR,—I have never changed my opinion on the subject of women's suffrage. I voted with great doubt and reluctance with Mr. Mill, and more out of sympathy with him than from agreement with him on the subject before us. I have always regretted the vote and explained the whole matter in a speech against women's suffrage in a subsequent session of Parliament. I cannot give you the date of the speech, but it is fully reported in "Hansard's Debates." I cannot give you all the reasons for the view I take, but I act from a belief that to introduce women into the strife of political life would be a great evil to them, and that to our sex no possible good could arrive. If women are not safe under the charge and care of fathers, husbands, brothers, and sons, it is the fault of our non-civilization and not of our laws. As civilization founded upon Christian principle advances, women will gain all that is right for them, although they are not seen contending in the strife of political parties. In my experience I have observed evil results to many women who have entered hotly into political conflict and discussion. I would save them from it. If all the men in a nation do not and cannot adequately express its will and defend its interests, to add all the women will not better the result, and the representative system is a mistake. But I cannot discuss the question in a note. I give you an idea merely of the view I take of it. There is more in my speech, but even that very lightly touches upon the whole subject.

I am, respectfully yours,

JOHN BRIGHT.

Theodore Stanton, Esq.

SOCIAL QUESTIONS.

THE UNEMPLOYED.

At a meeting in March, 1858, of the unemployed workpeople in Birmingham, a memorial to the Queen was passed, praying for an extensive system of free emigration. The chairman of the meeting was requested to ask Mr. Bright to present the memorial, and to his communication received the following reply:—

London, March 25, 1858.

DEAR SIR,—When your memorial reaches me or Mr. Scholefield, we will at once take the usual course with respect to its presentation to the Queen.

I am sorry to find that the "unemployed" should be so numerous in Birmingham as to induce them to unite, with a view to some public measure for their relief. At this moment the unfavourable condition of the markets of the United States, and of the continent of Europe, will account for much of the suffering which is being endured by the working men of England. I confess, however, that I can see no remedy for a large portion of the mischief complained of, so long as we find our taxes constantly on the increase, and our national expenditure augmenting.

We are now spending twenty millions a year more than we were spending only a few years back, and our military expenses have doubled since the year 1835, when the Duke of Wellington and Sir Robert Peel were in power.

This year I suppose we shall raise in taxes at least fifty millions sterling more than will require to be raised by an equal population, living, not in England, but in

the United States of America. Surely this will account
for much of the evils which you, and the memorialists,
and the working classes generally, suffer; and I am not
surprised that sensible men should wish to quit a
country where the burdens are so heavy, and the
political privileges of three-fourths of them are so few.
Every man who is not prepared to compel a better and
more economical government at home should emigrate,
or the pauperism of his day will be deeper, and more
without remedy, in the days of his children. I wish I
was able to come to Birmingham and talk to you about
these questions.

Yours very respectfully,
JOHN BRIGHT.

THE NECESSITY FOR EMIGRATION,
AND ITS CAUSES.

Read at a meeting held in Glasgow, on the 16th of
September, 1858, for the purpose of considering some
scheme to enable the working classes to emigrate to the
colonies. The special object of the meeting was for the
adoption of resolutions and of a memorial to her
Majesty in favour of such a scheme, and for the enrol-
ment of a band of pioneers for British Columbia.

Rochdale, September 1, 1858.

SIR,—I have to thank the council of your association
for the invitation to your approaching meeting. I
cannot be present at it, but I hope your discussions will
do good to those most interested in them. I have read
your resolutions, and I am not surprised that great
numbers of the working men are anxious to emigrate ;
and if I were younger and in their position, I should
strain every nerve to enable me to find a home in the
United States or in one of the British colonies.

I do not think you are quite correct in the assertions
of the resolutions. Generally, the waste lands in the
colonies belong to the colonies. Canada belongs to

the people of Canada, and Australia to the people of Australia—and I think any other arrangement would work badly. Any interference by the Home Government would do mischief, and would certainly breed disputes between the Colonial Governments and populations.

Again, I do not know that it is the " bounden duty " of the Government to adopt measures to enable a portion of our population to emigrate ; for if such a duty is laid upon it, I know not where it must end. Every man who thinks he can improve his position abroad may ask to be sent abroad, and, all men having an equal claim upon the Government, the difficulty may become, and soon will become, insurmountable.

I do not believe that it is the duty of the Government to provide means of emigration for the people, and therefore I could not support the main point in your resolutions. What I have long told the working men is this :—Here you have no political power, for the arrangements of the Reform Bill purposely excluded you. Here you are mixed up with the wretched confusion of European politics, and your sweat is pawned by the crimes of past generations. So thoroughly are you involved in European complications, that in any year you may have your taxes raised, and the demand for your labour destroyed, in pursuit of some phantom in which your rulers persuade you that you are interested ; your want of information unfortunately renders you easy victims to the delusion practised upon you. Not five years ago you rejoiced in peace, and there was a growing prosperity evident in every part of the country. Since that time we have sacrificed forty thousand English lives, and have spent one hundred millions of pounds sterling in one short war. You were consenting parties to that war; your comrades shed their blood in its worthless contests, and you have paid a portion of your day's labour and day's wages ever since, to defray the cost of it ; and your voice, so far as it was heard at all, was in favour of the war. What is gained by it ? Who has gained except the military class

R

and eaters of taxes'?   To working men, these wars with
Russia, with Persia, with China, bring only taxes, want
of employment, precarious and diminished wages, and
that pressure upon the means of living which urges them
to look to emigration as a remedy for the evils they endure.   And it is a remedy, and the only remedy, until
great changes take place in public opinion, and in the
law and policy of this country.

If you emigrate you may reach a country where land
is accessible to you, where there are no great hereditary
proprietors, as in Scotland, who dare to outrage heaven
and mankind by keeping 20,000, or 50,000, or 100,000
acres of land depopulated, that a handful of men may
enjoy the pleasures of the chase.   You may flee to a
land where laws of primogeniture are unknown, or known
only to be abhorred, and where the soil is left free to
the industry and enterprise of the whole people.   You
may find a home where such destructive delusions as the
" balance of power " are unheard of, and where the toil
of the nation of which you have become a part is not
absorbed to the amount of fifty millions sterling a year
to pay for wars that are past, and for preparations of wars
that are to come.   You may become a part of some
youthful and growing people, with whom a feudal pro-
prietorship of lands, national debts, great armaments,
oppressive taxes, and a sham representation, are but
traditions of a melancholy past, to be studied only as
rocks to be avoided in its new and more prosperous career.

If I do not see how the Government can be called upon
to provide the means of emigration, do not suppose I
think emigration unwise ; on the contrary, I feel assured
that, with the past and present policy of England,
labour will find its best reward in Canada, in the States,
or in Australia.   I would prefer that Englishmen should
stay at home—that our country should be well governed,
that its foreign policy should be just and rational, that
its burden of taxes should be light ; but seeing small
chance of such a state of things, I not only cannot blame,
but I must applaud the resolution of every man who is

determined, by his industry and his economy, to provide the means of conveying himself and his family to another, and to him and them, a more happy country.

Government cannot enable you to emigrate. Many of you can, by severe effort and saving, obtain the means to cross the ocean ; to many, I fear, this is not possible. I can only hope, for them, that our countrymen may become wiser, and that, under the influence of a more sensible policy and a greater economy in the national expenditure, we may be entering on a period of prolonged peace, during which even the poorest and most suffering of our population may make some progress in the way of comfort and independence.

I must ask your excuse for writing so long a letter, and the more, as it is opposed in some degree to your view.

I am, very respectfully yours,

JOHN BRIGHT.

Mr. Andrew Cumming, Glasgow.

STRIKES.

Written in answer to a letter Mr. Bright had received from a spinner and manufacturer in Blackburn, in which a complaint was made that education, literary and religious, had failed to teach the working classes wisdom in relation to their own interests.

Rochdale, November 3, 1860.

MY DEAR SIR,—I am glad to hear from you, and to learn that your health is better. I am, however, very sorry for the cause of your writing to me, and can understand the disappointment you feel at the small result of so many efforts to instruct the working population around you. It is not to be expected that the workmen in our population should be wiser than other classes, and we know well that other classes have, whenever able to do it, enforced combination prices, and endeavoured to make a scarcity in the articles in which they have dealt. The fact is, that among all classes there is a lamentable ignorance of the laws which ought to regulate labour and trade, and that the study of political economy is totally neglected in the education of the whole people. At this moment the views of a large portion of the highest class—I mean highest in position, in wealth, and in scholarship—are wholly unsound on these subjects, and, making allowance for difference of circumstances, they support precisely the same principles as those contended for by trades' unions. At first sight, nothing appears more clear to a workman than that it is a great advantage to him to be able to force his employer to give him higher wages; and for this end, an end apparently so desirable, almost everything will appear to the mind of the workman proper and justifiable. He considers the whole matter to be a struggle between capital and labour, and that anything is fair in his fight with the claims of capital. Hence the folly and injustice of many of the proceedings of the trades' unions, and the discord which arises between the class of workmen and the class of employers.

Along with the mischief which springs from ignorance on these questions, there is another source of evil, to which I think employers ought to turn their attention. The whole body of workmen, speaking in general terms, are excluded—purposely excluded—from the franchise. They have no political position, and therefore, practically, they have no politics. In this respect they are no more free than the labourers in Austria or in Russia, and consequently they have no inducement to consider political questions, and to examine or to suspect how far their condition is affected by the policy and acts of the Government of the country. They are shut out from the political world; they are told that they ought to have, and shall have, no opinion and no voice in the direction of public affairs; that they are an ignorant and a dangerous class; and that what are called the institutions of their country would not be safe if they were permitted to take any part in them. The inevitable result is that these men, growing every day in information, and in restlessness and discontent, rather it may be with their social than their political condition, and growing also in numbers and in the means of organization, maintain a contest with the only authority they see and feel, namely, with their employers, who are to them almost all they know and comprehend of superior power and of Governmental control.

The fact is, our system of political exclusion has this effect, it makes of the working classes a nation, separated by a gulf, passable only by few of them, from that other nation to which the existing constitution pretends to give, though it does not honestly give, political power. There is thus no real amalgamation of classes. The class receiving wages is shut out from the questions and the interests which occupy the minds and engage the energies of the employing class. Its members are limited to the consideration of their own individual, and local, and class interests ; and their mental activity is devoted to something like a servile war, because everything that is broader and greater is excluded from their view. So long as the employers of this county, and of the neighbouring counties, are content to allow the governing class to refuse the rights of citizenship to the industrious men, without whose skill and toil our national greatness could have no existence, so long will these men, whose general intelligence and whose energies are acknowledged by all, concentrate that intelligence and that energy on efforts to amend their condition within those limits of action which are open to them. If the capitalists practically assert that the workman is born only to labour, and that he is incompetent to take any part in those great discussions on public affairs which are so deeply interesting to the more fortunate and privileged of his countrymen, and so important to all—and if, unhappily, the workman should practically acquiesce in this view, and should abstain from efforts to invest himself with the rights of citizenship,—let us be assured that his activity will not cease—that his energies will not slumber. He may not read and think politics ; he may not canvass for and conduct elections ; he may not strive to influence the deliberations of Parliament, and to urge on or to check the action of the administration ; but he will not be idle, and his own condition and that of his class will not have lost all interest in his eyes. He will ignore the obstacles to his well-being which arise from violations of economic principles by the Government ; he will take no strong interest in the taxation of the country, or in the expenditure of the State ; he will conclude that the only mode of bettering his condition is in an advance of wages, forced from capital, it may be, at the risk of its destruction, and gained and secured only by combinations which in the long-run must be as injurious to himself as to the employer against whom he is contending.

I have never denied the legal or the moral right of workmen or employers to combine ; but I believe there is not one case in a hundred where it is wise to exercise this right. And, looking at the consequences of the strikes we have seen in this country, it is amazing that so many men of sense, so many men competent to works of skill and ingenuity, should take any part in them. I do not expect in our time that these deplorable transactions will come to an end, but I am persuaded that they would occur much more rarely, and be attended with less of bitterness and of that obstinate folly which now so often distinguishes them, if the wall of partition between classes were broken down by the admission of the great "labour interest" into the rights of citizenship. Then the same questions would interest us all ; the same grievances, where grievances exist, would be seen to affect us all ; the same great public objects would stimulate us all ; and instead of being as we now are, two nations in one country, having different ends and adverse sympathies, we should have objects and purposes in common, to the incalculable and permanent gain of the whole people.

I am not now propounding a new doctrine. I have held this opinion ever since I have considered social and political questions. I have as much interest in the harmonious working of our industrial organization, and in the welfare of my country, as any other man has, and I give it as my deliberate judgment, that it is the interest and the duty of all the employers of labour amongst us to confer upon the workman, whose labour we purchase, and whose wages we provide, those rights of franchise and of citizenship which we ourselves possess. Some men imagine that the existing exclusion can be perpetuated, and that it is safer to repress and exclude than to admit. This is the common delusion of those who shut their eyes to all that is passing around them, and who, in their timidity, adhere to a course which, more than any other, is dangerous and untenable.

The workmen are great in numbers, growing in intelligence, and their power of combination is without limit. They will contend *for* themselves, by themselves, if condemned to remain a separate and suspected order in our social system ; and this contest has in it the seeds of future and tremendous evil to them and to the great industrial interests of the country. I wish to unite all, to have no separate interests ; to blend all in a common sense of common rights, and thus to give peace and strength where now discord and weakness too much prevail.

I do not write this to you as though you differed from me in opinion on this subject, but I take the opportunity which your letter affords me of expressing to you the views I honestly hold, earnestly hoping they may one day become those of all the employers of labour in the manufacturing counties of England.

I am, very sincerely yours,

JOHN BRIGHT.

THE VACCINATION LAWS.

Read at a Conference of Anti-vaccinators held at Birmingham, on the 26th of October, 1874.

Dalguise, N.B., October 6, 1874.

DEAR SIR,—I cannot take any part in your Conference, nor will I express any opinion on the question in which you are interesting yourself except so far as to say that the facts which have come before me seem to be against you; but I have no objection to express my doubts as to the wisdom of compulsion, and I have always felt that the law which inflicts penalty after penalty on a parent who is unwilling to have his child vaccinated is monstrous, and ought to be repealed.

I am, truly yours,
JOHN BRIGHT.

Mr. Henry Pitman, Manchester.

THE VACCINATION LAWS.

A Leicester gentleman wrote to Mr. Bright, asking his opinion as to the enforcing of the Compulsory Vaccination Acts, the seizure of goods and the imprisonment of persons for refusing to have their children vaccinated, as to whether it was consistent with personal freedom that respectable men should be put in prison on any such matter of conscience. A case was also stated in which a workman in a condition of distress was apprehended by the police while his four children were at his knee saying their prayers, and the correspondent asked whether this was the sort of man for whom the State ought to provide prisons. Mr. Bright replied as follows:—

December, 1883.

DEAR SIR,—I fear I cannot help you in your complaint against the Vaccination Laws. I think compulsory vaccination doubtful, and the repetition of penalties as now practised monstrous. The repetition of penalties creates or intensifies the agitation against the law, and so long as they are inflicted I suspect we shall see only a greater hatred of the law.

As to compulsory vaccination, I am of opinion that if it had never been insisted on or enforced, vaccination might have been as general as it now is without the fierce opposition to it which now prevails in many quarters. The facts appear to me to be in favour of vaccination, but that it often fails of any good effect, and sometimes causes much evil and even death, is admitted even by its warmest supporters. To me it is doubtful if persuasion and example would not have been more effective than compulsion, but to inflict incessant penalties upon parents, and to imprison them for refusing to subject their children to an operation which is not unfrequently injurious and is sometimes fatal, seems to me a needless and monstrous violation of the freedom of our homes and of the rights of parents.

The instances of harshness and cruelty you mention shock me greatly. After so much contest for mildness in our laws, are such things still possible in our country?

I am, very truly yours,

JOHN BRIGHT.

THE VACCINATION LAWS.

Replying to the Secretary of the London Society for the Abolition of Compulsory Vaccination, who called attention to the repeated prosecution of Charles Hayward by the East Ashford Board of Guardians, Mr. Bright wrote as follows:—

Melrose, N.B., September 28, 1887.

DEAR SIR,—I think the compulsory clauses of the Vaccination Acts are a great mistake, and are the foundation of the bitter hostility now manifested in so many places, and by so many parents, to the practice of vaccination. Your Board of Guardians seem to be of a different opinion, and their plan of repeated prosecution is calculated to cause hatred of the law under which they deem it their duty to act. I hope their experience of the failure of their system may bring them to a more merciful conclusion. The results at Leicester, Keighley, and some other towns should make them more moderate in the working of the law. I fear I can do nothing in the sad case you have brought before me. If honest parents object to have their children vaccinated I would not compel them.

Yours very truly,

Mr. Wm. Young.   JOHN BRIGHT.

FUNERAL REFORM.

Written to a Birmingham constituent.

Rochdale, October 26, 1875.

DEAR SIR,—If your friends or any sensible people wish to reform the funeral exhibitions and expenses, let them observe and copy the practice of the sect to which I belong, that of the "Society of Friends." Nothing can be more simple, and nothing can be better. They would be wise also to follow them in rejecting the fashion of wearing mourning, which is always costly, and, as worn by many women, hideous. I am sorry to say, however, that the wearing of mourning has of late been rather increasing with " Friends," among whom are many who apparently do not comprehend or do not value the principles on which the practice of their forefathers was based.

I am yours, &c.,

JOHN BRIGHT.

THE "VIRTUOUS POOR."

At a meeting of the Haddington Established Presbytery in November, 1878, Dr. Whitelaw, in calling the attention of his colleagues to the condition of the virtuous poor of Scotland, but more particularly of those who were in communion with the Church of Scotland, read the following letter he had received from Mr. Bright on the subject :—

November, 1878.

DEAR SIR,—I do not see what law can do for what you term "virtuous poor," unless it is to assist them under the action of the poor law. The question which should be asked is, "Why are there so many virtuous poor?" It would take, not a letter, but a volume to answer this question—but in a letter one or two points may be indicated. If the law or laws make land a virtuous monopoly, as it is in the United Kingdom, and especially in Scotland, then we may expect that the population, divorced from the soil, will be in possession only of a precarious income or living, and that they will be subject to fluctuation and reverses which will inflict upon many of them the sufferings of poverty, even when their lives have been fairly prudent and virtuous. I cannot go fully into the question, but I am persuaded that enormous evil to the people comes from this cause. The public exactions and expenditure have much to do with poverty. To raise not less than eighty millions sterling per annum for purposes of government, to expend thirty millions of it in military preparations and means of offence and defence, the bulk of which is only rendered apparently necessary by a mistaken foreign policy, must act as a burden on the people, and must press multitudes of prudent and virtuous families to poverty.

These are two of the great causes and sources of the sufferings of the people. They are both capable of remedy, and the ignorance of the people—not of the working classes, but of the classes above them—is the only difficulty in the way. If you could persuade your General Assembly to look at these matters, and to thoroughly examine them, perhaps its members might make a discovery that would startle them, and benefit the people to whom they minister. I do not touch upon other questions. Some of them will suggest themselves to you. The great whisky question is one which your

friends there may consider with some advantage. If all the
ministers of the Scottish Churches were to banish whisky
from their houses, and the consumption of it from their
customs or social habits, they would do much to discredit
and to withdraw one fertile source of poverty and suffering in Scotland. Many of what you term " virtuous
poor " suffer much from the evil of whisky in connection
with members of their families. I am burdened with
correspondence, and so write hastily and briefly. I do
not suppose what I write will be of service; if you think
otherwise, you are at liberty to add this letter to the
other contributions of your friends.

I am, very respectfully yours,

JOHN BRIGHT.

Rev. Dr. Whitelaw.

THE MARRIAGE LAWS.

Written in reply to the Rev. Alfred R. Tucker, of
Bristol, who wrote to ask an explanation of Mr. Bright
concerning a passage in his speech at a meeting of the
Liberation Society at the Metropolitan Tabernacle, on
Wednesday, May 2nd, 1883. The following is the
passage in question :—" A handful of ecclesiastics . . .
condemn thousands of families to unhappiness during
their lifetime, and condemn thousands of children who are
wholly guiltless, *as I believe their parents are guiltless.*"

Mr. Tucker asked that " for morality's sake " Mr. Bright
would give an explanation of the words italicized.

Mr. Bright replied as follows :—

132, Piccadilly, London, May 7, 1883.

SIR,—I spoke of those who are married, but whose
marriage is by the existing law not legal in this country.
These marriages are legal in Canada and in the
Australian Colonies, and hence a man may have a legal
wife in the Colonies and another legal wife in England.
He may bring his Canadian legal wife to England,
where, when she touches our shores, she is not a legal
wife, and where her children born here are not legiti-

mate. If you can justify this, I will not argue with you. Excuse me if I do not discuss the main question with you. It is asserted, I believe truly, that the Queen is in favour of the change of law. It is known that the Prince of Wales is so.

In the Lords I learn there is a majority in favour of the change : last year the Bishops prevented it. In the Commons a majority of 150 or more support the change. When it becomes law your Church, Bishops and Clergy, will have to support it, which I doubt not they will do without much difficulty.

I only regret that they do not see the light before it is forced upon them. When I speak of a handful of ecclesiastics I refer to the members of Convocation who have been discussing this question.

Pray excuse this hurried note.

I am, very truly yours,

JOHN BRIGHT.

To Rev. Alfred R. Tucker, The Paragon, Clifton, Bristol.

THE FACTORY ACTS.

Written to a gentleman in the Fylde district, who had called Mr. Bright's attention to the criticisms of a Tory newspaper with respect to his opposition to factory legislation.

One Ash, Rochdale, January 1, 1884.

DEAR SIR,—I was opposed to all legislation restricting the adults, men or women. I was in favour of legislation restricting the labour and guarding the health of children. I could not therefore support Bills which directly interfered with and restricted the working hours of women, and which thus were intended to limit the working hours of men. I still hold the opinion that to limit by law the time during which adults may work is unwise, and in many cases oppressive. As to your Tory newspaper, you may remind the writer that I sought to give the workman two loaves of bread, when his party wished to give him only one.

I am, truly yours,

JOHN BRIGHT.

THE FACTORY ACTS.

In consequence of certain attacks having been made on Mr. Bright for his opposition to the Factory Acts, Mr. G. W. Medley, one of the Liberal candidates for Devonport, called his attention to them. Mr. Bright sent the following reply :—

One Ash, Rochdale, October 2, 1885.

DEAR SIR,—I cannot go into the whole question of the Factory Acts. My opposition was based entirely on the ground that they interfered with the labour of adults. I was at work endeavouring to give the labourers two loaves of bread in place of one and about three pounds of sugar in place of one, and in so increasing trade by the demand for labour that wages have generally risen more than one-half, and in thousands of cases to double the former rate. All this great reformation was violently opposed by the Tory party, and but for the changes we asked for and carried, the Factory Acts would long since have broken down, along with other things of even greater importance. I hope that if I am in the new Parliament I may meet you there. Your pamphlet is very good. I have read it with much pleasure.

Always sincerely yours,

JOHN BRIGHT.

TRADES' UNIONS.

A Salford workman having written to Mr. Bright to complain that himself and ten others had been excluded from the Trade Society to which they belonged, for having worked overtime on a break-down job, received the following reply :—

One Ash, Rochdale, January 24, 1887.

DEAR SIR,—I have read your interesting letter, but I abstain from writing anything on the subject of the action of trades' unions. In your case the cause has been singularly opposed to the true interests of workmen, and it is surprising that they should submit to it. I do not think anything I could say would be of the least use, and experience only can teach workmen how much or how little they gain by combinations which are supposed to be for their especial benefit. I believe strikes have done much more harm to labour in different trades than combinations have done good.

But workmen will not readily accept the opinion or the advice of anyone of what is called the capitalist class; they can only learn from their own experience. It is, however, pleasant to believe that in the conduct and contests of trades' unions greater moderation is shown and less of violence is seen than in past years—say 40 or 50 years ago.

I return your letter, as it may be of use to you in dealing with the question on which it has been written.

I am, yours respectfully,
JOHN BRIGHT.

Mr. J. Fairclough, 17, Peel Street, Salford.

JUVENILE SMOKING.

Written in reply to a letter from a Birmingham constituent, who had urged legislative action against juvenile tobacco smoking amongst the working classes.

February, 1879.

DEAR SIR,—I do not think such a law as you recommend would receive support in the House of Commons. We have rather too many laws already, and I prefer to leave such evils as you refer to to parental supervision and the effects of a better education among the working classes.

I am, yours, &c.,
JOHN BRIGHT.

PERSONAL INCIDENTS.

MR. BRIGHT'S REPRESENTATION OF MANCHESTER.

Read at a public meeting in the Free Trade Hall, Manchester, on Thursday evening, the 29th of January, 1857. The meeting was held to support the cause of Free Trade and Reform, Mr. George Wilson being in the chair. The letter was received with applause, and a resolution was afterwards enthusiastically passed, expressing sympathy with and unabated confidence in Mr. Bright, and requesting him to allow the continuance of his parliamentary connection with that city.

Mr. Bright had represented Manchester since July, 1847, when he was elected along with Mr. Milner Gibson. From 1843 up to that time he had represented the City of Durham.

Rochdale, November 5, 1856.

MY DEAR WILSON,—I mentioned to you a few days ago that I was about to leave England for a considerable time, probably for several months. My health, as you know, is greatly improved during the past six months —so much so as to afford strong reason for the belief that a further period of relaxation and change of objects and interests will so far restore me as to enable me again to attend to public business. I have consulted physicians of extensive practice and eminent in the profession, and their opinions all concur in this—that a complete rest from public labour for a longer period is necessary ; and that this, it may be hoped and believed, will give me renewed health and strength. Acting upon this advice, which my own judgment entirely approves, I am about to leave home for some months, and I

S 2

shall therefore, in all probability, not be able to attend the House of Commons during the next session of Parliament.

I think it my duty, under these circumstances, to write to you in your capacity of chairman of the committee which undertook the management of my election in 1852. I am very sensible of the kindness shown to me by my constituents, inasmuch as I believe they freely consented to my absence from Parliament during the past session. In absenting myself for another session, however, I feel that I am bound to enter into a more public and definite explanation with them.

Incapable as I am at present of performing any of the duties of their representative, it would seem to be my duty to resign my seat in Parliament, and to give them the opportunity of electing my successor. I feel, however, that the wishes and convenience of the constituency ought to be consulted before I decide. If we were at the beginning instead of being, as we are, very near the end of a Parliament, the interests of all concerned would probably be best promoted by my immediate resignation ; but as a general election is likely to take place during the year 1857, it may not be thought desirable to have two elections for Manchester during the same year. This is a point which I am anxious to refer to my friends in Manchester before I do anything which would make an immediate election unavoidable.

You will greatly oblige me, therefore, if you will take such steps as appear to you best to ascertain the wishes of my constituents as to the course I should take. I shall be guided by their decision, either to vacate my seat in Parliament on the opening of the coming session, or to retain it till the dissolution of the Parliament, which may come in the spring, and is almost certain to come in the autumn, of 1857.

I hope I am not too sanguine in believing that a few months more of rest—rest of the faculties which have had almost no rest during the past fifteen years—will restore to me the power, as I still have the will, to labour in that field in which so much of my life has been spent. If I am permitted to recover my former strength before the occurrence of a general election, I shall then hope for a continuance of the confidence which the electors of Manchester have so long placed in me ; if renewed health be not granted to me, I shall then withdraw from public life, remembering, as long as I live, how much I owe to the kindness and forbearance of those in whose name and on whose behalf I have acted for nine years past in the House of Commons.

Believe me, very sincerely yours,

JOHN BRIGHT.

ON LOSING HIS SEAT FOR MANCHESTER.

At the general election, in March, 1857, a strong effort was made by the leading Whig politicians in the city to secure the defeat of Mr. Bright and his colleague, Mr. Milner Gibson, the members for Manchester, on account of their opposition to the Russian War. Mr. Bright was seeking health on the Continent at the time, and he was represented in the election contest by his friend, Mr. Cobden. The result of the polling was that Mr. Bright and Mr. Gibson were defeated, Sir John Potter and Mr. J. Aspinall Turner being returned to Parliament in their stead.

Upon receiving by telegram the result of the election, Mr. Bright wrote the following farewell address to the electors of Manchester, which appeared in the *Examiner and Times* of the 8th of April, 1857 :—

TO THE ELECTORS OF THE CITY OF MANCHESTER.

GENTLEMEN,—I have received a telegraphic despatch informing me of the result of the election contest in which you have just been engaged. That result has not greatly surprised me, and so far as I am personally concerned—inasmuch as it liberates me from public life in a manner which involves on my part no shrinking from any duty—I cannot earnestly regret it. I lament it on public grounds, because it tells the world that many amongst you have abandoned the opinions you professed to hold in the year 1847, and even so recently as the year 1852. I believe that slander itself has not dared to charge me with having forsaken any of the principles on the honest support of which I offered myself twice, and was twice accepted as your representative. The charge against me has rather been, that I have too warmly and too faithfully defended the political views which found so much favour with you at the two previous elections.

If the change in your opinion of me has arisen from my course on the question of the war with Russia, I can only say that, on a calm review of all the circumstances of the case—and during the past twelve months I have had ample time for such a review—I would not unsay or retract any one of the speeches I have spoken, or erase from the records of Parliament any one of the votes I have given upon it, if I could thereby reverse the decision to which you have come, or secure any other distinction which it is in the power of my countrymen to confer. I am free, and will remain free, from any share in the needless and guilty bloodshed of that melancholy chapter in the annals of my country. I cannot, however, forget that the leaders of the opposition in the recent contest have not been influenced by my conduct on this question. They were less successful, but not less bitter, in their hostility in 1852, and even in 1847, when my only public merit or demerit consisted in my labours in the cause of Free Trade. On each occasion, calling themselves Liberals, and calling their candidates Liberals also, they have coalesced with the Conservatives, whilst now, doubtless, they have assailed Mr. Gibson and myself on the ground of a pretended coalition with the Conservatives in the House of Commons.

I have esteemed it a high honour to be one of your representatives, and have given more of mental and physical labour to your service than was just to myself.

I feel it scarcely less an honour to suffer in the cause of peace, and on behalf of what I believe to be the true interest of my country, though I could have wished that the blow had come from other hands, at a time when I could have been present to meet face to face those who dealt it.

In taking my leave of you and of public life, let me assure you that I can never forget the many—the innumerable kindnesses I have received from my friends amongst you. No one will rejoice more than I shall in all that brings you prosperity and honour ; and I am not without a hope that, when a calmer hour shall come, you will say of Mr. Gibson and of me, that, as colleagues in your representation for ten years, we have not sacrificed our principles to gain popularity, or bartered our independence for the emoluments of office or the favours of the great. I feel that we have stood for the rights, and interests, and freedom of the people, and that we have not tarnished the honour or lessened the renown of your eminent city.

I am now, as I have hitherto been,

Very faithfully yours,

JOHN BRIGHT.

Florence, March 31, 1857.

ON BEING ELECTED A MEMBER FOR BIRMINGHAM.

A vacancy having occurred, through the death of Mr. Muntz, in the representation of Birmingham, it was resolved at a public meeting held on the 4th of August, 1857, to put forward Mr. Bright as a candidate, and on being asked he consented to stand. He was elected on the 10th of August, in his absence—his health not having yet been thoroughly re-established—and without opposition. On the receipt of the news of his election, Mr. Bright sent the following address to the electors :—

TO THE ELECTORS OF BIRMINGHAM.

GENTLEMEN,—Your respected chief magistrate has informed me by telegraph that he has this day declared me to be duly elected one of your representatives in Parliament ; and I have learned from other sources that such was the feeling manifested in my favour, that no other candidate was presented to you at the hustings, and that, therefore, my election has been without contest or opposition from any quarter.

When I addressed you two days ago, I had no expectation of a result so speedy and so tranquil of the then impending struggle. I accept it as a conclusive proof of the bias of your political views, and of a confidence in me which I shall strive to maintain undiminished.

It is a matter of real regret to me that I have not been able to be with you during the past week, and at the hustings this day. I shall hope, however, that on some not distant occasion, I may be permitted to meet you in your noble Town Hall, and to become more intimately acquainted with a constituency from whom I have received an honour as signal as it was unexpected, and towards whom I can never entertain other feelings than those of respect and gratitude.

With heartfelt thanks for your kindness, which I trust I may have the health and the opportunity in some measure to repay, I subscribe myself,

Very faithfully yours,
JOHN BRIGHT.

Rochdale, August 10, 1857.

MR. BRIGHT'S REPRESENTATION OF BIRMINGHAM.

Before the election of Mr. Bright to represent Birmingham in Parliament, the report was industriously circulated that, even if elected, he would make the seat a mere temporary convenience, to be relinquished as soon as the constituency of Manchester regained its senses, and asked him to represent it once more. The rumour turned up again in 1858, and became so commonly talked of as to induce a gentleman connected with the Liberal party in the borough to write to Mr. Bright for an explanation. Mr. Bright replied as follows :—

Rochdale, May 26, 1858.

DEAR SIR,—I know nothing of the report to which you allude, and certainly I have said nothing to justify it. Remembering the circumstances under which I was returned for Birmingham, it is strange that anyone should imagine I could prefer any other constituency so long as I remain in the House of Commons, and so long as my opinions and course in Parliament are not opposed to the views of those I have now the honour to represent. I know no nobler constituency than that of Birmingham, and no member of the House of Commons owes more to a constituency than I owe to that on whose behalf I now speak and vote in Parliament.

I am, very respectfully yours,

JOHN BRIGHT.

MR. BRIGHT'S CANDIDATURE IN 1886.

The following letter was written to the chairman of the Liberal Committee of the Central division of Birmingham, on the eve of the general election of 1886 :—

Rochdale, June 21, 1886.

MY DEAR MR. JAFFRAY,—If it is the wish of the Council of the Central division of Birmingham that I should become a candidate for the representation of the division in the Parliament about to be elected, I am willing that my name should be submitted to the Council and the constituency. In November last I thought I had made my last appearance as a candidate for a seat in Parliament, for I felt that the time was near when I·might without blame retire from the political field. The events of the last three months have been so extraordinary, and the questions now before the country are of so grave a character, that I do not feel at liberty to withdraw from Parliament if my present constituency are willing to continue their confidence in me.

I thank you for your friendly letter, and am always yours,

JOHN BRIGHT.

ON HIS ACCEPTANCE OF OFFICE IN 1868.

Written in reply to a letter sent to Mr. Bright by a gentleman at Sheffield, congratulating him on being appointed President of the Board of Trade.

London, December 9, 1868.

DEAR SIR,—I must send you a short note, to thank you for your kind letter. It is a great pleasure to me to know that you and your friends in Sheffield are satisfied with the course I have taken in joining the new Administration. I have done it with extreme reluctance, but the pressure put upon me was more than I could withstand. I hope I have done what it seemed finally my duty to do. For your most friendly expressions and wishes accept my heartfelt thanks, and believe me always,

Very truly yours,
JOHN BRIGHT.

ON BEING ELECTED LORD RECTOR OF GLASGOW UNIVERSITY.

Written to the President of the Glasgow University Liberal Club:—

Stratford-on-Avon, November 22, 1880.

DEAR SIR,—I beg to thank you for your letter informing me of my election to the office of Lord Rector of Glasgow University. I am much indebted to you and your friends for the high favour that has been shown to me, but I cannot, I fear, reciprocate the enthusiasm of which you speak. If I am sensible of the kindness and good opinion of the students, and desire to rejoice in the success of your efforts, I am not less conscious that I have very little claim to the distinguished position in which I am placed. It is fortunate for me that the duties of the office to which you have called me, but to which I did not aspire, are light, and not immediately pressing. During its term I shall hope to have an opportunity of presenting myself before your constituency, and of delivering the address which is expected from me. I can now only ask you and those by whose support I have been elected to accept my grateful thanks for the confidence they have placed in me.

I am, &c.,

JOHN BRIGHT

ON RECEIVING AN INVITATION TO VISIT IRELAND.

Written in reply to the following invitation, signed by over twenty Irish Members of Parliament, which was sent to Mr. Bright in August, 1866 :—

SIR,—We, the undersigned, admiring your public character and grateful for your eloquent advocacy of the rights of our country, respectfully request your acceptance of a public banquet at Dublin on as early a day as your convenience will permit.

Rochdale, September 1, 1866.

MY DEAR MR. DILLON,—I am afraid you will think me long in answering your letter of the 21st ult., and in replying to the invitation to the proposed banquet, which has duly reached me. The invitation is a very remarkable one, and I cannot doubt it represents an important amount of public opinion in Ireland. To myself it is a testimony of approval and kind feeling which I estimate most highly, although it involves me in no small difficulty, for I have been hoping for a quiet autumn, with an absence of public meetings and of public labour. I am not confident that my coming to Ireland will be of any service, but as so many among you are of opinion that something may be done to make a more perfect union between the Liberals of Ireland and the Liberal party here, with a view to wiser legislation for your country and for ours, I have not felt myself at liberty to refuse the invitation which has been sent to me. I accept it with much gratitude to those from whom it comes, and with a hope that in doing so I may not be stepping beyond the bounds of what seems to be my duty. Some time during the month of October will, I hope, be convenient to all concerned, but I must ask you to leave the precise day to be fixed two or three weeks hence. About the middle of the month will probably be the best time for me, if there be no objection·to it on the part of my friends in Dublin.

With many thanks to you and to those on whose behalf you have written to me,

I am, very sincerely yours,
JOHN BRIGHT.

Mr. John B. Dillon, M.P., Dublin.

ON RECEIVING AN INVITATION TO VISIT THE UNITED STATES.

At the beginning of 1883 Mr. Bright received from Mr. Evarts a resolution unanimously adopted by the Union League Club of New York, inviting the right hon. gentleman to visit the United States as the guest of the club, which was to celebrate its twentieth anniversary on the 6th of February in that year.

Mr. Bright replied as follows :—

Rochdale, January 16, 1883.

MY DEAR MR. EVARTS,—I have received your kind letter of the 16th of December, along with a letter signed by yourself as President of the Union League Club of New York, and on behalf of the members of the club, inviting me to visit the United States, and to be present on the 6th of February next at the celebration of the anniversary of the foundation of the club in the year 1863.

The receipt of these letters and this invitation has caused me a very mixed feeling. I am pleased to think, and indeed to know, that I have many friends in your country who remember with kind feelings towards me the part I took in the discussions in England at the great crisis in your history, when the unity of your great Republic and your free Government seemed for a time to be in peril.

But if I am glad to have so many friends amongst you, I am grieved that the time has never come when I could visit a country and a people in whose greatness and welfare I have always felt the strongest interest. And now, when you send me the most friendly invitation, the obstacles in my way are not to be overcome.

Your celebration is fixed for the 6th of February. Besides the ordinary duties of a member of Parliament, I have special engagements for the spring—for March and May—which I cannot escape from or postpone. It is quite impossible, therefore, for me to accept your invitation for the coming month, and I cannot hope to take part in the interesting proceedings to which you have invited me.

But I must say something more. I never liked the sea, and my once strong appetite for travel has subsided, and I cannot but feel that the friendly welcome promised me on your side of the Atlantic would force me into a publicity from which I shrink.

What can I say, then, in reply to letters so complimentary, and yet, I cannot doubt, so friendly and sincere? That I am deeply grateful to you and to your and my friends on whose behalf you have written, and that I regret with a feeling not less strong that I am not able to accept the kind invitation you have sent me, and the most kind welcome you have offered and promised me. I write with difficulty ; but you will understand how hard it is to make a fitting, when an unfavourable, reply to such letters as you and your friends have addressed to me.   You will forgive me if I cannot come.   I can never forget your great kindness and the honours you have conferred upon me.

Believe me always, very sincerely yours,

JOHN BRIGHT.

ON RECEIVING AN INTERNATIONAL ADDRESS.

An International Address, arising out of the policy of the Gladstone Government in the Transvaal, which had received numerous signatures in Holland, Germany, Hungary, France, and Italy, was forwarded to Mr. Bright in March, 1881, by Mr. Karl Blind, to whom the right hon. gentleman returned the following reply:—

132, Piccadilly, March 14, 1881.

DEAR SIR,—I thank you for the memorial you have forwarded to me, and for the friendly letter from yourself on the sad question of the Transvaal difficulty.   I hope the prospect is one of peace, and not of further war, and that an arrangement may be made satisfactory to the Transvaal people, and honourable to this country. I scarcely need to assure you that whatever influence I possess is being and will be exerted in favour of peace. The conflict is one in which England can gain nothing, not even military glory, which is the poorest kind of glory, in my view, which men and nations strive for.   I hope the time may come when nations will seek and obtain honourable renown by deeds of mercy and justice.

This reply to your letter and the memorial is brief but, under the circumstances, I feel sure you and your friends will excuse its brevity.

Believe me to be, very sincerely yours,

JOHN BRIGHT.

Karl Blind, Esq., 3, Winchester Road, South Hampstead, N.W.

ON RECEIVING AN ADDRESS FROM FRENCH LIBERALS.

Another address with reference to the Transvaal difficulty was presented to Mr. Bright by Mr. Buisson, a French journalist resident in London. The address emanated from a number of leading French Liberals, and was signed by about thirty members of the French Senate, certain deputies and members of the Paris Municipal Council, the French Academy, &c. To this memorial Mr. Bright wrote the following reply :—

{London, March 23, 1881.

DEAR SIR,—I was glad to have the opportunity of speaking to you yesterday during your short visit, when you presented to me an address on the subject of the Transvaal war from the eminent French Liberals whose names I find appended to it. They have done me great honour in selecting me as in any manner worthy to be considered a representative of the friends of international justice, peace, and good-will between nations. I accept the address with much pleasure, and I can ask now to be permitted to rejoice with them in the happy settlement of a difficulty and of a conflict which has excited in their minds, as in mine, so deep a grief. I believe the English people will gladly sustain a Government which has restored peace by a course at once magnanimous and just, and I feel entire confidence that its policy will be approved in all foreign countries by "friends of international justice, peace, and good-will between nations." I ask you to convey to the eminent Frenchmen who have signed the address my warm thanks for the great compliment they have paid me.

I am, &c., &c.,
JOHN BRIGHT.

M. Buisson, Saville Club.

MISCELLANEOUS LETTERS.

ON BEING ASKED TO SUBSCRIBE
TO A BAZAAR.

A gentleman connected with a bazaar which was opened in Birmingham on the 10th of August, 1857, thinking that as the occurrence of Mr. Bright's election on that day had interfered with the probable profits, the honourable member might be induced from this circumstance to assist their funds, wrote him to that effect. Mr. Bright sent him the following reply :—

August, 1857.

SIR,—I am sorry if the occurrence of the election should have made your bazaar less productive; but if it has done so, I can hardly be held in any way responsible for it. I cannot undertake to subscribe to public objects in Birmingham, on account of my political connection with it. Since I have been in Parliament I have always abstained from subscriptions for objects connected with the constituency I represented, and I intend to continue that course. A contrary course would lead me to an expenditure which I could not consent to with any prudence, and might lead to an endeavour to secure public favour by means which I cannot practise or approve. I hope, therefore, you will excuse me if I find myself unable to add to your funds, and that you will rightly interpret the grounds upon which I act in this matter.

I am, very respectfully,

JOHN BRIGHT.

T 2

MR. MILNER GIBSON.

The Right Hon. T. Milner Gibson, who along with Mr. Bright was defeated at Manchester at the general election in 1857, was subsequently returned for Ashton-under-Lyne, and on the 28th of January, 1858, a *soirée* was given at the Ashton Town Hall to celebrate his election. At the meeting, the following letter was read from Mr. Bright :—

Rochdale, January 20, 1858.

DEAR SIR,—I regret very much that I cannot avail myself of the invitation to your approaching public *soirée*, so kindly forwarded to me by your committee. I need hardly say that it would have given me extreme pleasure to have seen my friend and late colleague—and may I not say still my colleague ?—among his new constituency. That you have filled up the vacancy which occurred in the representation of your borough by the return of Mr. Milner Gibson has been a subject of rejoicing in every house in the kingdom which is the house of an honest and intelligent reformer. To me it has given greater satisfaction than I have words to express ; for I, who for fourteen years have worked incessantly with him, may perhaps be more capable than almost any other man of appreciating his worth in the House of Commons. To refer only to one subject of legislation—the freedom of the press from taxes intended to crush or to cripple it—I would ask, to whom is the country so much indebted as to your member ? And what services can be greater in a nation pretending or aspiring to be free than to give it a free and cheap press, whereby the whole population may be informed from day to day of all questions affecting the public interests ? I am deeply grateful to you for the course you have taken, and hope I may still be able, though it may be with diminished force, to work with Mr. Gibson in behalf of the true interests of our country. I desire to thank the gentlemen of your committee for their kindness in inviting me, and yourself also for the kindly expressions contained in your letter.

I am, &c.,

JOHN BRIGHT.

Mr. William Hill, Ashton-under-Lyne.

THE USE OF INDIAN CORN IN ENGLAND.

Written to a gentleman in Cincinnati, who had addressed a letter to Mr. Bright, urging the importance of introducing Indian corn as an article of food for the people of this country.

Rochdale, October 10, 1873.

DEAR SIR,—I duly received your interesting letter of the 28th of April last, and I have submitted it to Mr. Buckmaster, who has been giving lectures on cookery at South Kensington, and have asked him to consider how far anything can be done on the subject of the use of Indian corn in this country. Hitherto nothing has been done, and there are great difficulties in the way, which it will take time to overcome. The greatest difficulty is that which attends all new things—the indisposition of the people to give a favourable or even an impartial attention to what is new. The chief hindrance to the use of Indian corn has always been the want of knowledge as to the various modes of cooking it. I speak now of those who are favourably disposed towards it. There must be men and women in this country who are familiar with this branch of cookery as practised with you, or, if not, it would not be difficult to engage some American man or woman cook who would undertake to instruct in it. I shall probably see Mr. Buckmaster again when I go up to London, and I shall urge him and those with whom he is associated to arrange for some provision by which all that is known in the States with respect to Indian corn may also be known in this country. We have always to import a large portion of our food, and it seems very strange that an article of such great consumption with you should be so very little favoured or known among us.

I cannot say more on the subject now, but I will not forget it, or your letter upon it.

Yours respectfully,
JOHN BRIGHT.

Mr. John H. Osborne,
8, Merchants' Exchange, Cincinnati, U.S.A.

MR. CHARLES SUMNER.

Addressed to a gentleman in Boston who had sent Mr. Bright a photograph of Mr. Sumner.

Charles Sumner, the distinguished orator and statesman alluded to in this letter, was born at Boston on the 6th of January, 1811. He began to practise as a lawyer at Boston in 1834 and in 1851 succeeded Daniel Webster as United States Senator. He took an active part as a public speaker in opposition to the annexation of Texas, and was identified with the peace and anti-slavery movements of the day. In the Senate he opposed the Fugitive Slave Act in a speech in which he declared, " Freedom is national, and slavery sectional." After the delivery of his famous speech, " The Crime against Kansas," on the 19th and 20th of May, 1856, he was assaulted, while in his seat, by a member from South Carolina, and was so severely injured as to be unable to resume his public duties for three or four years. On resuming his seat in the Senate, his first speech was on " The Barbarism of Slavery," on the 4th of June, 1860. He early proposed emancipation as the speediest method of ending the Rebellion ; and from 1861 to 1870 was Chairman of the Senate Committee on Foreign Affairs. He died suddenly on the 11th of March, 1874.

Rochdale, April 4th, 1874.

DEAR MR. KINSLEY,—I am much indebted to you for your letter, and for the photograph you have sent me. The portrait is admirable, and does justice to the great subject of it.   Mr. Sumner spent his last night in England under this roof, and left us for Liverpool on the morning of the day on which he sailed.   His health was very much shaken, and I was sorry his voyage was in the winter.   The news of your great loss has made me very sad.   I can imagine the feelings of sorrow it will have caused in the hearts of your countrymen.   In this country the press has done justice to your great senator. His unblemished life, his noble aims, and his great services to freedom and humanity are freely admitted and greatly honoured by our public writers.

Very sincerely yours,

JOHN BRIGHT.

THE TICHBORNE CASE.

Written to a correspondent at Sheffield, who urged Mr. Bright to support Mr. Whalley in his efforts to obtain protection for a man in New Zealand claiming to be Arthur Orton.

132, Piccadilly, London, July 15, 1875.

SIR,—You may rely upon it that Arthur Orton will not come from New Zealand.   During the trial 1000*l.* was offered for him, and nobody could produce him.   It was a large bribe, and I only wonder it did not bring over a score of Ortons.   The Arthur Orton is in Dartmoor, and nobody, I suspect, knows this better than some of those who are pretending to expect him from New Zealand.   I have read all the evidence and all the speeches of both trials, and the summing up of the Lord Chief Justice.   This last I have read again during last month.   And I have read more than once the evidence taken before the Chili Commission.   I know, therefore, as much about the matter as you can know, and much more than is known by nine out of ten of those who are clamouring for the release of the convict at Dartmoor.   I have before me now the handwriting of the real Roger Tichborne, of the real Arthur Orton, and of the convict, and this alone is sufficient to convince any man of common sense and observation what is the truth in the case. If you could see this handwriting, and if you could examine the evidence of the Chili Commission, the evidence of the convict's own friends, to whom he referred for proof that he was what he pretended to be, you could hardly fail to be convinced that your belief in the convict is wrong, and your sympathy with him wholly misplaced.

I mention these two points as conclusive against him. There are many other points in the evidence on the two trials which are fatal to his claims. He seemed to know the names of two dogs, but he did not know the name of his own mother. Mr. Turville, in Australia, asks him a last question, whether his mother was stout or thin. He said, "Stout, a tall, large woman." It is not denied that Lady Tichborne was leanness itself. Miss Nangles said she was more like a skeleton than anything else, and this was not contradicted by anyone. If you can believe in a man who did not know his own mother's name, and who stated that his mother, who is admitted to have been leanness itself, was "stout, a tall large woman," when he first came forward in Australia, and when he had no opportunity of picking up information and facts to support his case, I fear you are of that credulous nature that it may be useless to reason with you.

I can take no part in the proceedings of Mr. Whalley and his friends. To me the convict in Dartmoor is the greatest criminal of our time. His crime has extended over many years ; it is most base in character, and includes in it almost every crime for which evil men are brought to punishment.

You are much impressed, I dare say, by the declarations of those who traverse the country creating agitation on this question. I must ask to be permitted to value my own judgment at least as highly as that of these persons. One of them is believed to have invested money largely in the case, and pecuniary interest is not favourable to an impartial decision. Another suffers from a complaint which I call "Jesuit on the brain,"[1] and this seems grievously to distort almost everything he looks at. The third is the lawyer who failed, after a trial which lasted 188 days, to convince three judges and twelve jurymen, or any one of the judges or of the jurymen, that his client was anything but an impostor and a man most odious from his character and his crimes.

I shall be glad if you, and such as believe with you, will not ask me to correspond further on a question about which only honest men who are in entire ignorance of the facts can in my view differ in opinion.

I am, respectfully yours,

JOHN BRIGHT.

Mr. Mark Harrison, 1, Elliott Road, Sheffield.

THE FOREIGN CATTLE TRADE.

Mr. George Whitehead, of the Calder Vale Ironworks, Wakefield, wrote to Mr. Bright on the 2nd of September, 1875, to ask him whether the restrictions placed upon the importation of foreign cattle into our markets were necessary for the preservation of our English herds, or whether some other unworthy object was brought about to serve the interests of some selfish few. Mr. Bright replied as follows :—

Rochdale, September 3, 1875.

DEAR SIR,—I shall not venture to give you a confident opinion upon the matter on which you have written to me, but my impression when the Bill was passing through Parliament was that the country gentlemen were anxious to make it as restrictive as possible, and that its operation in the direction of protection made restriction popular among them. I have not much confidence in the legislation to prevent cattle

---

[1] The late Mr. Whalley, M.P., to whom Mr. Bright here alludes, had an exaggerated idea of the influence of the Jesuits on the private and public affairs of men, and this led him to the belief that there existed a Jesuit conspiracy to keep Roger Tichborne out of his estates.

disease, and I distrust it entirely when it is fixed at the point which meets the views of county members of Parliament.   High prices and high rents, by the help of legislation, were once greedily sought after, and will not be refused now if offered under cover of an Act to prevent the importation of diseased cattle.   An impartial inquiry into this question would, I suspect, discover that the restrictions imposed are needlessly severe, and that they tend sensibly to diminish the supply, and to raise the price of butchers' meat throughout the country.

I am, respectfully yours,

JOHN BRIGHT.

Mr. George Whitehead,
Calder Vale Ironworks, Wakefield.

KINDNESS TO ANIMALS.

Read at a meeting held in the Birmingham Town Hall on the 28th of November, 1877, when prizes publicly subscribed for were distributed to such of the Board School children as had succeeded either by writing essays or answering questions in connection with the subject of kindness to dumb animals.

Rochdale, November 22, 1877.

DEAR MISS GODDARD,—I cannot come to your meeting, but I am very glad your good cause excites so much interest as to enable you to hold a public meeting in its favour.   If children at school can be made to understand how it is just and noble to be humane even to what we term inferior animals, it will do much to give them a higher character and tone through life.   There is nothing meaner than barbarous and cruel treatment of the dumb creatures who cannot answer us or resent the misery which is so often needlessly inflicted upon them.

Wishing you a constant success,

I am, very sincerely yours,

JOHN BRIGHT.

CONSECRATED GROUND.

On the 20th of November, 1877, the Bishop of Peterborough delivered an address on the occasion of the foundation-stone of a new parish church at Loughborough being laid. In the course of his remarks the bishop said,—

" It was his fortune, or his misfortune, to have been in the gallery of the House when Mr. Bright was delivering what appeared to him to be an exquisitely beautiful and touching speech upon a sorely-vexed question—the Burials Bill. He never heard a speech more full of pathetic beauty and power ; but when speaking on that subject it occurred to the great orator to stop and to sneer at the observances of the Church of England, and, speaking of his own burial-grounds, to say, ' they have not been—what do they call it ?—consecrated.' He confessed, when he heard that, it seemed to him to be an entirely unworthy jeer, unworthy of the speaker, unworthy of the subject, and unworthy of the place—a jeer at the cherished religious feelings and observances of many who stood around him."

On reading the bishop's speech, Mr. Bright addressed the following letter to his lordship :—

Rochdale, November 23, 1877.

DEAR BISHOP OF PETERBOROUGH,—I have read your speech, and write to make one correction in it. You refer to my speech on the Burials Bill, to which you give too much praise, but you condemn what you term the " sneer " intended in my mention of the ceremony of " consecration." I assure you there was no sneer intended. The speech was entirely unpremediated. I had no intention of saying anything on the question when I went down to the House, and what I said arose from feelings excited during the debate. When I came to the word " consecration," it entirely escaped me, and for the moment I could not recall it. In my difficulty I turned to my friends on the bench near me, and said, " What is it called ? " or, " What do they call it ? " One or more of them answered "Consecration," and one or more laughed, I suppose at my ignorance or forgetfulness, and this laugh, which was somewhat ill-timed, made that seem a sneer which was never so intended by me.

This charge has been made against me more than once, but always, I think, in party newspapers, to which I did not think it needful to reply ; but coming from you, I write now to correct an error and misrepresentation which perhaps I ought to have corrected before.

You will not blame me if I do not believe in the virtue of "consecration." I cannot believe in what is called "holy ground" any more than you can believe in " holy water," and for the same reason, that there is nothing in it ; but it is not necessary to ridicule all that one cannot believe, although it is certain that ridicule has had its share in clearing the world of some portions of the superstitions which have misled and afflicted it.

I am, with great respect,
Very sincerely yours,
JOHN BRIGHT.

The Right Rev. the Bishop of Peterborough.

THE SALVATION ARMY.

Written to Mrs. Booth in reference to the opposition to which the Salvation Army was then exposed. In the case alluded to in the letter a sentence of one month's imprisonment with hard labour had been passed at the Petty Sessions at Whitchurch on four members of the Salvation Army for an assault on the police, who attempted to prevent their forming a procession. The chairman admitted that the assault was only a technical one, and on the case being submitted to Lord Chief Justice Coleridge, he stated that " hard labour was ignominious, and that the defendants might be religious enthusiasts, but such sentences were not to be tolerated for one moment." Sir W. Harcourt said he agreed very much with both of these opinions, and that he was happy to think that the sentence was under review by the Lord Chief Justice.

House of Commons, May 3, 1882.

DEAR MADAM,—I gave your letter to Sir W. Harcourt. He had already given his opinion in the House of Commons, which will be, to some extent, satisfactory to you. I hope the language of Lord Coleridge and the Home Secretary will have some effect on the foolish and unjust magistrates to whom, in some districts, the administration of the law is unfortunately committed. I suspect your good work will not suffer materially from the ill-treatment you are meeting with. The people who mob you would, doubtless, have mobbed the Apostles. Your faith and patience will prevail.

I am, with great respect and sympathy, yours sincerely,

JOHN BRIGHT.

To Mrs. Booth, 101, Queen Victoria Street, London.

THE OATHS QUESTION.

Read at a meeting of the Hebden Bridge Parliamentary Debating Society in February, 1883, in a debate on the question of permitting members of Parliament to make an affirmation instead of taking the oath.

One Ash, Rochdale, February 14, 1883.

DEAR SIR,—On the question of oaths, probably there is nothing in the New Testament more especially condemned and forbidden than oaths. To those who do not care about the New Testament this fact will be of no weight.

The practice of swearing to the truth of anything makes two kinds of truth or truthfulness. If oaths are of any avail, by so much as they make truth more certain, by so much they lessen the value of an ordinary statement, and diminish the probability of its truth.

If ignorant persons are not sworn, they think they may tell lies with impunity, and their lying is made to a large extent blameless in their eyes.

I think oaths and oath-taking have done more than any other thing to impair and destroy a regard for truth. If you wish to see the question treated more at large, you will find it in an admirable look, " Dymond's Essays on Morality," which you may obtain from any bookseller, or from Mr. Harris, 5, Bishopsgate Street, London.

I am, respectfully yours,

JOHN BRIGHT.

Mr. W. Pickles, Hebden Bridge.

THE WORK OF LUTHER.

Mr. S. Lloyd, of The Farm, Sparkbrook, having compiled a small volume on the work of Luther in the Reformation, as a remembrance of Luther on the fourth centenary of his birth, forwarded a copy to Mr. Bright, and received the following letter in reply :—

One Ash, Rochdale, September 3, 1883.

DEAR SIR,—I have read your little book on " Luther " with interest and with pleasure. I hope it may have a wide circulation. Every conflict does not need a Luther : our battles are not so fierce, and the strength and passion of the great reformer are scarcely called for in our time. Our triumphs are not after battles with " confused noise and garments rolled in blood ; " they come of discussion and gradual change of opinion, and not of great catastrophes— which is a thing to be thankful for. I hope, though we may not have Luthers, we may have teachers whose voice or pen may reach all corners of the land, and guide our people to a higher moral standard. There is a growth—we may wish it were more rapid—but must learn to have and to exercise more patience in this as in other things.

I thank you for sending me your little book, and am, very sincerely yours,

JOHN BRIGHT.

THE SUNDAY POSTAL DELIVERY.

Mr. Bright, having received an invitation to a conference proposed to be held with a view to the closing of all post offices and to the non-delivery of letters on Sundays, forwarded the following reply to Mr. Aston, of the Sunday Rest Association : —

One Ash, Rochdale, October 23, 1884.

DEAR SIR,—I cannot attend your proposed conference, or support the object for which it is to be held. To close all our post offices on Sundays would, in my view, be not only an intolerable inconvenience, but a great evil. To continue at least one delivery of letters in the day seems to me needful for the public service, and not unduly interfering with the labour and service of the letter-carriers.

The post office is our great means, not only of commercial but of family communication, and it is with reference to the " family " that I am most strongly opposed to your views. There are scores of thousands of young men and women in this country who are away from their homes and parents, engaged in cities and towns in the various occupations by which they live. To these Sunday is, to a large extent, a day of rest. It is a day on which their thoughts naturally turn to the homes they have left. It is the day on which the letter from the loving but absent father or mother is most frequently received ; and it is the day on which the absent son or daughter has the greatest leisure to write to the home circle.

If your plan were adopted, how many thousands of letters of wise and loving counsel from parents to absent children would be unwritten, or received under circumstances less favourable for good than if received and read and re-read during the quiet and leisure of the Sunday ? In cases of sickness or of death the closing of the post would often be a grievous inconvenience and a cause of great and prolonged distress. I have known two instances of it in my own family ; and what has happened in my case must have taken place in many others. I think the closing of the post in London on Sundays is a great inconvenience, and on the grounds to which I have referred, as to its effects on family correspondence, a great evil. But if the London system were extended to the whole kingdom it would cause an amount of confusion that would be intolerable. If I am not mistaken, the House of Commons did once pass a resolution in favour of your object, but was compelled to rescind it. I have no fear that you can succeed. If you obtain a momentary success, it must be followed by failure.

The one round of the postman in the day is not a heavy burden—not heavier than that borne by great numbers in almost every class in life. It is a great public service, an honourable labour, and it must be compensated for as other services are. There is not a word in the New Testament leaning to your views, so far as they are influenced by religious considerations. The Sabbath was made for man, and not man for the Sabbath.

> I am, very respectfully yours,
> JOHN BRIGHT.

Mr. T. H. Aston, Birmingham.

INTEGRITY IN BUSINESS.

In answer to a question as to how a man can succeed in business and yet be thoroughly a Christian, addressed to him by the Secretary of the Hackney branch of the Young Men's Christian Association, at the instigation of the members, Mr. Bright replied as follows :—

> November, 1884.

DEAR SIR,—I do not think I am specially qualified or in any way entitled to give an opinion upon the question with regard to which you have written. My own experience does not carry me further than other men. There are men who profit by practices of meanness and dishonesty in business, and I have heard of trades in which an honest man is said to be at a serious disadvantage in the competition to which he is subjected. But, on the other hand, I know many men who seem to me to prosper, in part on account of their high character for honour and justice, in their dealings as shopkeepers, manufacturers, or merchants. If a man is able to be strictly honest in all his dealings, in the quality of his goods, as well as in every business transaction, his character undoubtedly serves him in some sort as capital, because he gains the respect of those from whom he buys and those to whom he sells; and I believe this will in many, perhaps in most, cases balance, or even exceed, whatever gains may be secured by mean or dishonest practices to which some trades- men have recourse. That honesty is the best policy I firmly believe, as it is also the most righteous, and it will leave no stain upon the conscience. There are trades offering more temptations to dishonest practices than others, and parents may wisely consider this when seeking employment for their sons; and sons may likewise consider it when looking out for the business of their lives, and seek that trade which offers the least possible temptation. In my judgment the value of a high character for strict honour and honesty in business can hardly be estimated too highly, and it will often stand for more in the conscience, and even in the ledger, than all that can be gained by shabby and dishonest transactions.

Yours truly,
JOHN BRIGHT.

THE DOWRY OF THE PRINCESS BEATRICE

In May, 1885, the following resolution was passed by the All Saints' Ward Liberal Association, Birmingham, and was forwarded by Mr. Buckley, the secretary, to Mr. Bright: "That this meeting tenders its thanks to Mr. Labouchere for his opposition to an annuity to Princess Beatrice, and that a copy of this resolution be sent to him and to each of our three representatives, with a request that they will vote against any sum of money being granted for such purpose."

Mr. Bright replied as follows :—

Llandudno, May 16, 1885.

DEAR SIR,—I thank you for sending me the copy of the resolution on the subject of the grant to the Princess Beatrice, but I regret to have to say how much I differ from you in regard to the grant. The Princess is now the only unmarried daughter of the Queen, and I cannot believe that any considerable number of our people would wish her to be treated in a manner less generous than has been the case with her sisters, the other daughters of the Queen.

I gather from the concluding words of your resolution that your objection to the grant is on the ground of economy, on which you will permit me to say a word. The annual grant of 6000*l.* is less than one farthing per family amongst the seven millions of families in the United Kingdom, and therefore cannot be regarded as a burden that can be felt. I am astonished that Liberals and Liberal Associations should excite themselves over matters so small as this, and should be silent on the extravagance of Government and Parliament in other matters.

During the now nearly forty years of the reign of the Queen, I believe that more than 300 millions of pounds have been wasted in excessive military and naval expenditure, and in unnecessary and unjust wars ; and against all this evil but a faint protest has been made, even by Liberals and Liberal Associations. The blunders and crimes of successive Governments are overlooked, and the attention of working men is fixed on some trifle like this grant to the Princess.

If I had been in the House of Commons on Thursday last I should have voted for the grant. I would not have asked the House to cast a shadow over the mind of the Queen, and to tell her that in the later years of her reign Parliament was less generous to her family than in her earlier years. In years past I have spoken in Parliament against the magnitude of some of the grants to the Royal family, but I could not condemn this present grant on any grounds. I feel that in the course I am now taking, and which I now explain to you, I am acting in accordance with the general character of my countrymen, with whom whatever has a taint of unkindness and meanness is condemned. I feel confident that you will not blame me if I differ from you in this matter, but that you will rather approve of the course I have taken. Let our people look at the millions which are wasted, at the wars which are waged, and at the blood which is shed. This were a wiser policy than to excite themselves over a grant to the youngest daughter of the Queen, whose reign historians will deem illustrious, notwithstanding the blunders and crimes of successive Administrations. Forgive this long reply to your note, and believe me sincerely yours,

JOHN BRIGHT.

Mr. J. Buckley, Birmingham.

CLASSICAL LITERATURE.

In November, 1886, the *Pall Mall Gazette* published a number of letters from eminent men on the question as to whether English literature should be admitted to a place in the studies of the Universities, and as to whether it should or should not be associated with the study of Classical Literature. Among others was the following letter from Mr. Bright, written in answer to a correspondent who had asked "whether this great master of 'classical' English had not, after all, been somewhat of a classical scholar":—

November, 1886.

DEAR SIR,—Your letter has caused me some surprise, and has afforded me some amusement. You pay me a great complinent is asking my opinion on the question you put to me, which is one with which I do not feel myself competent to deal. As you know, I have not had the advantage of what is termed a classical education. My limited school time scarcely allowed me to think of Greek, and I should now make but slow steps in Latin, even with the help of a dictionary. From this it will be clear that my knowledge of or any success I may have attained in my own language owes nothing to instruction derived from the great authors of antiquity. I have read some of their works in English translations ; only recently I have read Mr. Jowett's translation of the Dialogues of Plato, and have been more astonished at the wonderful capacity and industry of the Master of Balliol than at the wisdom of the great Philosopher of Greece.

I suppose the youth of ancient Greece read the best authors of their own country, and the Roman youth the best authors of Rome. To have read Greek among the Romans would not have done so much to create and continue a classic Latin as to read and study the best books of Roman writers. So now, and with us, what can Greece and Rome do for English students more than can be done for them by the best writers of their own tongue ? Is there anything in the writings of the ancients that can compare in value for the youth of England with our translation of the Bible, especially of many of the Psalms and some of the Prophets, or with the unsurpassable grandeur and beauty of Milton ? If all existing Greek and Latin books were destroyed, is there not in our English classics sufficient material whereon to build a future of which our future need not be ashamed ? The learned men who were recently employed to revise the translation of the New Testament were, I presume, especially learned in the tongue of ancient Greece. No one has complained of their ignorance of Greek, but many have been surprised at and have complained of their failure in regard to English. They may have been profound in their knowledge of the ancient classics, but in English equal to the translation they were engaged to revise, they seem to me to have shown more of feebleness than of strength.

You ask me if I believe that the classics of the modern world are an equivalent, from an educational point of view, for the Greek and Roman classics? I answer that, as probably all the facts of history, or of biography, or of science, and all the reasoning to be found in ancient books, are to be found in modern translations, it follows that the study of the ancient languages is not now essential to education so far as the acquisition of knowledge is concerned; and that as the study of the best writers of English must be more effective in creating and sustaining what we may term classic English than the study of any foreign or dead language can be, it seems to follow that the classics of the modern world are, from an educational point of view, an equivalent for the Greek and Roman classics. The knowledge of the ancient languages is mainly a luxury. It is useful 'from the fact that science has enlisted it in its service, and it is pleasant to possess. and because it is pleasant it is a possession of value, with those who wander among ancient books, and whose association is chiefly with the limited class who are enabled by leisure and temperament to give themselves up to studies which are not open to the multitude.

I have written what has occurred to me after reading your letter. I do not feel competent fully to discuss the question submitted. I am one of the unlearned, having derived little or no nourishment from the fountain from which you have drunk so abundantly. If my answer to your question disappoints you, or seems to you shallow and unworthy, I am afraid it will add to the proofs you have of the insufficiency of an education in which classical learning has not been included.

I am, yours truly,

JOHN BRIGHT.

THE THIRTY-SEVENTH ARTICLE OF THE CHURCH OF ENGLAND.

In a letter to a gentleman in Glasgow, published in the *Christian Leader*, Mr. Bright referred to the above-mentioned Article in these terms :—" An Article of the Church of England makes all bearing of arms and all war lawful, and insists on this as a religious belief, and thus conscience is darkened and misled." In answer to this Mr. Bright received several letters, including the following from the Rev. Chas. Barnes, M.A., of Crewkerne, Somersetshire :—

Crewkerne, Somerset, March 10, 1888.

SIR,—There has been reproduced in many newspapers this week what purports to be a letter written by you on the 24th ult. to a friend in Glasgow, in which you write : " An Article of the Church of England makes all bearing arms and all war lawful, and insists on this as a religious belief, and thus conscience is darkened and misled." Your services and sacrifices of late in the interests of truth have been so many and great, that I am sure you would not willingly perpetuate the errors into which you appear to have here fallen. Doubtless, you refer to a clause of Article 37, which runs : " It is lawful for Christian men, at the commandment of the magistrate, to wear weapons and serve in the wars." So far, therefore, from the Article " making all bearing arms lawful," it is expressly provided that it be " at the commandment of the magistrate " (*ex mandato magistratus*). So far, again, from the Article " making all war lawful," it is only to be undertaken " at the commandment of the magistrate " (*ex mandato magistratus*)—at the direction of those responsible for the safety of the State. " *Christianis licet, ex mandato magistratus, arma portare, et* justa *bella administrare.*" Observe the epithet " justa." I quote here from the Latin version, which is at least of co-ordinate authority with the English. It is doubtful which is the original casting. We understand it, therefore, to be our duty to use the one version to elucidate and interpret the other.

You add that the Article "insists on this as a religious belief." You are right, if you mean that the Article is binding on the clergy. You are wrong if you mean, as probably you do, that the Article is binding on the laity. Our "Articles" do not constitute conditions of lay communion. Our Church "requires of its lay members no confession of their faith, except that contained in the Apostles' Creed." I have the honour to be, your obedient servant,

CHARLES BARNES.

To the Right Hon. John Bright, M.P.

Mr. Bright replied as follows :—

One Ash, Rochdale, March 14, 1888.

DEAR SIR,—I am glad to have your letter in reference to mine, in which I mention or quote from the 37th Article of your Church. I take the Article as I find it in your Book of Common Prayer : "It is lawful for Christian men, at the commandment of the magistrate, to wear weapons and to serve in the wars." I take this to mean at the commandment of any magistrate—that is, of any person who has authority to deal with affairs of State. It requires only that the wars should be sanctioned by the magistrate—that is, by the ruler for the time being—to justify any Christian man to wear weapons and to serve in the wars—that is, in any wars which the ruler or magistrate may undertake. The Christian man is not to trouble himself as to the justice of the quarrel. As a rule, every monarch or statesman going to war declares that the war is just, and this is to be accepted by those enlisted in his service. It follows, therefore, that according to the Article of your Church, any and every war which has the sanction of a magistrate or ruler is one in which Christian men may lawfully—that is, in compliance not only with human, but with the Divine law—engage themselves.

I object to this view of this solemn question, for it dethrones the individual conscience, and gives license to every crime with which war is everywhere and in all times associated. It is said that good men join the army, and in the crimes and murders which armies commit. I grant this, and I do not doubt that they derive much comfort from the 37th Article of your Church, which Article was inserted, not by good Christian men anxious for the good of the Church, but by monarch or statesman anxious that Christian principles and practice should never interfere with their schemes of ambition and conquest.

In the same Article it is declared to be lawful to punish Christian men with death for grievous offences, under which statesmen and judges and juries were comforted when they sent men to the gallows for stealing a sheep, or for forgery, or for stealing in a shop or dwelling house to some trifling amount, or for passing base coin.

The 39th Article declares that a man "may swear when the magistrate requireth," although there is no act or offence which a man may or can commit which is more expressly forbidden in the New Testament.

These Articles to which I am objecting have nothing to do with religious belief. They were introduced only for political purposes, and, in my view, they have for 300 years done much to pervert the minds of our people—not of Churchmen only, but of Nonconformists, who in many things continue the unsound opinion which in early times the teaching of the Church made common. You say these Articles are only of "religious belief" to the clergy; but you will hardly say that their influence is confined to your many thousands of ministers, and that what clergymen have to accept as doctrine to be believed may be wholly rejected by their congregations and parishioners. A Church free from the State might free itself from the fault and the dishonour of making very doubtful political ideas into articles of religious and Christian belief.

Yours very truly,
JOHN BRIGHT.

EXTEMPORE SPEAKING AND PREACHING.

The following letter, which was published in the *Evangelical Magazine* of January, 1874, was written to a student in a Nonconformist college, who had asked Mr. Bright's opinions on the art of public speaking and on reading sermons :—

DEAR SIR,—Your letter, written in May last, only met my eye a few days ago ; it has been at the Reform Club, and was not forwarded to me till quite recently. You ask me two questions, to one of which I can give a ready answer. I have never been in the habit of writing out my speeches, certainly not for more than thirty years past. The labour of writing is bad enough, and the labour of committing to memory would be intolerable ; and speeches *read* to a meeting are not likely to be received with much favour. It is enough to think over what is to be said, and to form an outline in a few brief notes. But, first of all, a real knowledge of the subject to be spoken of is required ; with that, practice should make speaking easy.

As to what is best for the pulpit, I may not venture to say much. It would seem that rules applicable to other speaking will be equally applicable to the pulpit. But in a pulpit a man is expected to speak for a given time, on a great theme, and with less of exact material than is obtainable on other occasions and on ordinary subjects. And further, a majority of preachers are not good speakers, and perhaps could not be made such. They have no natural gift for good speaking ; they are not logical in mind, nor full of ideas, nor free of speech ; and they have none of that natural readiness which is essential to a powerful and interesting speaker. It is possible, nay, perhaps very probable, that if reading sermons were abolished, while some sermons would be better than they now are, the majority of them would be simply chaos, and utterly unendurable to the most patient congregation. Given a man with knowledge of his subject, and a gift for public speaking, then I think reading a mischief; but given a man who knows little, and who has no gift of speaking, then reading seems to be inevitable, because speaking, as I deem it, is impossible. But it must be a terrible thing to have to read or speak a sermon every week, on the same topic, to the same people; terrible to the speaker, and hardly less so to the hearers. Only men of great mind, great knowledge, and great power, can do this with success. I wonder that any man can do it! I often doubt if any man has ever done it. I forbear, therefore, from giving a strong opinion on the point you submit to me. Where a man can speak, let him speak—it is no doubt most effective; but where a man cannot speak, he must read. Is not this the sum of the whole matter?

I thank you for the good wishes expressed in your friendly letter. My health is greatly improved, and I hope to be able to give some time to the House of Commons during the coming session.

I am, truly yours,
JOHN BRIGHT.

PUBLIC SPEAKING.

Written in reply to the Rev. G. E. Cheeseman, who had asked Mr. Bright's advice as to various methods of preparation for public speaking, namely: (1) writing speeches and reading them; (2) writing and committing to memory; and (3) sketching the heads of the topic and trusting to the inspiration of the moment for the words in which to clothe the thought.

Rochdale, October 15, 1888.

DEAR SIR,—As to modes of preparation for speaking, it seems to me that every man would readily discover what suits him best. To write speeches and then to commit them to memory is, as you term it, a double slavery, which I could not bear. To speak without preparation, especially on great and solemn topics, is rashness, and cannot be recommended. When I intend to speak on anything that seems to me important, I consider what it is that I wish to impress upon my audience. I do not write my facts or my arguments, but make notes on two or three or four slips of note-paper, giving the line of argument and the facts as they occur to my mind, and I leave the words to come at call while I am speaking. There are occasionally short passages which for accuracy I may write down, as sometimes also—almost invariably—the concluding words or sentences may be written.

This is very nearly all I can say on this question. The advantage of this plan is that, while it leaves a certain and sufficient freedom to the speaker, it keeps him within the main lines of the original plan upon which the speech was framed, and what he says, therefore, is more likely to be compact and not wandering and diffuse. Forgive me if I say no more.

Yes, one thing more. Edward Butler (I do not know him) has sent me a charming little book with the quaint title "For Good Consideration." It is published by Elliot Stock, Paternoster Row, London, and in it is an article, "Advice to Young Orators." I have read it and the whole book with much pleasure. I think it would interest you.

In regard to the questions you put to me, though I have spoken much, I am not sure that I am qualified to teach even what I have practised with some show of success.

I am, yours very respectfully,
JOHN BRIGHT.

Rev. G. E. Cheeseman.

INDEX.